Cruising the Canals & Rivers
of the Netherlands on
Orion

Cover Design, Photographs and Maps
by the author
Front Cover Photograph
by John Chapman

Additional copies can be obtained from:
www.eurocanals.com
orders@eurocanals.com

Cruising the Canals & Rivers of the Netherlands on

Orion

Tom Sommers

EuroCanals Publishing

2010

Dedicated to the three of us, who traveled
these towns and waterways together.

Acknowledgements

My thanks go to my friend Leo Bestgen who, in January 2000, urged me to "just do it" and also showed me how to create and publish a newsletter. Leo was a graphic artist and media freelancer who knew about photographs, writing, layout and printing, and taught me a little bit of what he knew. He said that I needed a trademark name and suggested "Euro-boats", "Euro-rivers", "Euro-waterways"; I countered with EuroCanals and that was it. Unfortunately my gratitude is posthumous, as Leo died at his desk in 2002.

A Christmas gift from my daughter Eizabeth, an 1849 map of the Netherlands, drawn by an English mapmaker, has been very helpful in my understanding and writing about the changes of the landscape and the waterways accomplished by the Dutch people.

About the Author

Tom Sommers began his canal-cruising avocation with a trip in 1966 aboard a classic wooden motorboat from Cayuga Lake, in the Finger Lakes of Central New York, through the New York State Barge Canal (Erie Canal) and the Oswego Canal to Lake Ontario and the St Lawrence River. Later canal trips included one across the length of the Erie Canal and down the Hudson River to the Statue of Liberty.

After early retirement from an engineering career, Tom moved to coastal North Carolina where he boated on the IntraCoastal Waterway and worked as a boat broker and as an advertising sales representative for a boating magazine.

In early 2000 Tom and his wife Carol acted on a longtime desire to live in Europe and cruise the canals and rivers. Their first year was in Paris, on the Canal St Martin, then on the river Seine near Conflans-Ste-Honorine, and later on the northern coast of Brittany. During these years they have traveled extensively along the waterways and visited France, Belgium, Germany, The Netherlands, Luxembourg, Switzerland, Italy and England.

Beginning with the monthly newsletter "Cruising the Canals & Rivers of Europe" in September 2000, Tom currently offers an e-book compilation of all of these newsletters and the subsequent waterway guides, as well as an extensive website describing the inland waterways of Europe (eurocanals.com). Previous books include the cruising guides "Waterways of France" (2007) and "Waterways of the Netherlands" (2009).

Table of Contents

List of Maps

Introduction & Short Glossary

This book is about meandering through the canals of Holland. It is very lovely country, and a major cruising area for Dutch boaters, as well as visiting boaters from Germany, the UK and even Australia, New Zealand and America.

We did not imagine there were so many pleasure boats in the world. As a Dutch friend in the USA told us before we left, "Holland is a very small country. It has a lot of people and they all have a boat!". I know that is an exaggeration but on a sunny weekend it certainly seems to be so. It seems not only does everyone in Netherlands have a boat but, everyone in Germany has a boat here too.

The writing includes my personal observations, some of which may not be of general interest, although I think they will be if you give them a chance. To understand why I am interested in what may seem to be unimportant or obscure, let me tell you a bit about myself.

My college degree was a combination of Mechanical Engineering and Industrial Engineering; pretty boring, right? That's what I thought at the age of 25, so I gravitated into Sales Engineering. That doesn't mean that I was a typical salesman, it meant that it was my job to help my clients who worked in factories select and engineer our products into their systems. It meant writing proposals and creating seminars which described how the products worked and how they might fit into the client's needs. It was this career, and of course my love of boating, which led me into writing the EuroCanals Guides, to describe the waterways of Europe to cruising travelers. My primary avocation is to understand the geography of the canals and rivers and turn that into clearly-drawn maps, which requires the graphic arts skills that I developed in creating my seminars.

It is those skills which, on this trip, attracted me to art, architecture and design. You will soon see my interest in the hundreds of different drawbridges in use in the Netherlands. You will also read about my interest in building design, especially modern architecture. Even the star forts, which you will read about early in the book, are of interest for design, not history.

After having lived in France for several years, and traveled in other European countries for shorter periods, I have found that it is best to use the local terms and customs as soon as possible. For instance in Holland I only used "good morning" until I learned "goedemorgen" and listened carefully until I could say "hoo de mor hen", or at least something close to that.

For that reason I am going to start right out in this book using the Dutch terms for certain things which came up all of the time on this trip, rather than use the English terms. These are listed on the next page; they should become familiar very quickly.

Similarly, all dimensions, as related to boat size, lock size and distance, will be given in meters. To convert meters to feet multiply by 3.3; thus 5.0 meters = 16.5 feet. To do this quickly, use "a little more than 3 X". To convert kilometers to miles multiply by .62; thus 10 kilometers = 6.2 miles. To do this quickly, use "about two-thirds".

Time will be shown as the 24-hour system. 09:00 is 9:00 AM, 12:00 is noon, 15:00 is 3:00 PM, 18:00 is 6:00 PM. Some non-Europeans complain about not being able to grasp the 24-hour time system, but I like it. Here is an easy calculation: Departing at 08:00 + 7 hours travel time = 15:00. To do the same thing in an AM/PM system it would "8AM till noon is 4 hours; subtract that from 7 leaves 3 hours, so it will be 3PM". Not too hard, but the first system is very easy.

Glossary of the most-used Dutch terms:
haven Probably the most common Dutch term used in this book; it means harbor (harbour), marina or quay designated for mooring. A commercial marina is called a **Jachthaven** (followed by a name.) A town dock can be **Gemeentehaven**, meaning municipal haven, or **Passantenhaven**, furnished for use by "passers-by" (visitors.) Some of these are free, others charge fees.
WV, WSV (name) Literally "Watersport Vereniging", a yacht/boating club haven. Another version is VVW.
sluis waterway lock; plural is **sluizen**.
molen mill, used for all classic Dutch windmills; plural is **molens**.
woonboot houseboat, either a purpose-built floating home or a barge converted for living aboard; plural is **woonboten**.
singel The moat, canal or stream around the perimeter of a fortified town.
buiten outer (as in buitenhaven.)
binnen inner (as in binnenhaven.)
brug bridge; plural is **bruggen**.
BB Literally "beweegbare brug", an opening bridge, liftbridge, drawbridge.
kade quay
markt street market
meer lake
VVV tourist office
noord, zuid, oost, west north, south, east, west

If the alert reader should notice that the names of waterways may be spelled differently on various pages, that is because the Dutch do it that way too. I was told that there is often an "old Dutch" version as well as the modern version, used interchangeably.

I hope that you will enjoy this cruise as much as we did.   *Tom Sommers*

Provinces of the Netherlands

The Netherlands is often casually called "Holland" but in fact there are twelve provinces. It happens that the two largest cities, Amsterdam and Rotterdam, are in the two provinces named Holland (Noord and Zuid Holland respectively.) These provinces include most of the places that draw foreign tourists, hence the common usage of "Holland". I will use that term occasionally, especially as related to the area of Noord Holland, Zuid Holland and Utrecht.

The chapters of this book are, in general, arranged by province, beginning in Zeeland and proceeding clockwise around the country to Limburg. Our route passed through each of the twelve provinces; in some cases we traveled extensively within the province, in other cases we touched it only lightly. The chapter titled "Heart of Holland" includes parts of Noord Holland, Zuid Holland and Utrecht. The most popular areas for visiting boaters are the lakes, rivers and canals of Heart of Holland and Friesland.

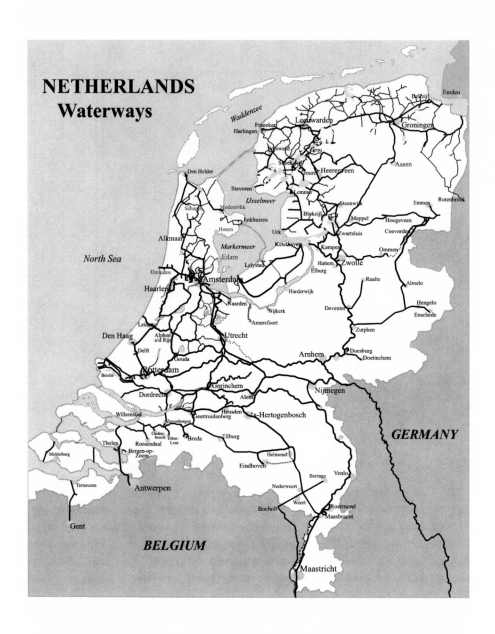

There are 269 waterways in the Netherlands, totaling 3,732 kilometers. These are the canals and rivers that could be traveled by visiting cruisers; in addition, there are hundreds, perhaps thousands, of small dead-end canals lined with boats and used by farms, residences and industry.

Zeeland... land of the sea, the delta of the rivers; the Dutch call them the *Grote Rivieren*. The mouths of the Schelde, Waal and Maas rivers, which come together here in a mix of channels flowing into the North Sea. (The Dutch name for the river Rhine is Waal and for the river Meuse is Maas.) The land hereabouts is made up of islands of silt from these rivers. We are in the town of Vlissingen (Flushing), formerly an important fishing village, now a commercial and recreational port. It is at the far southwestern corner of the country of the Netherlands, on the Westerschelde, the busiest river in Europe, with about 70,000 ship movements per year. The ships are headed to the commercial harbors here at Vlissingen, at Terneuzen and Gent, and on to Antwerp.

We are having our mid-afternoon coffee at a terrace table of the Grand Brasserie Evertson, on the edge of the boulevard overlooking the Westerschelde. In front of us is the small marina in the center of the old town. Our backs are to the sea, the Westerschelde and the North Sea, but our thoughts are ahead to the land, for we are thinking about the hundreds of kilometers of inland waterways that we will travel in the next months.

The Netherlands is by far the best country in which to search for and buy a boat for traveling the inland waterways of Europe; we have been told this by experienced cruisers and have seen it for ourselves while driving through Belgium, France and England. That is what brought us to this town, for we had bought our canal boat Orion, a Dutch steel cruiser, not far away and arrived here after a two hour cruise from the previous owner's dock.

Buying a boat

The search for a suitable cruising vessel had begun in France, where I was traveling throughout the country by car, making a preliminary survey of the waterways and the popular destinations for my cruising newsletter. As I went I looked for boats for sale, both for myself and on behalf of clients. I was very quickly disillusioned; France has very few brokers and not many boats for sale. The boats that I did inspect were generally shabby. In fact I came across "Avonbay", the legendary cruiser used by Hugh McKnight to travel along the entire network in the 1970s while writing the classic "Cruising French Waterways", at a broker's docks in Burgundy; it looked terrible, the wooden decks and the waterline were green with mold.

It all changed in the Netherlands. There were boats and barges everywhere, some showing *Te Koop* signs (For Sale). Several dozen brokers and buyer's agents offered long lists of vessels to consider. Almost every one of these boats was clean and well maintained (others were offered as "in process", projects for the buyer to complete.) It became not a question of finding a boat but of deciding which one.

Cruising the Canals & Rivers of the Netherlands

Some parameters needed to be established: length was the first question, it is the primary feature mentioned in sale listings: "10-meter Dutch cruiser" or "24-meter Luxemotor barge". I learned that barges longer than 20 meters must meet the most comprehensive technical requirements and operator's licensing tests. Another set of requirements apply between 15 and 20 meters. Below 15 meters the boat and the skipper are relatively easy to license and are least likely to be inspected in random checks from the waterway authorities. The ability to tie up at marinas and boat clubs is often limited to boats smaller than 13 meters (and in some cases 10 or 12 meters.)

Width (beam) is not usually a limiting factor, except in the case of catamarans (these can be very inconvenient or even impossible to use on the inland waterways.) Anything up to 5.0 meters beam will allow travel on nearly all of the waterways.

Draft is highly important, both water draft and air draft. After researching charts for all of the waterways of France, Belgium, Netherlands and Germany I settled on a general recommendation of water draft less than 1.5 meters, air draft less than 3.5 meters. Those limits would include about 90% of all waterways and also about 90% of all boats. The last 10% would require water draft less than 1.0 meters, air draft less than 2.5 meters; open boats with low draft are widely used on such waterways in Friesland.

Those are the numbers, but I also had my personal plans, as well as likes and dislikes, to consider. One important item was that I planned to eventually cruise in the Baltic Sea, to explore the Gota canal of Sweden and the Telemark canal of Norway. I settled on a Dutch steel-hull cruiser, open-cockpit/forward-cabin style, with round-bilge hull shape. The boat had been used for coastal cruising and in fact was equipped with GPS/chartplotter and maps from Denmark to Dunkirk. It measured 11.30m length, 3.55m beam, 1.15m water draft and 2.45m air draft. I would have preferred a more shallow water draft, but that goes against my desire for a coastal cruiser. For my needs, I considered this to be an ideal boat.

A Dutch surveyor and a notary worked with the broker to assure the technical status and to transfer the ownership and registration. I took possession at Terneuzen NL on the southern shore of the Westerschelde. We immediately traveled out

into the wide river and northwest to Vlissingen, finding a slip at the Jachthaven Michiel de Ruijterhaven. www.montparnasse.nl

Zeeland Province

Choosing a route

We are ready to begin our travels along the canals and rivers of western Europe, my wife Carol, our dog Johnnie and I spending nearly all of our time onboard, with only occasional trips back to our home in the USA. Since we are already in the Netherlands, a circuit of the country is the logical first step. But where to go, exactly? I had in my hand some of the maps that I had drawn using Dutch charts, road maps and aerial photos. They showed a network of canals and rivers, a maze of red and blue lines (red for rivers, blue for canals.) An obvious route didn't jump off the page, so we needed to decide on some destinations before selecting the waterways.

I did have the germ of a plan; I had been following the progress of a friend along the waterways of the Netherlands, through periodic postings on his blog. He wrote of stopping at a marina near Naarden, a very old town not far to the east of Amsterdam. Along with writing enthusiastically about the town, he included an aerial photo; I was immediately intrigued by what I saw, a twelve-pointed star of trees and berms enclosed by a moat, with another, wider, moat inside the star. Inside these defenses is the town, a walled oval protected by seven arrows of land pointing out outward into the larger moat. I had discovered "star forts". I had visited forts with this type of pointed exterior wall structure years before (such as Fort McHenry in Baltimore harbor, USA), but the aerial view of the dual moat system just knocked me out.

I soon began to notice other star fort towns and to mark them on a map of the Netherlands. There are now thirty-six stars on my map, and that may not be all of them in NL (two similar towns in France are Dunkirk and Lille.) So there I had it: I would choose a route which would allow me to visit as many of these towns as possible. Nearly all of them are located on navigable waterways and in some cases the moats (called *singel* in Dutch) are the waterways themselves and offer mooring places.

Cruising the Canals & Rivers of the Netherlands

From Wikipedia: http://en.wikipedia.org/wiki/Star_fort

A star fort is a fortification in the style that evolved when cannon dominated the battlefield. Ring fortifications of the Medieval era proved vulnerable to damage by cannon fire against a perpendicular masonry wall. Forces that could get close to the wall were able to conduct undermining operations in relative safety, as the defenders could not shoot at them from nearby walls. In contrast, the star fortress was composed of many triangular bastions, specifically designed to cover each other, and a moat.

Zeeland Province

Navigation Charts

The information that we needed to plan our travel is found on the charts published by ANWB, the Royal Dutch Touring Club. In addition to maps for highways, they publish the best and most current charts for the inland waterways in NL, showing the details needed for navigation. Paper charts can be purchased at bookstores and marinas throughout the country and at the many VVV (tourist information) offices.

The ANWB also publishes an annual *Wateralmanak Vaargegevens* (Waterways Almanac) that covers both the Netherlands and Belgium. *Deel 1* (Volume 1) describes regulations and certificate requirements and is required to be kept onboard all vessels. *Deel 2* provides detailed information on waterways, bridges, locks, marinas, authority contacts, etc. Both of these books are in Dutch; Deel 1 cannot be understood by most of us, but Deel 2 is very useful, the information is in symbols and numbers.

The charts and the Wateralmanak 2 are intended to be used together. Operating schedules for locks and bridges can be looked-up in the "Nummer kunstwerken" pages at the back of the almanac. Some towns are shown on a detailed local map. Many marinas and boatyards are described in great detail in the almanac. It takes a little practice but then items can be found quickly.

A very convenient and relatively inexpensive way to have all of these charts onboard is to download and install the digital version on a Windows computer (or in a Windows virtual machine in an Intel Mac, as I have done.) The Dutch software company Stentec updates the files each year and also makes available a sidebar panel with information on marinas, boatyards, locks and bridges; the latter includes photos, heights and opening time schedule, in an easy to read format. www.stentec.com

Vlissingen

Jachthaven Michiel de Ruijterhaven is a seaport marina, connected directly to the Westerschelde and thus tidal; floating pontoons adjust to the substantial changes in water level. On the northern quayside is a long row of restaurants and cafes with terrace tables; more can be found around the corner on the main street. Aside from a few modern apartment buildings, the street view is typical Dutch: two, three or four stories lead to a pitched roof with dormer windows or a stepped gable, each narrow building a different color of brick finish. A late afternoon walk through the nearby streets was very enjoyable and gave us the opportunity to stock the boat with coffee for our first daily cup. We will fully provision later, probably in Middelburg, and we are looking forward to breakfast tomorrow in one of the cafes on the quay.

On the south side of the marina an observation tower (65 meters high) gave us an opportunity to see exactly how we would travel the next morning, out into the Westerschelde, then turning back through a lock to enter the Kanaal door Walcheren. (We are on the island of Walcheren, *door* means "through".) Our first destination is Middelburg, just 7.7 kilometers north but in that distance there are five bridges, four of them less than 1.7 meters height clearance when closed; each will open on a fixed timetable. With the lock passage time to consider we will allow about two hours for the trip and depart at about 09:00.

The light morning fog didn't deter us from continental breakfast at a table on the quay, and soon we were off. Dealing with the rising water in the lock was easy, once we realized that floating planks lay along the waterline; Orion has a waterline rubrail extending forward from the stern about one-third of the boat length. We lowered a pair of fenders forward of the rubrail and used a single line, attached at the bow and held on the stern cleat, around the bollards set into the lock wall; we moved the line once to a higher bollard as the water rose and the job was done.

BB Bridges

Then our first encounter, of which hundreds will follow, with the Dutch BB bridges. BB is the term used on charts; it stands for *beweegbare brug*, a bascule bridge which is hinged at one end and lifted by a pair of counterweighted arms. In some cases there is a bridge mechanism on each bank, so that the span is split in the middle and the sections lift to each side. The sight of these arms standing above the countryside will become as common to us as the sight of the many windmills that we will pass by. Most are graceful, some are utilitarian; newer bridges are often sculptural.

The chart shows the data for each bridge, such as: BB H15 W193 VHF22 877. H15 is the clearance under a closed bridge, in decimeters, thus 1.5 meters; sometimes the passage can be done without opening the bridge, but our height is 2.45 meters so we need the bridge to open. W193 is the width of the channel, again in decimeters, thus 19.3 meters, no problem there. The VHF channel allows radio contact with the bridgekeeper (not required.) 877 is the identification number for the bridge, with full details, including the operating schedule, listed in the Wateralmanak 2 published by the ANWB.

The bridges and locks utilize a traffic light system: during closed hours a light panel will show two red lights; during opening hours they show a single red light. Boats should not enter, even if the gates are open or bridge is up. When they are ready to open, each panel will show one red plus a green light, indicating that they are about to open. When the red light goes out and only the green is showing you are clear to proceed.

It is important not to enter a lock or go under a bridge, even if it appears clear, if only one red and no green light is showing. This is telling you that boats on the other side of the lock or bridge have priority and you must wait for them.

Beyond the first bridge we traveled with three sailboats from the UK; two had been in the lock with us, another joined from the inland haven VVW Schelde, a boat club that welcomes visiting boats overnight. (This is common in the Netherlands, we will use the facilities of such clubs many times.)

The canal is a straight line between high grassy banks topped by a long row of trees. There wasn't much to be seen, as flat land lay below the berms on the banks. A few of the occasional industrial walls on the outskirts of Vlissingen are well decorated by graffiti, which seem out of place in these otherwise perfectly clean and green surroundings. Several bicyclists passed by on the east side, on a paved path; again, these are a harbinger of thousands of cyclists that we will see along the waterways.

It was the bridges that drew my attention; the designs and colors are striking. Each of the three BB bridges lift a span of 20 meters (66 feet) so the mechanism is tall and heavily built, painted white and a deep red. One bridge, swinging open rather than lifting, was just for bicycle and foot traffic.

It wasn't unexpected, for I had been prepared by viewing the chart, but our arrival at the first star fort town, Middelburg, showed no signs of the anticipated fortifications; the canal had cut off the entire eastern side of the star and new channels had been cut into the center of town. A long glass office building was first to be seen on our left, followed by an impressive BB bridge. There are two bridges lifted at once, one for road traffic, with a bicycle lane on each side, and another for pedestrians. After a second, swing-type, bridge we found the dock of Jos Boone chandlery on the left side, where we fueled the boat and bought replacement bottles of propane, as well as some new fenders for locking.

Middelburg

Two hundred meters further into town we arrived at the reception dock for WV Arne www.wvarne.nl As it was our plan to move on to Veere later in the day, we arranged to tie up at the *winkel* (shopping) pontoon for a few hours. This gave us time to gather provisions and, as it was a Thursday, to find both fresh fish and produce at the street market. Carol already knows that, at this time of year, she should watch for fresh asparagus.

We used our dinghy to follow the inner canal (tour boats take visitors on this route) and get to both the street *markt* and a supermarket and return to our boat, then took our bicycles for a brief ride along the outer chain of *singel*. Here we found De Hoop, our first up-close view of a classic Dutch *molen* (windmill.) The singel outlines the stars that had so intrigued me when seen in aerial views, but from the bicycles they were just a pleasant waterway meandering through residential neighborhoods.

Veere

In late afternoon we headed north along the second half of the canal to Veere, passing through a lock into the Veerse Meer and then to the town harbor for an overnight mooring near the center of the village, a much smaller and quieter town than Middelburg. The Jachtclub Veere offers full facilities, including wifi and a wastewater pumpout station which we used to make sure that our tank was empty; since it is small, 70 liters, we will need to keep on top of pumping it often. www.jachtclubveere.nl

(Wastewater holding tanks are now required on all new boats in the Netherlands, but they are not yet common, nor are pumpout stations. They are not required on older boats, however it is illegal to discharge toilet water. Large marinas are required to offer pumpout service by 2011.)

We moored across the narrow harbor channel from the village but a footbridge gave us quick access to the very picturesque streets. It's hard to imagine that the Dutch towns which we visit in the future will be any more pleasant than this one. We have a family joke that, as we travel and find a place that we like, Carol and I say at the same time "Let's move here". It's not just a joke, we have done it several times in our life. Veere is one of those places, although we will force ourselves to stay only overnight. We do need to return, for we are missing the Power Horse Competition held during the last week in August; we would like to see those magnificent horses at work.

The old red or white brick houses of the village are low, two stories topped by a variety of gable designs. Every street and front stoop was immaculately clean, as expected. Behind our mooring, to the west, I found the berms of the star fort (again the canal had taken away those on the east.) No fortifications remain, just the grassy berms and star points with singel beyond. Cobbled roads and paved paths meander through open fields, backyard gardens, orchards and country cottages. And a windmill, De Koe. The village does have a suburb, a peninsula with a few streets among dense woods. The bike path here enters a tunnel of shrubs in some places; houses can only be glimpsed through the trees.

Although we were now ready to cook onboard, we wanted to enjoy this town as much as possible, so we walked to De Peperboom for dinner, two blocks away from the harbor and near the *Grote Kerk* (large church.) The restaurant was a good choice, offering excellent seafood in a historic building or on a terrace. www.peperboom.nl

Veerse Meer - Oosterschelde

The Veerse Meer was no doubt once one of the channels made by the rivers, now it dead-ends near the sea just 5 km to the northwest; we could easily have anchored there for a beach visit. But instead we traveled a curving path to the east to join the Oosterschelde, historically the second channel (along with the Westerschelde) of the Schelde river from Antwerp to the sea. Today farmland connects the peninsula of Zuidbeverland to the mainland, cut only by a straight-line canal. Our destination was Tholen, on the northeastern end of the Oosterschelde at the Schelde-Rijnkanaal.

We cruised on open water, 20.5km on the Veerse Meer to a lock at the junction with the Oosterschelde, then 26.5km to another lock and a short section of canal into Tholen. This took a full day. We made no stops, although there were several harbors and docks along the way if necessary. There are shallows, channel markers showed the proper path. The northwest current of the North Sea brought rain showers alternated with bright sunshine.

Holland is a land of water and air. The land is a country risen from the water, a country floating at anchor, where sunlight seems to be filtered by a carafe of pellucid water. The sky carries white clouds in front of bold blue. The water surface reflects the light up to the clouds, and the clouds reflect it back to the earth. The light that comes from above is mirrored, reflected and intensified; it has endless movement and change.

The day passed easily, with many leisure sailboats and motorboats on the open waters and a few commercial barges once we were on the canal. We tied up in the municipal harbor of Tholen in mid-afternoon, right where the eastern side of the fortifications were located before the modern world replaced them with a canal and harbor. The western half of the star remains, so we put our legs back on land for a good 2km walk along the star-points of the singel and back through the center of town. The restaurant Hof van Holland was near the dock and looked very impressive, but too formal and

9

dark for our taste on this day, so we cooked our first dinner aboard. Seafood, of course, as we are still in Zeeland.

But not for much longer. Tholen is an island and thus part of Zeeland but right across the canal is the mainland, the province of Noord Brabant. Tomorrow we will travel on to Willemstad and from then on we will be on "inland" waterways.

Waterway	From	To	KM	Hours
Kanaal door Walcheren	Vlissingen	Middelburg	7.7	1.5
Kanaal door Walcheren	Middelburg	Veere	6.7	1.2
Veerse Meer	Veere	Oosterschelde	20.5	3.0
Oosterschelde	Veerse Meer	Tholen	26.5	3.3

Noord Brabant Province

Volkerak

Our morning travel from Tholen was 18 km northbound on the Schelde-Rijnkanaal, an easy canal with no locks and three fixed bridges, all offering 9.85m clearance, to the Volkerak, a wide and open waterway between the mainland of Noord Brabant and the islands of Zeeland.

There is plenty of time for thinking, almost three hours with little to do but watch for green channel markers on the right, red on the left, and the occasional commercial barge going in the other direction. So I reviewed where we had been and what we had done in the past three days. We were busy getting settled into the boat and into our travel routine, so we had skipped some of the sightseeing. Such as the museums; nearly every town in Europe has at least one museum and the larger cities have several, covering art, history and culture. Sometimes the cultural themes are quaint or even bizarre, but they are almost always interesting and entertaining.

The tourist office, in the Netherlands called VVV (their signs are usually easily seen on arrival in a new town), is the source for information on the museums and other sights. I always gather brochures and take notes, so now I can review what we have missed. In Vlissingen it was the MuZEEum of local history, the 19th-century maritime displays at Het Arsenal and the Reptielenzoo Iguana, home of reptiles and insects. In Middelburg it was the Zeeuws Museum, in a 14th-century abbey. In Veere we missed a tour of the Grote Kerk and the view from its tower. I'm sure that these would have been very interesting and I promise to take the time in the future to visit such places!

Once on the Volkerak we could turn immediately inland on small rivers into the heart of Noord Brabant province, perhaps to travel to the cities of Roosendaal, Breda or Tilburg. But we bypassed the Steenburgse Vliet and the Mark & Dintel river routes and continued on to the Hollands Diep. There we will be truly on the big rivers, for the Waal and the Maas have joined to form this wide flow.

Four side-by-side locks serve the junction of the Volkerak and the Hollands Diep; the complex is one of the largest in Europe. We used the *jachtsluis*, the smallest of the four, on the northern side of the channel. It is still plenty big, at 16m wide X 145m long, but much smaller than those for barges, at 24m X 326m. Entering the lock was no problem, we just followed other pleasure-boat traffic and blended in. An 8-lane autoroute passes overhead; on the south side of the channel is a row of sleek modern wind generators. Just around the corner to the east is the very old town of Willemstad, a popular stop for waterway cruisers and for me a mostly undisturbed star fort, marred only by the channels cut for the marina and the town dock. In fact the marina includes two docks which lie along the point of a star.

Cruising the Canals & Rivers of the Netherlands

There are only as many locks in all of the Netherlands as there are on just one of the major canals in France, but some of the locks operate in unexpected ways, so I will write a bit about what to expect in the Netherlands.

How Locks Work:

Step 1: A vessel bound upstream enters the lock and secures lines to bollards.

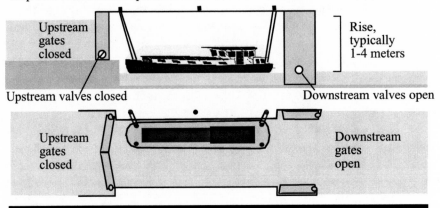

Step 2: Downstream gates and valves are closed after all vessels have entered. The lock fills with water through the open upstream valves, lifting the vessel.

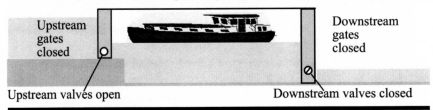

Step 3: The upstream gates are opened, allowing the vessel to exit and proceed.

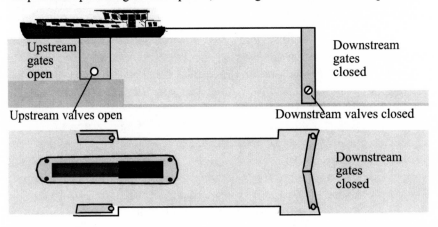

(For vessels bound downstream, the process is reversed.)

Noord Brabant Province

The first "pound lock", a basin of water impounded between two gates, was invented in China in 984 AD. The practical details that make locks work as they do today was developed by Leonardo da Vinci, who introduced the apparatus in France in 1495. The key to his design are the mitered gates which close tightly and are held in place by the pressure of water due to different water levels.

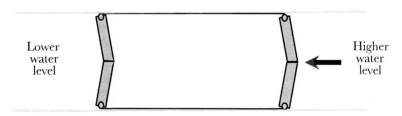

Lower water level

Higher water level

When you are in a lock that is filling or emptying, the first sign that the cycle is complete will be the slight opening between the mitered ends, indicating that the water levels have equalized, allowing the gates to open.

In most countries the rivers flow downhill, from the mountains to the sea. Canals may cross between rivers, but the water that flows through the canals goes into the rivers, eventually flowing to the sea. Not so in the flat country of the Netherlands, where the rivers do flow toward the sea as they enter the country, but later that flow is countered by tidal waters that come well inland. Other waterways flow in the direction that Dutch authorities direct, not necessarily as nature intended.

This is controlled by locks. In countries such as France locks are usually a long series of steps up an incline. In the Netherlands locks are often installed alone, to adjust for only slight differences in water level or to hold back the tide. In some Dutch locks a boater may go through the full lock sequence and then wonder why, as the water level appears unchanged; this may be true, as the purpose of that lock may be only to separate salt water from fresh water.

That is the case here at the *Volkeraksluizen* lock complex; a small amount of fresh river water is fed through the lock to keep the water in the Volkerak and the Schelde-Rijnverbinding Kanaal fresh.

Willemstad

We had eaten our lunch onboard while cruising the Volkerak and were ready for a walk through Willemstad as soon as we had tied up at the short-stay dock. It didn't take long to decide that this town would be a good place for a two-night stay, and that we would have a "fancy" dinner out tonight at the Restaurant Bellevue, facing right on the harbor. I moved the boat to the nearby marina docks while Carol and Johnnie made our dinner reservation (for two; Johnnie usually dines onboard.)

Cruising the Canals & Rivers of the Netherlands

The short-stay quay and the overnight moorings are operated by the town government, thus we were dealing with the Gemeentehaven Willemstad. And were very happy, a modern marina with good facilities at 37 (euro) cents per meter per night. <u>havenwillemstad@moerdijk.nl</u>

One of the reasons for staying two nights was that the next star fort town on my list, Klundert, is just ten kilometers east of Willemstad and two kilometers inland, easily accessible by bicycle along country roads. So we will cycle the outer ring of star points at Willemstad tonight before dinner, walk the inner ring after dinner and tomorrow off to Klundert.

From Willemstad haven it is just a short walk back to the Volkeraksluizen lock complex for commercial barges; it is interesting to watch the operation of some very large barges.

We started off in that direction on our bicycles, then down the path of the outer star fort ring, through a narrow but dense cover of trees. Occasionally we could glimpse the church spire and the gabled roofs of the taller houses, whetting our appetite for a walk through the town streets. The path took us on three-fourths of the outer ring, past four star points, until we intersected the main road, Landpoortstraat, and found that if we continued it would be a dead-end; at least that's the way I interpreted the sign in Dutch: *Let Op! geen doorgaande wandel route* (Attention! no through walking route.)

We rode into the center of town and came across one of the strange but now routine features of our travels: on many trips and in many places we have encountered a wedding party on the streets, or the bride, groom and a photographer on the rocks by the sea or at some other picturesque setting. This time it was the photo shoot; just as we rode around a parked truck making a beer keg delivery, the bride stepped into our path, followed by the groom and a man carrying a large camera on his chest. We managed to avert disaster as Carol and the bride first screamed, then laughed. The group continued on, no doubt to the picturesque setting of the singel with its beautiful grass berms, a perfect backdrop. I learned later that the 17th-century Mauritshuis at Willemstad is often used for weddings.

I had almost caused the potential accident by sightseeing as I rode, looking down a row of very charming small houses across from the green moat which surrounded a large fenced block. The moat was of course covered in algae; the fenced block, with a thick growth of trees, surrounded the Koepelkerk, the domed church that we had glimpsed from the bike path. From the front gate of the church we turned back to the haven on Voorstaat, the main shopping street. The bike path ran down the center of a paved median, bordered on each side by the typically European rows of poplar trees cut back regularly so that the leaf umbrella was all low and uniform.

Carol has warned me not to write too much about the star forts, because most people will not be as interested as I am. I know that, even our Dutch friends in the USA have never heard of them. The shape is really only apparent when seen in an aerial view and often very little remains of any fortifications. But not here at Willemstad; this is a very historic town and the fortifications have been utilized for centuries; the walls were opened and the garrison left town only after World War I. The Germans built concrete bunkers on the riverfront star point during World War II. The reasons are obvious on a navigation chart, for the town is located at the "corner" of the Volkerak and the Hollands Diep, the primary shipping route between central Holland and the sea at Antwerp or Zeeland.

When you are walking or cycling the paths on the fortifications it makes a wonderful park, with grassy berms, lots of trees, a long waterway but seen in short ponds, a perfect home for ducks and swans. The singel contains the town center in a very pleasant way. At Willemstad there are only two roads that cross the singel to connect into the town, at the haven on the north and on the southeast, into a suburb of new homes. The town has the feeling of isolation from the modern world, without the use of stone walls. Willemstad has some beautiful buildings, five of which are historic landmarks. This town is an excellent example of the star fortress.

The Restaurant Bellevue was actually well above our usual choice, both in terms of elegance and price, but we avoided the overly-formal dining salons by using the terrace tables and kept the cost reasonable by ordering from the à la carte menu: "Dutch Shrimp" croquettes, "Wild Zeeland" oysters and two very good soups: tomato with basil and lobster with tarragon and olive oil. Total cost, with wine by the glass, 70 euros.   restaurantbellevue.nl

On the next day we found the town of Klundert to be unremarkable but we did enjoy a pleasant bike ride along the south shore of the Hollands Diep past plowed fields, bright green pastures scattered with sheep and tiny villages of brick farmhouses. The weather was typical of Holland, scattered clouds with blue skies and strong rays of sunlight.

At the point where we turned away from the water toward the town we took a brief look at a marina; Jachthaven Nordschans can be used as a mooring for Klundert, but the town is over two kilometers south and the marina is primarily intended for long-term docking of sailboats.

In Klundert we rode around the star points on the north and south ends of the canal which bisects the town; as usual they are attractive combinations of grass, trees and water, always with a good path. We returned to the boat directly from the southern tip of the fort, following narrow roads across the fields, a longer route but not one oriented directly into the strong west wind as on the Hollands Diep.

Johnnie

For those readers who are dog-lovers, I will explain a little more about Johnnie. He is 15 years old, a Tibetan Terrier. He is very intelligent, loyal and silent. You would never hear him bark unless someone stepped onto the boat unexpectedly. He has many good traits, the one most important while traveling is that he can "hold it". He is comfortable to wait until we get to our destination, or on a long day at a brief stop during locking, to sprinkle the flora. He goes with us on all walks and to dinner, but on a day when we are riding the bikes he is happy to stay aboard for an undisturbed rest.

Hollands Diep/Amer

We departed Willemstad early the next morning, as there was a steady rain and we would be going upstream against more than half of the flow from two of the major rivers of Europe. There are no locks and the three fixed bridges provide about 10m clearance, so the only delay would be the current. We expected to encounter heavy commercial traffic, but the channel is very wide; it is the widest section of the inland waterways of the Netherlands. We have noted, from the chart, that we must pass on the northern side of a long, narrow island starting about 9km into the trip; the area on the south side is restricted to commercial traffic bound for a heavy concentration of industries on the mainland. The destination is Drimmelen, 27km east, on the Amer river.

I haven't yet made use of the onboard electronics but intend to do so today. Radar would be useful in this situation but we do not have it, only a radar reflector, which looks like a toy and doesn't offer much protection at the top of a mast only ten feet above the water. The boat does have a Lowrance 3300c GPS/chartplotter; it is a discontinued product, I don't know how old it is, but it will provide me with GPS data. The digital charts which have been installed are coastal but there is one that will take us past the above-mentioned island. This will be helpful as the rain is heavy enough to make visual navigation difficult. We also have a Uniden VHF radio with ATIS capability (Automatic Transmission Identification System); we have tuned it to channel 10 to hear the barge skippers but we can understand very little and I didn't intend to use the radio unless necessary.

As it turned out, there was very little current against us. We easily cruised at 8 km/hr (on European inland waters distance is measured in kilometers and speed in km/hour.) We could see barge traffic in plenty of time and made only slight changes to our heading to stay far enough away, sometimes using the "wrong" side of the channel markers, where there was still plenty of depth. In good weather and on a weekend there might have been a sailing regatta to avoid, but that was not the case today.

Four kilometers past the three Moerdijk bridges we angled right, to a due east path, bypassing a group of barges anchored in the river, to enter the mouth of the river Amer. To me this is the mouth of the river Maas, however the Dutch often use other names for the same waterway in different areas. Thus the Meuse river becomes the Maas when it enters the Netherlands from

Belgium, then is called the Bergse Maas west from Heusden and finally the 12km-long Amer west from Geertruidenberg. Oh well, it's their country!

Nearly all of the commercial traffic follows the main channel to the northeast, which is obvious from the silty color to be the flow coming from the Rhine; that portion of the river is named the Nieuwe Merwede. We continued into the Amer, a broad natural river that was originally the southern drainage of the Biesbosch marsh area. We immediately saw on the south shore the harbor at Lage Zwaluwe, where there are marinas and a boatyard if necessary. Since it was not yet noon we stayed with our planned destination at Drimmelen. Either of these towns are a good base from which to explore the Biesbosch national park, which we would be doing for the next few days.

There are several havens, boatbuilders and boat service yards at Drimmelen, in two harbors. We passed the first harbor and entered the second; we had called ahead and tied up quickly at the Biesbosch Marina. www.biesboschmarinadrimmelen.nl

Biesbosch National Park

The rain had stopped so we walked over to the village for lunch and to investigate the many services available for visitors to the Biesbosch. First we visited the Biesbosch Visitors Center to get our bearings and to pick up a navigational map; this is essential, as only certain waterways and mooring places are designated for visits by boat. Later Zijlmans Watersport kept me busy for several hours; I had heard many compliments for the motorcruisers that they build here and I asked for a tour of the boatworks. Then I walked the docks, inspecting their *occasions* (occasion, as in opportunity, is both the Dutch and French term for "used boat for sale"; the term is also applied to cars) and their rental fleet of canoes, kayaks, small motorboats and sailboats. www.zijlmans.nl

We had been canoeists for many years, so we decided to rent a canoe that we could take with us into the park and paddle the shallow and narrow waters. We have always enjoyed the sighting of birds and small mammals that can be approached in a quiet way. Often we have taken our own canoe up an estuary as it gets smaller and smaller, sometimes touching the bank on each side at the same time with our paddles.

The Biesbosch National Park is a green maze of several rivers, islands and a vast network of narrow and wide creeks. The area is one of the largest natural areas in the Netherlands; it is one of the few remaining fresh-water tidal areas in Europe. The Nieuwe Merwede canal divides the National Park equally between the provinces of Noord Brabant and Zuid Holland. The part in Noord Brabant is called the Brabantse Biesbosch. The part in Zuid Holland is divided into the Sliedrechtse Biesbosch and the Dordtse Biesbosch. The park covers an area of approximately 9,000 hectares.

Cruising the Canals & Rivers of the Netherlands

The vegetation mainly consists of willow woods that developed after decades of neglect. These marshy woods alternate with grasslands and reed-lands that have run wild with weeds. The area had known many traditional forms of land use: agriculture, hunting and fishing. Remnants of those days are still there, like the so called 'salmon hut', huts of willow workers and farm workers, duck decoys and the quays and grass dikes with their characteristic pools.

The tidal influence of about two meters was reduced significantly in 1970 after the closing of the open sea connection on the Haringvliet (the waters west of Hollands Diep.) Certain plants and animals disappeared while others took their place. The Biesbosch has always been an important area for birds to rest, forage and breed. This watery area is of such international importance to waterfowl and waders that a large area, the Brabantse Biesbosch, has been officially recognized as a 'Wetland'.

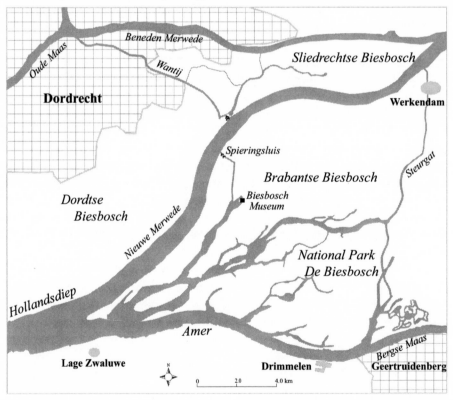

Departing from Drimmelen early in the morning, we went downstream about 4km on the Amer and entered the park on the Gat van de Kerksloot, which passes between two large drinking water reservoirs. The *gat* (a gap or narrow opening, a "cut" through the land) had plenty of depth, over 4 meters, and we easily found a mooring pontoon at a wide point where

18

the gat branched into a series of small waterways. The pontoon was unoccupied and so we claimed it for the day and overnight. Taking our lunch, the three of us set off in the canoe on a route which would take us three or four kilometers into the densely wooded section named *Doktershoek* (Doctor Corner; I never found the story behind the name.)

It was just as we had hoped. We paddled along ever-smaller streams, passing a few other boats tied to the shore in a small bay and occasional motorboats traveling in the other direction, until we found the branch named Vlooiensloot. Soon the channel was only as wide as our canoe was long and the trees arched overhead so that we were paddling in a green tunnel. Many times we stopped paddling and just sat there, enjoying the overhanging moss-covered branches, the quiet and the occasional bird song. Eventually we were halted by a beaver dam; we were very familiar with beavers and their dams, as we had watched them take over a small stream on our own property in western New York state, USA. We were unable to see any, as midday is not a good time for beaver sightings; it's best just as the sun goes down. All of the surrounding ground was marshy and we couldn't walk far into the woods, so we turned the canoe around and returned to the boat along the same route. As we entered the main channel we were startled for a moment by the sight of an approaching two-deck tour boat, but it was traveling slowly and left almost no wake.

We initially had some concerns about the security of our boat, but we really were not surprised to find it just as we had left it (we had taken the precaution of locking our bicycles inside the salon.) The evening was very enjoyable as we sat in the cockpit watching a continual parade of ducks feeding along the shoreline. A few barges could be heard passing along the Amer but the heavy traffic on the Nieuwe Merwede, which makes a steady drone, was too far away to be heard. The night was very still and we appreciated being alone for the first time.

In the morning we moved back up the Amer to an area just across the river from Drimmelen, where we could tie up at a nature walk and then canoe through open savannas for a few hours. Later, after crossing the river into Drimmelen's old harbor, we returned the canoe and set off again to the west, almost to the junction with the Nieuwe Merwede, then turned northeast to our planned mooring at a place named Keet. There we again spent a night alone, other than a few hundred sheep in nearby fields, and this time we did have the drone of barges through the night. But it was steady and not too loud, so we slept well.

There was a reason that I had selected that mooring, which was that in less than an hour we could cruise to the Biesbosch Museum. Displays and videos show how the man from that period earned his living in the area and how by his actions the appearance of the Biesbosch was determined. Cane cutters, rush weavers, hunters, duck and cherry farmers in remote farms earned a meager living. This ancient culture disappeared after the elimination of the high tides which regularly flooded the area.

From the museum it was a short trip north to the Spieringsluis lock, haven and restaurant area. At Spieringsluis I didn't plan to pass through the lock or stay overnight in the haven but I did want to see both places and I had read that the lunch in the restaurant would be good (and it was, as usual in Holland limited to soups, salads and sandwiches, but very good.)

Back on the boat and in less than two hours we were tied up on the Rietplaat, an island in the middle of the Biesbosch National Park. The island is very small but there are walking paths, a beautiful pond in the center of the island and a sandy beach along one side; for us a small version of paradise, especially when other boaters left in late afternoon. We were to spend our third night (and last in the Biesbosch) in isolation.

The island is in the Gat van Kampen; the same waterway became, on our way out of the Biesbosch, the Gat van de Noorderklip, Ruigt of Reugt, Nauw van Paulus and the Steurgat. The last brought us out, via the Spijkerboor, to the river Amer. We stopped at another *natuurpad* for a short walk in the forest near the De Dood bird sanctuary before setting off in earnest for our next destination, Heusden.

We re-entered the river at the point where the Amer becomes the Bergse Maas, with a major change of scene from nature to a large electrical-generating plant at Geertruidenberg with three huge cooling towers. Coal is brought to the plant by barge, dozens of them were in the haven. I skipped the star fort at this city, perhaps a future trip will take me on the Wilhelminakanaal from here to the upper Maas river and we can visit then.

Bergse Maas to Heusden

The Bergse Maas is like a superhighway; the river is uniformly wide, with no islands, it is a smooth sweeping path. There is a reason for this, as the river is not natural, it was dug, and completed only in 1904, to connect the Maas river to the Amer. Views stretch far over the adjacent fields, as the dikes were set well back from the river, creating a broad floodplain to absorb large amounts of water. The path of the river bypasses the Oude Maasje, a small arm of the Maas from Heusden to Geerdtruidenberg. Portions of the old waterway are navigable by small boats; it is scheduled for renovations.

There was both pleasure-boat and commercial traffic on the river, but it was light. Nothing to do but an occasional tug at the wheel. It brought us to Heusden in mid-afternoon, a town that is easy to spot from the river because of the two tall black molens standing on a high fortified wall at the waterfront. We moored at the WSV Heusden; they offer 20 spaces for *passanten* in the singel of this star fort town, plus the pumpout service that we needed. wsvheusden.nl

Noord Brabant Province

Carol is always on the watch for a good butcher; she found one here at Jansen's on the Vismarkt square, near our marina and just off the small old harbor. The bakery was pretty good too, for an afternoon coffee and pastry. We looked at the Restaurant De Klepperman and decided that their menu was broad and would give us the opportunity for something different, at reasonable prices. We returned in the evening and were happy with our choice. restaurantdeklepperman.nl

Cobbled streets and bike/walking paths took us around the preserved fortifications; this town is a beautiful example of the star fort, with some of the brick guard towers rebuilt. We hadn't seen windmills for a while, there were none in the Biesbosch, but our walk around the stars of Heusden brought us past three. These were interesting because, rather than having a rotating cap atop a fixed base cone, the entire structure looks like a box and is perched atop a pivot point, so that it can be turned to face the wind.

Breakfast the next morning at Heusden was something we had been waiting for, an onboard buffet of Dutch/German cold meats, cheeses and bread, accompanied by good strong coffee and finished off with yogurt and fruit. Soon we were off, north across the Bergse Maas river.

Our destination was the city of Gorinchem, ten kilometers northwest. To get there we entered the Heusdenskanaal, 1.5km long, and then the Andelse Maas river, 14.5km, to the river Waal. (The official name of this river is the Afgedamde Maas, meaning "dammed-off". It is commonly known as the Andelse Maas, for the town of Andel.)

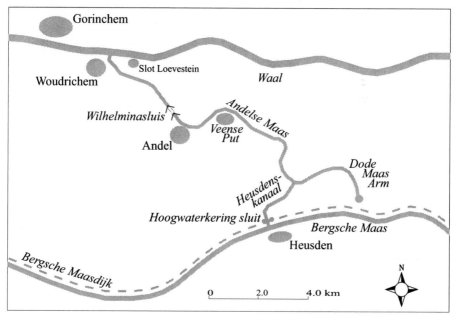

Cruising the Canals & Rivers of the Netherlands

The Heusdenskanaal is obviously a creation of the Dutch, not nature, as is the Bergsche Maasdijk, an earthen berm which runs along the north shore of the Bergse Maas river. (Bergsche is an old-Dutch version of Bergse.) The canal cuts through the dike, under a guillotine-type gate which is lowered at times of high water in the river. We soon came to the Andelse Maas at a T-intersection, the river coming from our right and our destination to the left. But we took an excursion, to the right, to see this arm of the river. (I have seen it on the map, of course, but I need to see it for myself.) We passed a small town and a variety of boats moored at private docks, then came to the expected dead-end: a sandy beach and adjacent parking lot, a public recreational area. Carol accommodated my foolishness by handling the boat while I hopped off, waded ashore and walked up on the dike.

Here I could clearly see what they have done, closing off the old river, which is now named the Dode Maas Arm. Not surprisingly, "Dode" translates as "dead". They have built a new canal, with a storm gate (a *Hoogwaterkering sluit*, a high-water gate) and then closed the original river path with a dike. A perfect example of the Dutch working to control the waters which define their country. Uncontrolled, the Maas in earlier times had crossed over the low-lying land during high water periods and joined with the Waal. Now the river authorities have the ability to close off the flow.

Andelse Maas

With me back on board, we restarted our day and enjoyed a pleasant cruise past green fields, a few towns and an industrial complex looking quite out of place in this environment. Many more small boats were docked along the river, in front of the owner's home or at town docks. The water here is slightly tidal, most of the docks are floating pontoons. A car ferry crossed in front of us from Aalst to Veen, reminding me to watch the chart for warning of these crossings. We had passed two ferry crossings on the Bergse Maas but the ferry boats were not in the river at the time, so I hadn't taken much notice. On the shore at Aalst there is a large shipyard; Neptune Marine builds the Elling line of motorcruisers and ocean yachts here. A sleek white Mediterranean-type yacht up on blocks appeared to be near completion.

The river loops around the Veense Put, a lake on the south side of the river; both an island along the river, which forms the edge of the lake, and a causeway leading to it are lined with side-by-side cottages, each with its own dock and boat. This river is the very epitome of boating country.

The land is flat, and looking across it you can see low villages just barely appearing on the horizon, usually with just the one major spire of the church.

After an hour we came to a lock complex. There was no other traffic on our side of the lock and we had not called on VHF (the chart shows channel 22 for this lock) but the light was green so we went directly in and secured the boat; as usual Carol handled our single line while I remained at the helm. We waited a few minutes for two other boats to join us; the lockkeeper must have known that they were coming. We had not seen them previously because of the curves in the river; perhaps they had called the lockkeeper on VHF or cell phone.

This lock, I learned later, is unique in the Netherlands because it does not have stone or concrete walls; grass banks are the walls of the lock chamber, with a structure of wooden beams erected along each side for the boats and barges to tie against. The structure consists mostly of open spaces between the beams, giving a pleasant view as opposed to the usual closed-in feeling.

Another few kilometers of tree-lined riverbanks to Woudrichem, where we intended to stop for lunch. There is a private harbor adjacent to the factories and then a narrow cut which leads to a second harbor, WSV Woudrichem. For overnight mooring we would stop here, but for a short stay we continued north to the edge of the river Waal and then turned back into the singel canal, part of the original star fortifications. A row of historic barges lined the north bank of the canal; we found the visitor's docks on beyond the barges and tied up at the Gemeente Woudrichem.

This is one of the best-preserved star fort towns and is worth exploring. The ramparts of the old town remain, so we walked them the long way around to arrive at Restaurant De Gevangenpoort, situated in the only remaining gate, just above the junction of the Andelse Maas with the Waal river. Although quite a formal place, they do offer simple lunches at reasonable prices. But after our heavy breakfast we needed no lunch so we didn't go in, especially with Gorinchem just a few kilometers further on.

An excursion that we did not take at Woudrichem is to cross the Andelse Maas by passenger ferry (from a dock near the boat club) and walk a short distance east to the castle Slot Loevestein, a small version of the star fort genre (no docking for private boats.)

We returned to Orion and exited the Woudrichem harbor, pausing at the end of the Andelse Maas to watch for passing barges; there were several, traveling in both directions. The few minutes that we waited gave me time to think of the families living on these working river-cruisers; one had a line of laundry hung out to dry, two others had personal cars stored on the back deck, over the living quarters. I once watched a car being driven from a barge to the quay on precarious-looking wooden planks. Other barges use a hydraulic crane to do the job more elegantly.

We found a gap and moved out into the river; immediately were swept along in the silt-laden flow of the Waal. We had a short ride on the fastest current yet, about 4 km/hr (during high water it can be as high as 6 km/hr.) In just two kilometers, we arrived at Gorinchem, our first stop in Zuid Holland province.

Cruising the Canals & Rivers of the Netherlands

Waterway	From	To	KM	Hours
Schelde-Rijnkanaal	Tholen	Volkerak	18.3	2.3
Volkerak	Schelde-Rijnkanaal	Willemstad	17.4	2.2
Hollandsdiep/Amer	Willemstad	Drimmelen	27.0	3.4
Bergsche Maas	Drimmelen	Heusden	24.0	3.0
Andelse Maas	Heusden	Woudrichem	16.0	2.0

The Great Rivers

Grote Rivieren

Our voyage had started in salt water, on the edge of the North Sea, but for several days we were in fresh water, actually French water, flowing hundreds of kilometers north from France. Soon we would cross into another flow of fresh water, from Germany. The delta of these waters has literally formed the landscape of Holland and they will be our traveling path for the next few weeks. The Dutch call this area the *Grote Rivieren*, the Great Rivers.

My interest in star forts is just an infatuation; my real interest is in rivers, where they come from and how they get to the sea. Rivers are the basis of the European waterways; most of the canals were built to either connect one river to another or to provide a navigable path alongside a non-navigable river. This part of the Netherlands is a great place for me to indulge this interest, because although I can look at a map of Europe and see the Rhine and Meuse rivers flowing north, it isn't as easy to understand how they cross central Holland.

Many rivers around the world split their flow into more than one stream when they flow out to the sea over a flat plain. But it is very unusual, certainly unique in western Europe, that two major rivers come together in a single delta where their flows cross, join and otherwise present a complex picture. That happens here in the Netherlands, with the Rhine and the Meuse.

The sea plays its part as well. Tidal effects can reach halfway across the country. Boaters need to be aware of fresh and salt water, stagnant water and water influenced by tides. Attention to current is of major importance, not just the rate of flow but also the direction of flow, which may not be as it would seem on first glance at a chart. The delta in Holland consists of a diverse and extensive system of large and small waters that together form a whole, a small universe of waterways.

In this chapter I am hoping to make some sense of how these rivers interact. For boaters the most important thing to know is the direction of flow, because the current can be strong in normal weather and stronger yet at times of high water. For instance, lower-powered boats often have difficulty going upstream on the Gelderse IJssel. The skipper needs to recognize that, when told a story about "fighting our way up the IJssel" that the direction is in fact south, not north.

I have rewritten this chapter several times, but still the descriptions can be very confusing; a serious reader will need to refer to the map often. Carol thinks that I should add a warning: "If you are not a river nut, skip this chapter!"

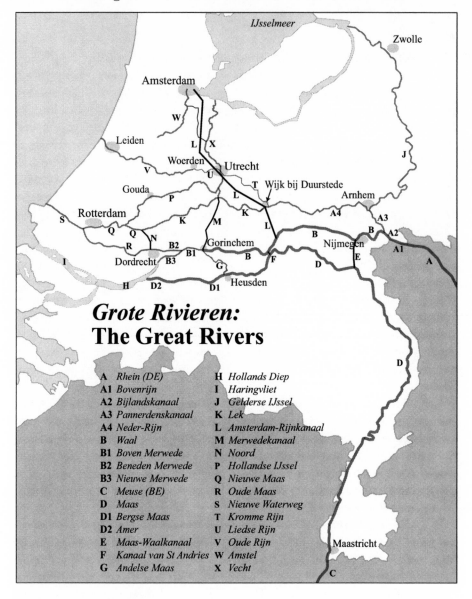

Grote Rivieren: The Great Rivers

A Rhein (DE)	**H** Hollands Diep
A1 Bovenrijn	**I** Haringvliet
A2 Bijlandskanaal	**J** Gelderse IJssel
A3 Pannerdenskanaal	**K** Lek
A4 Neder-Rijn	**L** Amsterdam-Rijnkanaal
B Waal	**M** Merwedekanaal
B1 Boven Merwede	**N** Noord
B2 Beneden Merwede	**P** Hollandse IJssel
B3 Nieuwe Merwede	**Q** Nieuwe Maas
C Meuse (BE)	**R** Oude Maas
D Maas	**S** Nieuwe Waterweg
D1 Bergse Maas	**T** Kromme Rijn
D2 Amer	**U** Liedse Rijn
E Maas-Waalkanaal	**V** Oude Rijn
F Kanaal van St Andries	**W** Amstel
G Andelse Maas	**X** Vecht

Note: The Schelde (Scheldt) is a major river which flows into the delta from Antwerp, Belgium, however it does not mix with the waters of the Rhine & Meuse and thus is not included in the "Grote Rivieren" discussion. The Oosterschelde and Westerschelde through Zeeland are not part of the outflow of the Great Rivers.

The Great Rivers

Map	Waterway	From	To	KM
A1 A2	Bovenrijn/ Bijlandskanaal	Germany	Pannerdenskanaal	10
A3	Pannerdenskanaal	Waal	Gelderse IJssel	6.0
A4	Neder-Rijn	Gelderse IJssel	Amsterdam-Rijnkanaal	50
B	Waal	Pannerdenskanaal	Gorinchem	86
B1	Boven Merwede	Gorinchem	Werkendam	8.8
B2	Beneden Merwede	Werkendam	Dordrecht	15
B3	Nieuwe Merwede	Werkendam	Hollandsdiep	18
D	Maas	Belgium	Heusden	227
D1	Bergsche Maas	Heusden	Geertruidenberg	25
D2	Amer	Geertruidenberg	Hollandsdiep	12
E	Maas-Waalkanaal	Maas	Waal	13
F	Kanaal van St Andries	Maas	Waal	2.1
G	Andelse Maas	Heusdenskanaal	Waal	17
J	Gelderse IJssel	Neder-Rijn	IJsselmeer	118
K	Lek	Noord	Amsterdam-Rijnkanaal	62
L	Amsterdam-Rijnkanaal	Waal	Amsterdam	72
M	Merwedekanaal	Gorinchem	Utrecht	35
N	Noord	Dordrecht	Lek	8.6
P	Hollandse IJssel	Nieuwegein	Nieuwe Maas	46
Q	Nieuwe Maas	Oude Maas	Noord	24
R	Oude Maas	Dordrecht	Nieuwe Maas	30
S	Nieuwe Waterweg	Oude Maas	North Sea	21
U	Liedsche Rijn	Utrecht	Harmelen	6.0
V	Oude Rijn	Harmelen	North Sea	38
W	Amstel	Aarkanaal	Amsterdam	26
X	Vecht	Utrecht	IJsselmeer	40

Rijn/Rhein/Rhine (Dutch/German/English)

The Rhine river rises in the Swiss Alps and flows north, forming the western borders of Liechtenstein and Austria, then fills the Bodensee (Lake of Constance) between Switzerland and Germany. Kilometer measurements start at the German city of Konstanz, as the river leaves the Bodensee, and continue to the North Sea, at KM 1031. The river flows west as the northern border of Switzerland (except for some minor incursions of the Swiss border into Germany) then north, forming the eastern border of France as it passes by Strasbourg. The head of navigation for vessels on the waterway network is 21km upriver from Basel, Switzerland. The Rhine is canalized along the French border, then at Iffezheim (Germany) it continues as an open river, with no locks, to the Dutch border. The first kilometer post in the Netherlands is KM 856.5, near Lobith.

The main stream of the Rhine flows almost due west across Holland as the Waal. The flow is unhindered by weirs or locks, all the way to the sea. In the late 18th century the Pannerdensch Canal was dug to connect the Waal with the Neder-Rijn/IJssel junction at Arnhem. This short canal is for the convenience of shipping but it also plays a major role in the removal of rainwater and meltwater by directing it onto the IJssel and thus to the IJsselmeer, as well as down the various Rijn river branches described below. Managers can also open gates to allow water into the smaller rivers, such as the Linge, as well as flooding the open spaces and fields between the two major waterways to protect the towns downstream.

The Neder-Rijn originally branched northwestward from the Rhine while still in Germany; near what is now the city of Arnhem NL it split off a north-flowing river, the Gelderse IJssel, then continued west. The main flow southwesterly from the town of Wijk bij Duurstede became the river Lek, which flows on to Rotterdam and the sea. There are two weir/lock installations on this flow, one on the Neder-Rijn and another on the Lek.

There are smaller branches of the Rhine which are interesting; we will travel on some of these later, without noticing that the water actually came from the Rhine. For instance, on an 1849 map of the Netherlands the "R.Rhine" branches to the north off of the Neder-Rijn at the town of Wijk bij Duurstede, just slightly east of the Amsterdam-Rijnkanaal intersection. It passes through the city of Utrecht, then Woerden, Alphen aan den Rijn, Leiden and on to the sea at Katwijk. This stream is named the Kromme (twisting) Rijn east of Utrecht, the Leidse (to Leiden) Rijn from Utrecht to Woerden and the Oude (old) Rijn from Woerden to the sea

There are other, smaller branches of the Rhine which feed the river Vecht and even the Amstel, thus the flow of the Rhine goes as far north as Amsterdam. The river Hollandse IJssel, a branch of the Lek until it was closed off by a dam in 1292, flows from the Utrecht area to Gouda and Rotterdam.

The Great Rivers

Meuse/Maas (French/Dutch)

The Meuse river doesn't have as impressive a source as does the Rhine; the Meuse begins as a tiny stream in the agricultural fields and wooded rolling hills of eastern France, 180 kilometers to the west of the Rhine at Strasbourg and 100km northeast of Dijon. It traces a convoluted, sinuous path until it becomes the Canal de La Meuse, flowing north between the Champagne and Lorraine regions of France. Navigation on this canal begins at the Canal de La Marne au Rhin, the east-west waterway from Paris to Strasbourg, and continues 272 km to the Belgian border. Still named Meuse in the French-speaking province of Wallonie, it is joined from the west by a major tributary, the Sambre, another river from a French source. The river enters the Netherlands at Maastricht, becoming the Maas river. The overall length of the Meuse/Maas is 935 kilometers. Kilometer measurements in the Netherlands start from 0 at the BE/NL border and end at the junction with the Hollands Diep, KM 262.5.

The Limburgse Maas is the section between the cities of Maastricht and Nijmegen. It is non-navigable from Maastricht to Maasbracht; fifty kilometers of tight curves on the natural Maas are bypassed by the 35km straight-line Julianakanaal. At KM 165, south of the city of Nijmegen, the Maas-Waalkanaal connects the two rivers at the point where the Maas turns to the west.

Now the three rivers, Maas, Waal and Neder-Rijn, flow westward across the Netherlands, through a valley between higher land on the north and south, their paths almost parallel. They are connected to each other again as the land flattens to sea level in the center of the country; the Amsterdam-Rijnkanaal connects the Neder-Rijn with the Waal, while the Kanaal van St Andries connects the Waal with the Maas, at the point where their natural paths almost touch. Another north-south connection is centered on Gorinchem, where the Andelse Maas connects the Maas to the Waal and the Merwedekanaal connects on to the Neder-Rijn/Lek.

The names of the rivers change here: Maas becomes Bergse Maas at km post 226.5, Waal becomes Boven (upper) Merwede at km post 952.5 and Neder-Rijn becomes Lek as it crosses the Amsterdam-Rijnkanaal at km post 929.

West of Gorinchem the Waal splits into the Beneden (lower) Merwede, flowing due west to Dordrecht, and the Nieuwe Merwede, flowing southwest into the Hollands Diep. The Nieuwe Merwede was dug by opening up small kills and ponds through the Biesbosch in 1874 to give the Waal quicker drainage into the Hollandse Diep, as an alternate to the constrained channels past Dordrecht and Rotterdam.

The Maas, known as the Amer for its last 10km stretch along the south edge of the Biesbosch, joins the Nieuwe Merwede as they both flow into the Hollandse Diep. Thus the Hollandse Diep brings 60% of the flow from the Rhine and the Meuse into the Haringvliet and then into the North Sea. The dam and lock at the mouth of the Haringvliet separate the sea from the rivers; water managers use the lock to keep the Haringvliet fresh water or to allow some tidal flow in from the sea.

At Dordrecht the Beneden Merwede changes its name to Oude Maas after a three-way junction with the Noord. The Noord joins the river Lek to form the Nieuwe Maas. West of Rotterdam the Oude Maas flows into the Nieuwe Maas, the two becoming the Nieuwe Waterweg to the North Sea.

The Historical Changes of Course

The St. Elizabeth flood of 1421 created the Biesbosch and substantially altered the ancient course of the tidal rivers. The waters of the Waal and Maas were redirected from their courses past Rotterdam and Dordrecht to the more southern estuaries as an outlet to the sea. Only the water of the Lek flowed through the northernmost riverbed, which later was called the Nieuwe Maas. Originally the Nieuwe Maas continued southwest from Rotterdam and joined the Oude Maas to enter the North Sea near Brielle. Due to silting at the mouth of the Nieuwe Maas, a cut through the dunes at Hook of Holland was required to make a new connection to the North Sea; this connection was called the Nieuwe Waterweg. The original mouth of the Nieuwe Maas river near Brielle was dammed in 1950. The completion dates of some of these waterways show a bit of the history:

1872 Nieuwe Waterweg, Rotterdam to North Sea
1874 Nieuwe Merwede, Gorinchem to Hollands Diep
1892 Merwedekanaal, Gorinchem to Lek river and Utrecht
1904 Bergsche Maas/Amer, Heusden to Hollands Diep
1927 Maas-Waalkanaal, connecting Maas and Waal at Nijmegen
1952 Amsterdam-Rijnkanaal, Waal and Neder-Rijn to Amsterdam

Locks/Current/Water Levels

The flow in the Maas has been tamed by a lock at the Belgian border, a bypass canal with three locks and another six locks on the Maas below Maasbracht. In comparison, the Waal river and the IJssel are open, there are no locks at all and the current is therefore faster. The Neder-Rijn/Lek has two locks but the current is similar to the Waal. The current in each river will vary with the season and with the amount of rainfall in each watershed; When planning a trip, attention needs to be paid to the time of year and the weather conditions far upstream. "Normal" flow rates are approximately:

Maas	3-5 km/hr
Waal & Neder-Rijn/Lek	4-6 km/hr
IJssel (normal)	5-6 km/hr
IJssel (high water)	7-8 km/hr

The Great Rivers

Tidal waters

Tidal effects are seen on the Maas and the three Merwede rivers as far inland as the Andelse Maas, on the Lek up to the Hagestein weir/lock east of the Merwedekanaal and up the Hollandse IJssel to Gouda. However, tidal water does not mean salt water; locks and flood gates control the flow direction of the rivers and the connecting waterways such that fresh water/salt water separation is maintained. The Westerschelde, Oosterschelde and Grevelingenmeer are salt water, while the Volkerak, Haringvliet and Hollands Diep are fresh water. At Rotterdam, the Nieuwe Waterweg and the havens of Europoort are salt water but the Nieuwe Maas and Oude Maas are fresh water.

Websites

The Dutch people have worked for centuries to "manage" these waters, building dikes, groins, dams, locks and even digging entirely new paths. For the past 2000 years, the inhabitants of the Netherlands have often had to cope with flood disasters, both from the sea and from the rivers. History and current status can be viewed on these informative and useful websites:

> History and management of floods from the sea
> www.deltawerken.com

> History and management of inland waterways
> www.rijkswaterstaat.nl/water

Charts

The Great Rivers are shown on these ANWB charts:

ANWB *L* - Grote Rivieren Oost
(German border west to Amsterdam-Rinkanaal)
ANWB *K* - Grote Rivieren Midden
(Amsterdam-Rinkanaal west to Dordrecht)
ANWB *J* - Grote Rivieren West
(Dordrecht west to the North Sea)
ANWB *M* - Limburgse Maas
(Maastricht north to Nijmegen)

Gorinchem

We departed from Woudrichem into what I thought at the time was the Waal river; I later realized that this was the point where the name changes to Boven Merwede. We quickly reached the mouth of the river Linge and turned north; we immediately saw the slot in the concrete wall of the *jachtensluis*, which will take us into the Passantenhaven Lingehaven. This lock is much smaller than those that we have passed through in our first ten days of travel, only 4.5 meters wide and 32 meters long; our boat fills half of the lock. Another similar motorcruiser followed us in from the river, the lockkeeper closed the outer gate with no delay and moved us through into the haven in just a few minutes.

The lockkeeper is also the harbormaster; he directed to an open slip and then gave us the full run-down on the facilities of his haven and of the neighborhood.

The Lingehaven is an enlarged section of the river Linge at the southern end of its cut through the city. The harbormaster pointed out that the fixed bridge above the haven is at 2.8 meters clearance, so many boats need to exit the way they came in, even to continue north; the alternative Merwedekanaal passes through the city with BB opening bridges. We will be okay on the Linge, at 2.45 meters height. More slips are located beyond this bridge. There are 85 slips in all; water and electricity are available at the docks, a new building houses showers, toilets and laundry facilities. With all of these services and an interesting medium-sized city around us, we decided to stay here for a few days.

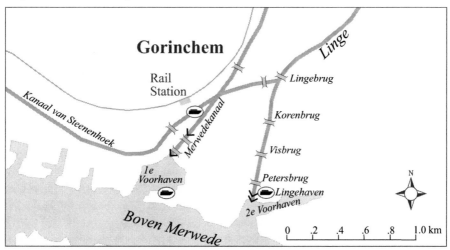

Gorinchem is on my star-fort list but we came here because it is a popular stop for waterway travelers, both because of its location and its services. It is a major waterway junction on the Great Rivers, centrally located in the Netherlands; travelers pass through here to go to or from each of the four quadrants of the country. It is a great place to stop and regroup, whether you are coming or going. Quite a few foreign visitors winter onboard here, before setting off to the south for Belgium and France.

To the southwest is Zeeland and the Flanders province of Belgium, with routes south into France. To the northwest is Zuid Holland, Noord Holland and Utrecht, encompassing the most well-known destinations in Holland. To the northeast is the river IJssel, the only waterway on that side of the country connecting to Friesland, Groningen, Drenthe and Overijssel provinces. To the southeast is the river Maas (and an alternative canal route) leading south into the Wallonie province of Belgium and to the northeastern corner of France. Along with the various river routes, the Merewedekanaal leads north from Gorinchem directly to Utrecht and Amsterdam.

The city is big enough to have a lot to offer, while still small enough for a feeling of community with the three marinas. Each are within walking distance of restaurants and shops, as well as a fully-stocked chandlery near the Lingehaven.

Dutch/English Language

Writing of the friendly harbormaster reminds me to say something about the language. The language used in the Netherlands is "Nederlands" (Dutch); it is related to, but not the same as, Deutsch (German.) It is used on all written signs and documents; some of these will include a translation into German, because of the large number of visitors from Germany, but not a translation into English. But English is widely spoken as a second language and some English slang words are used on business signs. The harbormaster spoke to us in very clear English.

Personally, I have become reasonably competent in reading written Nederlands, at least to get the gist of a sign or document. But even when I practice a spoken word it almost always cannot be understood by a Dutch person. Gorinchem is a good example: I had been advised to say "khorekum" and thought I could do it fairly well, but it has only led to blank looks from my Dutch friends. It's even worse when I attempt to say the town of Grou, which draws laughter (it is something like a deep-throated "hrow".) I have given up trying to say the name of the city 's Hertogenbosch, using instead the alternate name Den Bosch, pronounced pretty much just as it is written.

Roger Van Dyken, author of "Barging in Europe", says this about VHF radio communications: "Lockkeepers in any (European) country are highly proficient in what they do, but that does not mean it extends to use of the English language; most are accustomed to talking in rapid and clipped "professional" exchanges developed over years of conversing with barge captains, so as to render it largely unintelligible."

In fact some lockkeepers and bridgekeepers do not speak English, but in practice it doesn't matter. The red/green light system described earlier is used everywhere and is a reliable indicator of what you should do. Also there are usually some local boaters traveling nearby, just "do what they do".

It will be helpful to pay attention to the wording of waterway signs and to become accustomed to them. International symbols are used, they should be learned and a poster can be kept handy but there are also useful signs in text, such as wachtsteiger (waiting post, as at a lock) and bezoekers (visitors.)

Earlier in this book I reported on seeing a sign: *Let Op!* meaning Attention! The first time that I had seen one of those was while driving a rental car through a parking lot and saw such signs at each "speed bump' (ridge of asphalt placed across the lane.) I followed the advice of the sign and at each point I "let up" on the accelerator pedal.

Gorinchem

By the time that we had gotten settled into our slip we were ready for a short dog-walk and then an early dinner; while coming from the river into the lock it was impossible to miss Restaurant de Poort right at the lock entrance (poort means city gate, not a harbor.) So we planned to return there after walking east along the old walls of the fort. There are steps up from the haven promenade to the top of the wall, where the view reaches south across the wide river. Following the turns in the ramparts, we were soon at the impressive Dalempoort (Dalem Gate), the only remaining gate of the original four built when the wall was completed in 1609. It is a well-preserved brick building, a two-story square topped by a steep tile roof and clock tower, cupola and finally a weathervane. The arched opening under the gate leads to a small cobbled lane which crosses the singel on a narrow bridge and then turns east, a two kilometer link to the village of Dalem.

A short distance along the wall brought us to the grassy star-point home of the De Hoop molen, protected by two ancient cannon aimed toward the river. Beyond the river we can see the line of trees which mark the ramparts of Woudrichem; surely these are the two closest star fort towns that I will visit. A classic barge passed by between them, westbound on the river.

Our turnaround point was the highway to Dalem; half a dozen bicyclists are riding into the city from the village, another group headed out; wewere starting to get used to this common sight in Holland.

On the other side of the road I noticed a sign which reminded me of another comment on language: the sign read *Fietspad* which helped me jump to the conclusion that it meant "footpath". But I realized that is wrong, for the footpath is a smaller walkway to the right, marked by a symbol of an adult and child walking hand-in-hand, while the wider path to the left is in fact a bicycle path. I can't translate the text below the fietspad sign, but I interpreted it to mean "no pedestrians allowed". (...pad = path, pathway)

Cruising the Canals & Rivers of the Netherlands

The Netherlands is well-known for the ubiquitous bicycle paths, in cities and in the countryside. The fact that all is flat here of course stimulates cycling in the first place, however the Dutch seem to make a point out of creating the infrastructure as well. If you find yourself cycling where there is no bicycle path, you are in principle allowed to bike on the street but of course you have to use common sense. Sometimes it is obvious that you shouldn't! You will know that you are on the wrong path if you hear:

"Dit is een voetpad. Hier mag je niet fietsen!"

("This is a foot path. You are not allowed to bike here!")

(Fietsen = to bike Fietser = bicyclist Voetpad = foot path)

The view from the restaurant De Poort is very nice, however we have just seen it all up close; the food is mediocre and somewhat overpriced, so we didn't return during our stay; there are enough other choices along the central-city streets.

The next day was Sunday, a good opportunity to walk the streets of the city without car, bicycle and pedestrian traffic. People were out, of course. We followed a small well-dressed group who have crossed the Petersbrug near our dock on their way to church. The church is in the same central square as the Gorcums Museum, whose banners invited us to the current art and history displays.

One-half block off the square we found a very beautiful tall, narrow building which later research showed to be *Dit is in Bethlehem*. The facade is highly decorated with stone carvings and multicolored shutters; it contains several sculptures, one them a Christmas scene with the words which became the name of the building. It dates from 1566 and had previously housed the museum, which moved to the old city hall when a new structure was built elsewhere.

Wandering north through the streets we eventually came to the northern ramparts and the windmill Nooit Volmaakt; it was built in 1717 and rebuilt after a fire in 1889, unfortunately, as the name says in Dutch, the work was "Never Perfect".

We walked back to our boat along the Linge river. Moored on the banks of the river outside the ramparts, near the windmill, are ten sailing barges of various sizes and styles, an informal museum of barge history that can be viewed from a path on the riverbank and from the bridge Korenbrug.

The east bank of the river is a promenade; boats are moored the length of the river on this side, while across the narrow river are the backs of houses which line Kortendijk and Langendijk streets. Seeing the back doesn't mean that we were seeing the "bad" side of these houses, they are quite good-looking and of course well maintained. Some have balconies, or at least large windows, overlooking the river; a few have a small dock. I hesitate to call it the "Venice of the Netherlands" but it does remind me of that city, in the way that the houses are directly on the water, no street or sidewalk in front, and the brick walls run straight down into the water.

On our side of the river we strolled along a cobble-paved quay, lined with flower-boxes and urns, overflowing with vines in blossom, along the quay and on the railings of the bridges. Yellow black-eyed Susan vine (it is thunbergia, Carol tells me) are the theme throughout. It was a very welcoming scene.

To our left is a row of trees, with parking for cars and bicycles, then a brick-paved street lined by brick townhouses and shops. This is not only a nice place to visit, it would also be a very comfortable place to live. (I did spot a *Te Koop* sign on one of the houses backed up to the river, however the house was not even as wide as our boat.)

As we walked along these ten blocks we enjoyed seeing the continuous passage of boaters on their Sunday cruise. Some of them will turn around at the lock, they are just doing their sightseeing on the water, as we are on the sidewalk. Others will pass through the lock into the river, perhaps to visit Woudrichem.

Later in the afternoon, as we relaxed aboard Orion, we saw the electric rental boats returning. These small open *sloepen* are rented from a dock in the Lingehaven and used by families or groups to tour the city or to travel out on the river Linge (range is seven hours, at about 6 km/hr.) We considered doing this, as we do have plans for a round-trip into the countryside on the Linge, but it seemed an unnecessary expense because we already have a suitable boat, and we saw a sign at the rental office showing a sad-faced dog with the words "ik mag er niet in" meaning "I may not". No dogs, no us!

The rental boats do not require a skipper's license, so I was amused when I viewed their website www.ecorecreatie.com and translated the page with this result from Google: "From Gorinchem port may be at risk Arkel, Kedichem, Heukelem, Leerdam and Fort Asperen". These towns on the Linge may be at risk but I don't think that a whole lot of damage can be done!

Monday is market day, from 8:00 to 12:30 in the central Grote Markt square. We went early to get the best choice of biologische (organic) fruits and vegetables. Carol enjoys her olives, so she was glad to find a booth with a wide selection. Household goods, tools and even window drapes were offered in other booths. Since we had not eaten, just our first coffee onboard, the waffle vendor was a great find.

A walk around the western edge of the city was our afternoon agenda. We started out on the aptly-named Buiten de Waterpoort (outside the water-gate) with the stone rampart on one side and a park between us and the main river. It was a short walk to the riverbank, where we sat and watched several commercial barges rumble by. A few years earlier we had lived for six months on the Seine west of Paris, where this same scene was on our daily schedule.

From there we toured the marina WV De Merwede and decided that this is also an excellent place to moor in Gorinchem, although not as interesting and pleasant as the Lingehaven.

We continued around the points of the star fortifications, at the outside base of the two-tiered grass berms. At the fourth point we came to the lock used by barges and large boats to enter the Merwedekanaal. As expected it was large and modern but the ultra-modern, swoopy, structure for the lockkeeper's station was even more impressive, not the usual utilitarian box. From the quarter-view it resembled a Darth Vader mask. I noticed that a series of vertical columns of boxes inset into the wall held bollards, along with a bollard atop the lock wall above each column. This is the most convenient for our system of securing to a single bollard, moving higher or lower as necessary.

North of the lock we could look westward across the water and see a long row of permanently-moored *woonboten* (houseboats), one of many such groups of residences to be seen in the Netherlands. There was one more star point, then the windmill Nooit Volmaakt which we had seen the day before, so we turned back through the city streets, past townhouses and shops to the Lingehaven. We passed the museum and did want to visit, but it was closed on Monday. We decided to go there Tuesday morning, then leave for our excursion on the Linge.

Gorcums Museum proved to be worthy of a morning's visit. A "timeline" of the city's history shows how the city developed from a simple settlement on the river to important fortress. Napoleon called the city "the key to Holland." Exhibitions of work by many artists are displayed; not Rembrandt, Van Gogh and Vermeer of the big-city museums, but less well known local artists such as Abraham Bloemaert, Gerard van Kuyll and Jan Meerhout. On the first floor of the museum the Artotheek leases contemporary art to individuals.

After seeing most of Gorinchem on our walks we agreed that this city is an excellent place to visit on a cruise and would be ideal for an over-winter stay onboard. The municipal government encourages this, as the haven is empty of short-stay boats during the winter. The facilities are available year-around and the rates are reasonable. Their website has full information: www.veerdienstgorinchem.nl/lingehaven_nieuws.htm

Linge river

We left the city northbound on the Linge river; as we passed by the classic barges I took advantage of a fueling station on the east side, topping off our diesel tank. The canalized river leads past an industrial area and under an autoroute, a highway and a rail bridge then breaks out into green fields and woods. There is a long loop around some lagoons, probably where sand had been extracted, then we were eastbound: on our left is the short canal at Arkel which connects to the Merewedekanaal, followed by three marinas for local boats. A dike on our right allows us to see only the church steeple in the town of Spijk but on our left there are fields dotted with sheep, with the dike located further beyond. Soon we realize that this will be the continuing pattern, for the towns and agricultural fields are protected from high water on the river by dikes but they are back from the river itself. The river turns through meadows and woodlands which are occasionally flooded. There is a town dock and a picnic area at Heukelum, which we didn't need and passed by.

But we did stop soon after at Leerdam, because our son is a glassblower and cast-glass artist and we wanted to see this "glass town". There was space at the town dock and we set off on a walking tour. We didn't need to view any of the demonstrations and exhibits, having seen glassblowing done many times. We just had a general curiosity about the town; it is a tourist attraction where buses bring visitors by the hundreds, so we didn't linger.

We cruised just a bit further around the next curve in the river to Asperen, where we tied up for the night at a small riverside park. The view on the other side of the river was of woods, wildflowers and fields irrigated by a grid of tiny canals. A walk along the village waterfront after dinner brought us to a lock and bridge; we learned that the road leads to Fort Asperen, which we planned to visit the next day.

I had read about Fort Asperen and quickly became interested. It's not a star fort, in fact it is a round tower, one of several built much later than the star forts, in 1840-1860. It is part of the Nieuwe Hollandse Waterlinie, the defense system in which the Dutch purposely inundated fields so that approaching armies could not pass.

The Netherlands has two historic "Water Lines", the Old and New. The (old) Hollandse Waterlinie was started in 1672 to protect Amsterdam against the invading armies of Louis XIV, when lowlands south of the Zuiderzee were put under water. With armed forts guarding the narrow country lanes the relatively small Dutch army could successfully stop the invasion. In the 19th century Netherlands was under French administration; during this period Napoleon laid the foundations for a new defensive system of the future "Kingdom of the Netherlands". The main defense was the flooding of certain areas to a depth of 30 to 50 inches. This was enough to keep men and horses from easily crossing the fields, but was shallow enough to prevent the use of boats.

Fort Asperen, Fort Vuren and other forts were part of the Waterlinie, stretching from Naarden and Muiden on the Zuiderzee to the Biesbosch at Werkendam. On April 12, 1940 the order for inundations was given for the last time, but the Nieuwe Hollandse Waterlinie was not resistant to modern warfare. The German Luftwaffe crossed the 19th-century defense work without problems and dropped their parachutists far behind the Line. Thus the military usefulness of the water line was over.

Our history lesson completed, we headed further upstream on the Linge. Now we were in dairy country, with black and white cows in most of the fields rather than, or along with, the ubiquitous sheep. We stopped for lunch at the dock of the restaurant De Twee Gezellen in Rumpt, a good choice not just for the very good food but also the opportunity to see a charming, peaceful village. www.detweegezellen.nl

In this region most of the houses are built on ground lower than the dikes and so the river is not a part of the view, but here there was a row of beautiful houses set right atop the dike, overlooking the river and the fields on the other side. Our after-lunch walk was not long in distance but took quite a while, as we enjoyed the sights of houses and gardens.

Three more sweeping S-curves in the river and we were at Geldermalsen, the upper limit of navigation on the Linge. We tied up at municipal docks near the downtown shopping district. This is an unremarkable town, more like the suburb of a major city than a town in the countryside; we stayed here overnight and in the morning started back down the river.

Above Geldermalsen the river is navigable (for small boats only) another two kilometers, then again for three km on a tributary, the Korne, to the village of Buren. Out of interest I followed the line of the Linge east on the map and was surprised to see that it begins over 50 km away near the intersection of the Waal and Neder-Rijn rivers. At the Amsterdam-Rijnkanaal it supplies that canal and also crosses under on its path to the west; in periods of high water this junction is used to relieve the Waal by dumping water into the Linge.

Soon after leaving Geldermalsen we stopped for a brief tour of the Jachtwerf van Rijnsoever Deil BV, which I had seen previously as we passed by. This is a boatyard that builds custom sailing barges, which seems rather unusual on this narrow river in dairy country. The completed barges are to be found sailing the open waters of the IJsselmeer and other inland seas.

The rest of the day was a nonstop cruise down the Linge, then at Gorinchem we turned west onto the Kanaal van Steenenhoek, which parallels the Boven Merwede and then joins the Beneden Merwede. Although we weren't far from Dordrecht, our planned destination, we stopped overnight at WSV De Snap, a boating club marina at the end of the canal, just inside a lock at the river. There is a busy (and noisy) autoroute nearby, but better that than the busy boat traffic into Dordrecht; we will tackle that early in the morning.

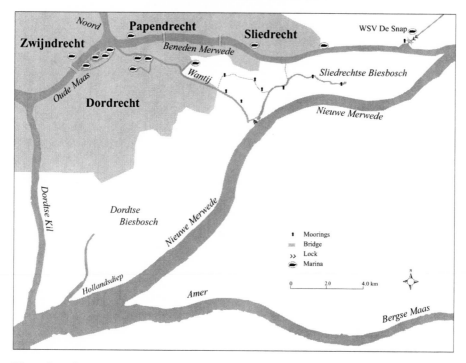

Dordrecht

Dordrecht is perhaps the most heavily-industrialized area of the Netherlands, especially if the neighboring cities of Zwijndrecht, Papendrecht and Sliedrecht are included. The island of the Dordrecht municipality is surrounded by five well-used waterways: Beneden Merwede, Nieuwe Merwede, Hollands Diep, Dordtse Kil and Oude Maas. A smaller waterway, the Wantij, cuts through the eastern side of the island, separating off the Sliedrechtse Biesbosch. Another major waterway, the Noord, flows north from the old city center, between Zwijndrecht and Papendrecht (...drecht means ford, river crossing.)

The combination of waterways and industries means that these waters may be the busiest in the Netherlands. But that doesn't mean that pleasure boaters don't use them as well, they do, in the hundreds. There are four yacht clubs in the old city area of Dordrecht alone, and several more scattered around the four cities. The clubs welcome visiting boaters.

We planned to stay one overnight and wanted to tour the narrow streets of the old city, between the Oude Maas and the arc of two tiny canals, so we looked only at the harbors nearby, inside the canals. The most famous landmark is the Grote Kerk, so we selected the docks of WSV Maartensgat, which is in the Leuvehaven, a small harbor next to the church. For better or worse, the entrance to the harbor is right behind the water taxi terminal, adding to the traffic to be watched out for. At least those boats would help lead us to the entrance.

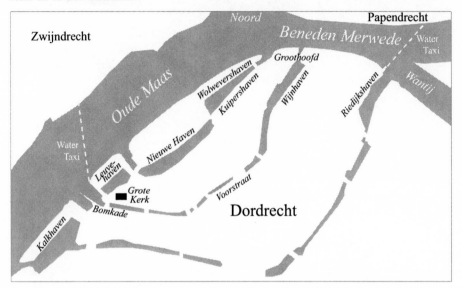

It turned out that traffic was busy but orderly, so we simply kept to the right and watched carefully, turning across the channel behind one of the water taxis crossing from Zwijndrecht to Dordrecht. It was a little stressful but easy enough.

The harbor is entered through a lifting bridge, the Mazelaarsbrug, which is operated by the harbormaster. Rather than ask for an opening immediately, we decided to tie-up temporarily at the wachtsteiger on the Bomkade (...kade means quay); we could leave the boat there for a short stay while we walked over to the docks and looked over our assigned slip. Carol waited there while I went back for the boat, as the bridge was lifting. Within 15 minutes of leaving the river we were settled at the dock. This harbor is sometimes locally called the Lange Geldersekade haven, after the street on the south side; the street on the north side is the Maartensgat. Their website is www.maartensgat.nl

The Grote Kerk tower rises directly from the south quay of our harbor, so we first went there and climbed to the top to view the layout of the area we will be walking for a day or so. The view of the rivers that we had just piloted was of course excellent, but even more important was to see the various harbors, the canals and the streets of the old city.

The city lies along the southern banks of the Beneden Merwede/Oude Maas rivers, a smooth curve with its crest at the point where the river Noord splits off and flows north to Rotterdam. This is the Groothoofd (waterfront), the northern tip of the old city of Dordrecht. Immediately to the west is the entrance to the historic commercial harbor, known as

Wolwevershaven on the north quay and Kuipershaven on the south quay. Barges enter through the opening bridge (BB) Damiatebrug. Although connected by water to the next harbor at the western end, traffic is blocked by the low fixed bridge Roobrug.

That next harbor is named Nieuwe Haven on charts and called Tweede Haven (second harbor) locally. Boats enter from the Oude Maas into the western end of the harbor, through BB Engelenburgerbrug, on a small entrance channel which can be difficult to see when approaching the way we did, westbound. A landmark is the modern brick building on the right-hand side of the opening, a four-story brick structure with three steep gables, and usually a red fireboat moored on the left side. This is the largest of the harbors in the old city, home of the Kon. Dordrechtsche R & ZV, the royal rowing and sailing club, which describes itself as "A friendly marina in the historic center of Dordrecht". Visiting boats are welcome. www.kdrzv.nl

The next harbor to the west is ours, the Leuvehaven. It is not connected by water to these first two, but at the entrance on the Bomkade, where we first stopped for a few minutes, the inner canal Voorstraat passes under the Leuvebrug. The canal arcs through the city, back to the river at the Groothoofd. The northern section of the inner canal, near the river, is the Wijnhaven; two more marinas are located here, WSV Drechtstad and WSV 't Wantij.

A second canal passes through the old city: the outer canal follows a similar arcing path, starting on the west in the commercial harbor Kalkhaven and ending in the Riedijkshaven, at the mouth of the small river Wantij. The water taxi to Papendrecht is based here, but there are no marinas at either end of this canal.

We set out to see each of these harbors on foot, starting along the Nieuwe Haven northside street. This is a large marina to be nestled into an old city; a footbridge crosses the middle of the harbor, the Lange Ijzeren Brug (long iron bridge.) There are a variety of boats; motorcruisers, sailboats, sailing barges and Luxemotor barges. At the far end of the harbor we found the Eetcafe 't Vlak and stopped to read the menu. It is a tapas bar, on the ground floor of a handsome building which we later found was built in 1616. Tapas are Spanish, a wide range of small dishes of meat, fish and salads. This seemed good to us, we would return for dinner.

Walking on to the northeast we followed the Wolwevershaven, enjoying the sight of more than a dozen classic barges, both motor and sail. This is definitely the best side of the harbor, the Kuipershaven on the south side is now a parking lot. There is a landmark on that side, a boat lifting structure that appears to have been in service for a good many years. A sign stretching across the top states: "Machinefabriek L. STRAATMAN Ketelmakerij".

Cruising the Canals & Rivers of the Netherlands

At the river end of the harbor is a very beautiful opening bridge, the Damiatebrug. The span is split across the middle, forming a slight v-shape; the two halves are lifted to each side by graceful black arms. It seems dainty as compared to many other of these bridges, which have a massive look.

We walked over the Damiatebrug and out to the 3-rivers junction on the Groothoofd. It is a beautiful sweeping view, you can look far down the Noord river to watch the barges chug on toward Rotterdam. The waterfront here is marked by two landmarks easily seen from the rivers, the old hotel Bellevue and next to it the archway of an old city gate under a tall red-brick tower with a green-roofed cupola, topped by a sharp spire..

Turning back along the Taankade we passed by a long line of boats moored on both sides of the Wijnhaven, most of them smaller boats than those in the Nieuwe Haven. Although the Boombrug at the harbor entrance is an opening bridge, the next two fixed bridges have clearance of 2.0 and 2.7 meters, restricting the size of boats moored along the Voorstraat canal. But we have already seen hundreds of boats owned by the residents of Dordrecht, this is surely a typical Dutch water-oriented city.

Soon we could no longer walk on a promenade beside the Voorstraat, for the houses are backed up to the canal on both sides. We stopped at each of the bridges and at the edges of Arij Scheffer's Square to see that I spoke too soon about Venice when I was in Gorinchem; here it really does look like that city, as the walls reach down into the water from both sides. The reflections of the houses on the water make the view especially beautiful.

Since we now could not follow the canal, we instead zigged and zagged on narrow brick and cobble-paved curving streets; many of the houses are the quaint old step-gable Dutch design. We didn't know exactly where we were going but the occasional glimpses of the Grote Kerk tower gave us guidance. A row of very handsome townhouses on the Grotekerksplein led us directly to our dock, the end of a most enjoyable two-hour circuit of the central part of the old city.

Our dinner at Tapasbar 't Vlak was excellent, our desires for different dishes soon exceeding our appetite. We ate at an early hour, which worked out well as this is a famous "party" bar, too lively for our lifestyle during the late evening. Photos of some of the bar's carnival events held on the water of the Nieuwe Haven looked to be fun, if viewed from a safe distance. hetvlak.nl

The next morning we made a lengthy visit to the Grote Kerk (Dordrecht Minster). Although dark and grim-looking on the outside, the interior is bright and very attractive. Details such as the choir gates, the pulpit and the strikingly beautiful organ are unique. The stained glass windows of course feature scenes of the rivers, complete with barges.

Zuid Holland Province

We had noticed two places of interest during our walk on Nieuwe Haven: Carol wanted to tour Huis van Gijn and I was interested in the Museum 1940-1945. So we split up, easily done as the two museums are side-by-side on the northern quay. Huis van Gijn is a restored manor house, furnished as it was in the 18th century, with a garden along the side and rear. The World War II Resistance museum is privately operated and very small, but interesting to me; I have read the history of Holland during the war and have seen a number of Dutch movies depicting the activities of the resistance, so some of the exhibits were of events and places that were somewhat familiar to me.

In mid-afternoon Carol walked over the marina on the footbridge and then across the Voorstraat canal to the Albert Heijn supermarket; she found some staples that we needed, and a beautiful sea bass for our dinner. That evening we enjoyed our fish dinner onboard and decided to travel to Brielle the next morning. Although this will call for a half-day cruise off of our route up through Holland, I wanted to see what looked to be a picture-perfect star fort town. There is a lot more to see and do in Dordrecht, but to be honest this relatively large city was not to our taste, we needed to get back out into the countryside.

Oude Maas to Brielle

On the map Brielle seems a long distance away, near the North Sea coast, but it was an easy 4-hour trip: 25 kilometers downstream at a good clip on the Oude Maas, pushed along by a 5 km/hr current, then 14 km on the Voedingskanaal and Brielse Meer. We passed by occasional industrial areas but most of the river was lined by trees and agricultural fields, along with a few towns. There was one lock, at the entrance of the Voedingskanaal but it was showing a green light as we arrived; the rise was about one meter, accomplished for us alone very quickly. The canal is a true man-made waterway, unvarying in width and dead-straight at first, then a slow curve toward the north. There are high dikes along each side, it is what I call a "ditch" canal. But the view is pleasant enough, trees and shrubs are plentiful on the dikes. To the north we can sometimes see the towers of piping and chimneys of the oil refineries and petroleum storage tanks; if we didn't want to think about the large industrial zone to our right, we simply kept our eyes to the left.

Soon enough the canal widens into what had been an estuary. It is now closed off at the sea and is a pleasant inland lake, the Brielse Meer. The presence of quite a few marinas and moorings on the lake shore and in the adjacent creeks shows that the lake is a popular recreational venue for the local boaters, in this case probably largely from nearby Rotterdam.

Our own destination was Brielle, a star fort town with its thirteen star points undisturbed. The entrance channel passes between two of these points, then splits into two legs that end inside the town. Visitor's moorings are offered by Maritiem Centrum Brielle on the south quay of the right-hand fork, the Noord Spuihaven. We followed an eight-man rowing team practicing in the entrance channel, no problem because they were faster than us!

Brielle was built as a port on the sea, at the mouth of the Maas river. Fortifications are intact around the periphery; the interior is entirely built-up, with just a few small parks, but the star points provide open spaces and walking paths. A berm about ten feet high surrounds the town. Road access cuts the berm at several points; some of these cuts can be closed off by thick wooden gates. The houses are brick, in various shades of red, yellow and white, but the roofs are invariably of red tiles.

Soon after we moored at our assigned space along the quay, we were off for a two-hour walk, following entirely around the thirteen points. We only stopped when we saw that we were back at the entrance channel and had to come into the town to find a bridge crossing. Leaving Johnnie on the boat, we toured just about every street in the town on our bicycles. For dinner we went to the nearby 't Swarte Schaep (the Black Sheep), a quaint eatery with a good choice of fish, meats and salads. The online reviews were mostly highly enthusiastic, and we would agree after filling up on tasty pork ribs. swarteschaepbrielle.nl

You might ask how we were able to go online; the answer is WiFi, we have been able to connect to one network or another wherever we have stopped. We haven't yet gotten set up to connect to 3G wireless service, just as well because that will cost a fair amount and so far we haven't had to pay for a connection. We do have a prepaid Sim-card in our cell phone, but we haven't tried to connect through the phone. Eventually we will set up an account and use a "dongle" in the USB port of the computer, which will allow us to connect as we travel. I have in mind to do this in Utrecht, I am certain that I will find English-speaking assistance there; we have visited this university town previously.

Our visit to Brielle was brief, but we had seen the town well and saw no reason to stay longer. The only way out was to reverse the way that we came in, back to the Oude Maas, with the Hartelkanaal and EuroPoort on our northern side. Before we left I used Google Earth and Wikimapia to see what is there behind the dikes at the "Gateway to Europe". EuroPoort is the world's busiest port by some measurements. It offers the deepest draft of all continental European ports. The facilities nearest to Brielle, close to the sea, are the petroleum unloading and storage facilities for just about every major oil company: Shell, Exxon/Mobil, Kuwait and many others that I had never heard of. Inland there are a great many short canals leading to the wharves of freight warehouses and to more oil and chemical processing plants along our left side. When we reached the Oude Maas and turned north we passed the

Shell and BP refineries on our right side, then turned east on the Nieuwe Maas with more refineries continuing alongside.

Schiedam

I had a reason to stop at Schiedam, having been driven all over that city by a yacht broker during our boat search; I now wanted to see these waterways and harbors from the water. Finding the proper channel entrance was difficult; I had noted that we needed to pass on our right side the 1e Petroleumhaven and the 2e Petroleumhaven then the Eemhaven, all marked "No Sport" on the chart. On our left we would see sport marinas in the Spuihaven, then the narrow opening of the Schie river. On Google Earth I had noted that there is a park on the waterfront between these two, so that is the landmark that I was watching for. When we got there I could see the park easily enough, as the rest of the northern bank is industrial. We crossed the channel, watching for openings in the barge traffic, and breathed a sigh of relief as we entered the narrow cut of the Schie.

This would be only a brief tour of Schiedam, as I have made a reservation for a slip at the Veerhaven in Rotterdam. I know, just a while ago I wrote that we were tired of the city of Dordrecht, now we are touring Schiedam and staying overnight in Rotterdam; the two of these together form a major metropolitan area. My excuse is that we did have an overnight at Brielle, which is definitely in the countryside, actually almost at the edge of the North Sea.

Other travelers may want to use Schiedam as access to the western side of Holland, on a route which includes Delft, Den Haag (The Hague), Leiden and Haarlem. The river Schie twists through Schiedam, making for an interesting cruise, then becomes the Delftse Schie canal after connecting with the Delfshavense Schie, which is the Rotterdam leg of the river. (This is the only waterway that passes through Delft, a stop on many wish lists.)

Schiedam does mean "dam on the Schie" as does Amsterdam mean "dam on the Amstel" and Rotterdam mean "dam on the Rotte". Another example is Zaandam, I can't think of any others.

We proceeded slowly at first, as there was a lock just ahead showing a red light. There is no VHF channel listed for this lock, so not only couldn't I call but I also couldn't listen for other barge traffic. Complicating things were the two large barges on my left and six or seven smaller barges on my right; as we get closer I could see that these all appear to be moored, not just waiting for the lock. I slowed almost to a stop, but it was only a minute or so before the green light was added to the red and the gates began to open. Two Dutch-flagged motorcruisers exited the lock and I started forward as soon as they had cleared the narrow channel between the moored barges.

Coming out of the lock we were welcomed by the molen Nolet, the first of many that we will see today. We proceeded straight along the

Buitenhaven (outer haven) and then the Lange (long) Haven. These havens do not have slips, there are scattered barges moored parallel alongside the quay on both sides. We had four opening bridges and one lock to pass through; they operate on demand but close for the lunch hour, we cruised slowly to see the sights but didn't dawdle, so that we we could beat the closing time.

Being the type of person who hates to turn around and go back on the same route (we just did that at Brielle), it seemed on first glance at the chart for Schiedam that I could make a circle through the city and return only 400 meters above the first lock. But it was not to be, more careful research showed that there are low fixed bridges which prevent this idea.

This particular research took some effort, no jumping to conclusions. The paper ANWB chart shows all but one bridge (of seven) to be BB, opening bridges. The non-BB bridge at the eastern end of the Korte (short) Haven is shown as H17, or 1.7 meters clearance, too low for us (and too low for all but the smallest open boats.) Using my electronic copy of the same chart, I could zoom in and I see that the western end of the Korte Haven is shown open, no bridge present. But looking at the actual situation on Google Earth (which has excellent resolution at this location, as it does in much of the Netherlands) I clearly saw what appeared to be a low fixed bridge. A photo from Google Earth Street View confirmed that the bridge is fixed, a low stone arch with a paved street on top; there is no passage on the west end, therefore no circle route, as the chart had led me to believe.

But I am still puzzled, as I can see on Google Earth that there are several sailing barges moored in the Korte Haven; how did they get there, past a very low bridge? Again a Street View photo has the answer: the bridge is an iron footbridge, split across the middle and able to be opened manually. The Korte Haven is home of the WV De Schie, which accepts visiting boats, so I assume that the bridge will be opened by the harbormaster on request.

Our short visit did not call for this, so I looked at more Street View 1photos. I found that we could pass through the Beurssluis lock and immediately turn back to our left into a short closed canal, where we tied up at bollards for a few hours.

I had wanted to take Carol out for lunch at *Lepels Eten en Drinken*; who wouldn't want to go to a place dedicated to eating and drinking? I had been there with a boat broker and found the location on the Korte Haven, the food and the environment to be perfect. But it was Monday, a closed day according to their website. Google Maps helped me select the Restaurant de Noordmolen, open at noon on Monday and located in the row of five molens along the Noordvestsingel, one of the sights that I had already planned to visit. The restaurant's website stated that they are located in the tallest (33.3 meters) historic windmill in the world.

When we found the proper molen, we thought it would be too closed-in and gloomy inside, so we passed it up. But we did enjoy seeing the row of molens along the arcing singel. We went back to the boat and made our own lunch, saving 60 or 70 euros. After lunch we walked down the Lange Haven and crossed through to the Nieuwe Haven.

That is the harbor which held a special attraction for me, it was where I saw the first Dutch boat that I really wanted, the "Matja", a converted bunker boat. I did not make my offer in time and it was sold to another buyer. But I was so taken by this harbor inside a city that I had always wanted to return and walk the quays, without the pressure of being with a broker. This time it wasn't as scenic as I had remembered, I think that some of the trees had been removed. But we had a nice walk, passing by yet another historic molen, De Walvisch. That makes seven molens in Schiedam.

On our way back to the boat we crossed the Schie on a bridge which brought us to the front of the Stedelijk Museum of art and local culture. The first building to the right, on the quay, is the Cooperatie Museum, of the Dutch trade cooperatives. A few steps down the quay is the Jenever Museum. This city is famous for the distilling of jenever gin; at one time there were 19 windmills to mill the grain for 400 distilleries. Those numbers have now greatly diminished, but the Branderij in the museum is described as "A place with a long history and the only distillery in the Netherlands where more malt wine gin is distilled according to original recipe. Come in, try and buy a bottle of Old Schiedam".

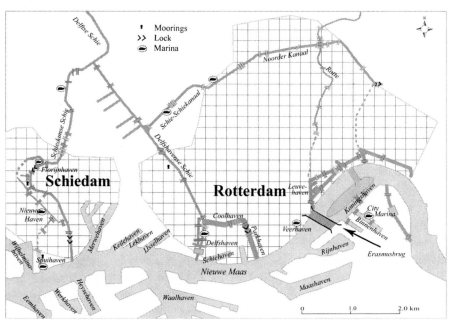

Cruising the Canals & Rivers of the Netherlands

Rotterdam

We didn't linger at the museums, wanting to get on to Rotterdam by the end of the afternoon. We were soon back on the Nieuwe Maas headed east. Both sides of the river are lined by low industrial warehouses, the continuous long line broken occasionally by the modern tall boxes of office and residential buildings, and by a forest of cargo cranes jutting up in all directions. We will be looking first for the entrance to the Rotterdam leg of the Delftse Schie canal, at the Parkhaven. It will be easy to find because the well-known Euromast tower stands on its eastern quay. The tower is visible well before we get there; a thick concrete column supports the ring of windows in an observation level, then a thinner shaft doubles the tower height up to a group of TV/Radio and telecommunications antennas.

We aren't planning to enter this canal, it is our landmark to lead us to our own destination, the Veerhaven, where we have called ahead for a slip; the conversation was unclear, but I think he said that we can be accommodated. The harbor is a short distance east of Het Park, the park area around the Euromast. We only have to follow the line of trees on the waterfront until we see the narrow opening for the Veerhaven. There are other landmarks, on our right we know that we should not pass the tall rounded office tower of the Port of Rotterdam authority, nor should we pass the futuristic bridge Erasmusbrug, which is just one-half kilometer east of the harbor entrance.

There is an alternative marina, the City Marina Rotterdam, east and south of the Erasmusbrug. This is a much larger marina, with full facilities, but the Veerhaven is the historic harbor and is close to most of the places that we want to see, including Het Park, which is convenient for our dog walks. The city guide map shows seven museums within a short walk from the haven.

We turned in past the fleet of historic sailing ships and found an open slip. Later the harbormaster arrived and told us that our choice would be fine for a two-night stay. www.veerhavenrotterdam.nl

Veer means ferry; the current ferry quay is on the river, just outside the harbor entrance. The Veerhaven website has this to say: "The ferry port offers home to sea going ships with a historical character. The fleet consists of former cargo ships like schooners and coasters, also loggers, cutters and fishing boats. Wooden and steel ships from home and abroad. In addition to operating vessels you will find there are a number of classic yachts. They are all sailing ships and mostly privately owned. Most owners live on board their ships. Besides its regular fleet Veerhaven welcomes visitors year- around."

Now the ferry fleet are high-speed water-taxis, which operate on demand and respond to a telephone call to take visitors to over 30 locations or on a tour of the city's waterways. We could easily walk to the areas of our interest and wouldn't be needing the taxi, but we did see them frequently pass by our mooring.

Carol and I are both fans of modern architecture (not so our dog Johnnie, he will lift his leg anywhere, old design or new.) That is what drew us to Rotterdam; we can appreciate the historic buildings that we have seen all over Europe, but we get especially excited when we can see interesting and innovative designs. This is the place to find many well-known buildings and a few surprises. The old city was devastated by bombing raids in 1940; rather than rebuild replicas of the old buildings, the city has forged ahead into world-leading designs. There are numerous architecture firms, progressive design museums and spectacular structures. These were the focus of our walking tours.

The closest museum to our dock is the Belasting & Douane Museum, the "Tax & Customs" museums; we skipped that one. But also nearby is the Wereldmuseum, the World Arts Museum, with extensive collections of ethnographic art brought back by the Dutch traders. Carol suggested that she would go there (it is open until 10:00 in the evening) while Johnnie and I looked over the historic and the modern boats in the next harbor, the Leuvehaven and further east in the Oude Haven, adjacent to the Maritiem Museum.

A curious sight at the Oude Haven, where the traditional barges are surrounded by sleek modern office towers, is the Witte Huis (white house), a skyscraper when it was built in 1898, at 11 stories. It was one of the few structures in this area to survive the 1940 bombings. There must be hundreds of windows in this building, each with a colored-tile panel beneath and each covered by a zebra-stripe awning. Even more startling is to come around the corner of the Witte Huis and see the Cube Houses.

I had been watching for them, as I had read articles and seen photos. Seeing them in person was still a shock, I hadn't known that they overlook a small harbor filled with old sailing barges. The houses are true cubes, but turned 45 degrees so that they sit on a corner point, atop a three-story hexagonal pylon. They are assembled into groups, on my first view I counted a horizontal row of 12 cubes; there are 38 cube houses in total. City streets and tram lines pass underneath the elevated row of cubes.

Immediately next to these strange homes (as they say, a great place to visit but you wouldn't want to live there) is the Pencil building, designed by the same architect, Piet Blom. It is a six-sided tower with a point at the top resembling a pencil. Aside from the pencil shape, another interesting feature is that the windows, which otherwise might be normal vertical rectangles, are shaped in a U at the bottom. These draw the eye such that the pencil shape is not seen right away.

These structures are located at the flying-saucer-shaped Blaak train and metro station. Next to the pencil building is the Rotterdam Library, very much in the style of the Pompidou Center in Paris, a glass and exposed steel structure with large-diameter orange-colored ventilation tubes.

This had been quite an unexpected adventure; I had thought to go on a search for such architecture on the next day, but there it was hitting me right in the face. I returned here the next day with Carol, along the Blaak, a wide boulevard of city streets and tram lines where we had an open view some of the less famous but still interesting architectural designs. The Plein 1940 is on this route; the 6.5 meter-high bronze sculpture in the center of this open square represents a man without a heart and symbolizes Rotterdam without its historic heart after the Second World War.

On our return we wandered a few blocks into the city and crossed a wooden footbridge over a still river, contained by concrete walls. I remembered the map and realized that this must be the Rotte river. It was totally covered by bright green algae, justifying the translation of its name as "rotten". A much more inviting stream ran down the Eendrachtsweg, a strip of grass, trees and stream that took us back to the Scheepvaartkwartier, the maritime section of the city around our harbor. The tables outside Restaurant Zinc drew us there for lunch, a very pleasant meal at this simple, rustic family-run eatery.

Neither of us are keen on observation towers, even if they do feature a Michelin-starred restaurant, but we did enjoy a restful afternoon in the park under the Euromast. The three of us stretched out on the grass and just did nothing for a few hours. In the morning we would be off again.

Nieuwe Maas and Lek

The most beautiful architectural design in Rotterdam has to be the Erasmusbrug, an elegant and extremely simple design. The main span across the Nieuwe Maas river is a suspension bridge, supported by thin cables from a single tower of steel. The tower is an inverted V; the two legs lay back at an angle to pull against the cables, then kink to vertical and meld into a single point. Two thick cables pull in the other direction from near the top of the spire to anchor the tower into a concrete caisson. It is wonderful thing to see; from the water we had the best view. We were off early, so the shallow arc of the roadbed and the cables supporting it were backlit by the morning sun.

There is a bascule bridge on the south end of the Erasmusbrug for passage through the Koningshaven, but the clearance under the cable span is 11.5 meters and under the Nieuwe Willemsbrug which follows is 10.5 m, so we didn't need the open bridge and stayed in the main channel. To our right as we passed under the bridge we noticed a tall office building which appears to be leaning such that it might fall over on its glass eastern face; not to worry, it is "propped up" by a steel shaft pushing back on the falling building. An amusing and clever piece of work by the architect.

Zuid Holland Province

The river made a long S-curve as we headed upstream out of the metropolitan area. The major autoroute A16 traversed overhead and then on our left, the northern bank, we could see the Hollandse IJssel river flowing southwest from Gouda. We continued to the right to stay in the Nieuwe Maas.

The sights on both sides of the river were a mixture of green spaces, industrial zones and a few high-rise residential buildings. Five kilometers on from the Hollandse IJssel we came to the junction with the Noord, the short (13 km) river which flows north from Dordrecht, closing the loop on our excursion to the west. We were now on the river Lek, leaving the name Nieuwe Maas behind. Kinderdijk was our first landmark for today, one kilometer ahead on the right-hand side.

Kinderdijk is the largest group of old windmills in NL. The 19 molens were built around 1740 to drain the polder. There is no mooring on the south bank near the site but there are two marinas on the north bank and a ferry for access. We would like to visit but it seemed quite a bit of trouble for a day stop, and we could already see groups of tourists walking the dikes. So we contented ourselves with a view from the river, which is not so good because the windmills are at a lower level, in the polder. We could see only the long line of the tops and sails of the windmills. Perhaps a visit later when we may be staying overnight in one of the marinas. Our decision is confirmed when we see behind us, headed toward the ferry slip, a three-deck tour boat roughly a city block long, filled with tourists. Not our cup of tea, thank you.

The Lek is a smaller river than we had been on lately, it has a narrower floodplain and irregular banks. The river's path is a continuing series of curves, most of them slight but a few are long S-loops. All along the river there are cribs (groins, short stone dams in the river bed). From the A16 bridge to Vianen, a distance of 43 km, there are no bridges over the Lek, but there are five ferries to be on the lookout for.

This is truly in the agricultural area, polders on both sides stretch off into the distance. The fields are served by a grid of major and minor irrigation canals. The river is tidal and diked on both sides, but there are small wetlands and pastures on the river side of the dikes, making the sightseeing unspectacular but pleasant. Stone groins lay perpendicular to the banks on both sides, some of them extending far enough out into the river to require the skipper's attention to the channel.

As I had estimated, we traveled 30 km in just under 4 hours, against about 3-4 km/hr current on the rivers. Eight km/hr is a good average speed for quick estimates. I hadn't yet decided where to stop overnight, we were coming to two towns that almost face each other across the river; they both have moorings available, but I wanted to investigate which one to use overnight.

Nieuwpoort - Schoonhoven

Nieuwpoort: A well-preserved star fort town directly on the south bank of the Lek, this is an interesting short stop for a return to the 17th century. The canal is no longer in use but it provides a walkway through the center of town and a return via the dikes of the star-shaped walls along the singel.

Schoonhoven: Just across the river on the north bank, this is the historic "Silver Town" of the Netherlands. Shops and craftsmen are located throughout the old district, especially in the Watertower, an interesting and often-photographed building.

Nieuwpoort is actually 1.3 km further upstream than Schoonhoven so I decided to stop at the latter first. Schoonhoven barely qualifies for my list of star fort towns; there is a singel around just two remaining star points, on the northeastern corner of the town. A narrow singel and accompanying park form three stars along the western edge, but they show no sign of the original fortifications, just a shaded walkway.

We had turned into the Gemeente Schoonhoven just before the ferry dock and tied up at the town quay, inside a narrow dike along the river. This haven is tidal (1 meter normal tide) and very exposed to wash from passing barges on the river, not very promising for an overnight (local small boats moor inside a flood lock, which leads to two narrow canals that stretch straight across the town.) The one part of the original fortifications that remains is the Veerpoort (ferry gate) which is the entrance into town from the docks. It is a massive structure of stone blocks, bricks and a steep tile roof, the design is very detailed and impressive. As we entered the haven we couldn't miss the welcoming sight of the hotel/cafe Belvedere, so we immediately headed there for lunch. Even though we had just come in from several hours on the river, it was fun to watch the passing barges.   www.hotelbelvedere.nl

One block south along the river and a few turns inland is the Watertower, a red brick building with yellow brick decorative details and a tall cylindrical cupola-topped tower, now used as shops and galleries by silver craftsmen. We were interested in seeing these shops as our home in the USA is in Santa Fe, New Mexico, which is also a significant silver town; natives of the Navaho and Pueblo tribes sell their silver jewelry on the plaza, joined by newcomers of all backgrounds who make and sell their designs in galleries surrounding the plaza. The work here at Schoonhoven was familiar to us, although of course the style is quite different.

We walked away from the tower to the west for our circuit of the star ring. Our first discovery was the common garden area for the residents, located on a man-made island in an enlarged singel, accessed by a footbridge, an excellent way to make use of the moat. We circled the town to the north and east, finding another interesting use of a star point, as a cemetery. The walkway does not complete a circle, stopped by residences and commercial buildings, so we turned to the interior and back to the boat. My plan was to simply follow the street that we turned in on, the Lopikerstraat, then follow the Oude Haven canal back to the haven. I later found, on the town's website, that this is the exact route recommended for a shopping tour of the jewelry stores! I had failed to bring blinders for Carol, so our progress was slow but she managed to keep expenditures under control.

Late in the afternoon we crossed over to Nieuwpoort, with an eye on the car ferry being loaded nearby. The ferry goes straight across the river but we were headed further upstream, so we passed by quickly, skimming along the ends of five groins on the southern bank before turning into the WSV Nova Portus haven. The docks are just off the river but stone harbor walls diminish the wash significantly, so we thought we would be comfortable there at night. The town lies behind the grassy berms of the old fortifications; there are open wetlands on both sides of the haven, suiting us just fine. Facilities were very simple but the nightly rate was only 0.75 euro/meter of boat length, as compared to the more usual €1.00 or more.

The Buitenhaven/Binnenhaven canal was our route to the town hall and dam straddling the old canal at the Hoogstraat (High Street) intersection. We had already enjoyed a substantial meal at the Belvedere but couldn't resist the charming Eetcafe de Dam; we decided to walk Johnnie through some of the wetlands and then return here. There is no formal gate at the eastern end of Hoogstraat but a row of graceful stone columns on each side of the roadway marked the bridge over the singel. The view from there was truly beautiful, as the late afternoon sun reflected from the water and highlighted the bright green grass on the slopes of the old berms; outside the moat the park walkways lead on to open fields.

We turned toward the river and fell in with a local gentleman and his very friendly pointer. After much sniffing by the dogs and where-are-you-from questions from the man, we walked together past ponds with white swans and green/brown ducks. As we walked we learned that the man's name was Ton (tone), the same as a Dutch fiend of ours in the USA, and that his dog was Piet (pete). There was a bit of banter about Ton and Tom. Before we knew it we had returned to the haven, saying goodbye to our new friend.

The cafe offered sidewalk tables but the typical Dutch wooden interior drew us to seats at the bar, where we quickly reacted to the polished taps in front of us suggesting Hertzog Jan pilsener. That was followed by a series of appetizer dishes which we shared, our own version of Tapas. We couldn't resist the chocolate soufflé, especially when we saw this warning on the menu: Let Op! 20 min bereidingstijd (Attention! 20 minutes preparation time.) eetcafededamnieuwpoort.nl

Early the next morning we took Johnnie for his walk and then returned him to the boat, for we were off to a bird sanctuary, no dogs allowed. We cycled down the river and then in across the fields to the

Ooievaarsdorp Het Liesvelt; pairs of nesting storks, some with chicks visible, can be seen on platforms. We rode into Nieuwpoort and went up, then down, the two other streets which parallel the main street of the canal, just to view the homes and the star points on the southern end of town. We had a quick lunch on the boat, then set off upstream into the province of Utrecht. Today would be our last on the Grote Rivieren, the Great Rivers of Holland.

Vreeswijk

A short (20km) section of the Lek took us from Nieuwpoort to Vreeswijk; it was an uneventful trip of 2.5 hours. We came out onto the river eastbound behind a line of four barges but kept well back and just followed along, using their same path to avoid the groins. The scenery was almost entirely countryside, wetlands along the river and agriculture beyond the dikes. The sole exception was the town of Ameide on the south bank, where we could see most of the town from the river. Usually the towns are back some distance from the river or down behind a dike, but here we could see the houses and shops along the waterfront and could even read the sign for the "SalonModern" and joked about stopping for a haircut. (Actually that was on our list for Utrecht, we will spend a week there.)

Soon after Ameide I got a lesson in dealing with barge traffic; after being lulled into passively following the barge ahead of me, I suddenly saw two side-by-side barges coming downriver. Obviously one of the oncoming barges was passing the other, but their speeds were almost the same so it took a long time to complete the pass. The river twists and is always in a curve here and so on one of the relatively narrow curves there was a squeeze of three barges, one headed upstream and two downstream. After clearing the barge headed upstream, the middle barge moved over toward my side and I needed to take quick avoiding action, moving closer to the bank than I had been traveling. It wasn't really a close call or dangerous, but it did wake me up and remind me to stay alert.

Because of this I saw the highway bridge ahead sooner than I might have otherwise, the arch of trusses showing over the brushy sandspit on a curve. I had been expecting the bridge, it is for the A2 autoroute and marks the approach to the towns of Vianen on our right and Vreeswijk on our left.

I had studied the chart so I knew that I would see a small haven on the north bank just past the bridge, where I didn't intend to stop, then a ferry crossing, then I needed to quickly cross left through traffic into the Merewedekanaal. There is a lock very close to the entrance of the canal. While I watched the left side to see where I was going, Carol helped by watching for traffic, especially wary of a possible ferry boat crossing perpendicular to our path. The river narrowed quite a bit, compressing all of this into a tighter space. One thing that helped is that the groins on our right are each marked by a tall tree right at the end, so it is easier to see them in peripheral vision.

I was not as panic-stricken as this may read, but we were both very alert as we made the junction, passing between two oncoming barges but with no active ferry boat, and relaxed a bit as we glided into the canal and saw the lock gates open but two red lights showing.

It is against the regulations to enter a lock with two red lights, even when the gates are open and the lock is empty. So we tied up on a long wachtsteiger and consulted the ANWB Wateralmanak. To do this I noted the number of the lock from the chart (742d) and looked in the back of the book, in the section "Nummer kunstwerken" which referred me to page 256, the description for the Merwedekanaal. There I found the information for "Sluizen" and learned that the lock is in operation today (Thursday) from 0600 to 2200 hours. I could see the lockkeeper's booth but no one seemed to be there. The book shows a telephone number so I called it; I had difficulty understanding the man that answered but he apparently realized that an "Englisher" was asking to use the lock, for soon I saw him walking on the lock wall. The light turned green and we went in. As we left the temporary mooring I noticed a sign that seemed to say that the wachtsteiger is for commercial barges only; too late for that now!

The Willemsbrug just ahead shows a clearance (on the chart) of 2.3m, too low for our boat, but apparently the lockkeeper also controlled this nearby bridge, as it displayed red/green lights and began to rise. By the time we arrived the bridge was fully open and the light was green only, so we passed right through. As the ANWB Wateralmanak had informed me, there is no charge for the use of the lock or the bridge.

Vreeswijk is an historic barging center because of its central location. A section of the old river branch Vaartse Rijn, now with boat access from the river blocked by a flood gate and fixed bridge, passes through the center of town. Water traffic uses the new Merwedekanaal on the west side or the even newer Lekkanaal on the east, which is the wider, straighter canal used by barges.

We proceeded up the canal passing barges and cruisers moored along the Handelskade on our left and a long row of some very nice-looking floating residences on our right. I use the term "floating residences" rather than "houseboats" to differentiate them from the also-common barges converted to houseboats for full-time residences. These are actual houses built of wood; by necessity they are long and thin, the long side tied permanently to the bank. Both types are covered by the Dutch word *woonboten*.

The Merwedekanaal curves along the row of houses and at the end is the intersection of the Vaartse Rijn and the northern end of the old town. This point was my cue to make a sharp right turn into the Passantenhaven Vreeswijk, our destination. There are 40 slips here, at the rate of €0.70/meter per night. Apparently we could also find a space in the town along the narrow Vaartse Rijn but we found it simpler to just stay here. The whole town is only about ten blocks long, a very pleasant stroll with classic bridges, beautiful old Dutch houses and sidewalk cafes.

The Oude Sluis (old lock) is now connected to the Lek only by an underground culvert but it is interesting to see the oval lock and gates closely surrounded by small brick houses. Classic barges can be viewed along the Vaartse Rijn canal; a barging museum and working boatyard has recently been created, where you can bring your own barge and do the work yourself or have it done by the skilled staff.   www.museumwerf.nl

Restaurant Rotisserie Zott is located in a renovated old white-brick building; along with modern dining rooms and bar in the building they also serve at tables on the river quay at a handsome white liftbridge. We had an excellent dinner of cod marinated in lemon and coriander, veal from the rotisserie and pumpernickel bread with truffles and olive oil. It was a very elegant meal in a charming location.   restaurantzott.nl

The old town of Vreeswijk is an island, in both senses of the word, at the south end of the urban area of Utrecht. We left it behind after an enjoyable visit to head north into the city center. The combined Merewedekanaal/Vaartse Rijn was our route between a long series of low industrial buildings on our right and an equally-long barrier of tall trees on our left, protecting a residential area. Several towns, including Vreeswijk, have been merged into the municipality of Nieuwegein, a suburb of Utrecht. The city is notable for two reasons: first, a short canal connects our waterway to the Hollandse IJssel river, leading southwest to some interesting towns and to Gouda. Second, Nieuwegein is the home of Hatenboer Yachting, one of the largest charter-boat fleets in the Netherlands. It is possible to moor at the quay here, but our plan was to go into Utrecht, for a stay at the Singelgracht haven.

Waterway	From	To	KM	Hours
Heusdenskanaal/ Andelse Maas/ Boven Merwede	Heusden	Gorinchem	18.3	2.3
Linge	Gorinchem	Geldermalsen	35.0	7.0
Kanaal van Steenehoek	Gorinchem	Beneden Merwede	8.9	1.3
Beneden Merwede	Werkendam	Dordrecht	14.3	1.4
Oude Maas/Voedingskanaal	Dordrecht	Brielle	40.0	3.5
Nieuwe Maas	Oude Maas	Lek	24.0	3.0
Lek	Noord	Vreeswijk	40.0	5.4

Utrecht

To get into Utrecht we crossed the Amsterdam-Rijnkanaal, a broad straight canal which resembles an autoroute. We convoyed with two local cruisers to negotiate the locks on each side of the ARK; the crossing was accomplished just in front of two southbound barges bearing down on us side-by-side. The southern part of Utrecht is almost entirely office and industrial zones but the waterway is lined on both sides by trees, not an unpleasant short cruise into the city.

The Merwedekanaal branched to the left while we continued arrow-straight on the Vaartse Rijn. Small boats used for local outings and liveaboard barges were moored along the quays. Three BB bridges opened for us; their operating hours needed to be checked in advance, but the morning between 9-12 is fine, so our convoy traveled along quickly (and still at no charge.) At the southern end of central Utrecht the two other boats continued into the downtown on the Oudegracht, as we turned left into the dead-end Catharijnesingel, the southwestern arm of the Stadsbuitengracht, the moat of the star-fort.

We proceeded as far as we could go, to the blocked-off end of the canal alongside Catharijnesingel (...street). We found wooden docks on both sides, shaded by trees and with a grass slope up to street level. The docks are fixed, since we were no longer in tidal waters so we could tie-up tightly. There is a bus stop just a few steps away. We were allowed to stay here for three days, then we moved to a new location, the Nieuwe Haven, for another three days.

The old city of Utrecht is surrounded by a new modern city and suburbs; it is (almost) separated from them by the singel of the original star fort, which defines the perimeter of the central city. The (almost) part is where Orion was moored. The Catharijnesingel moat comes to a dead end right in front of the boat at its mooring. It has been filled in, paved and turned into a boulevard complex, with four roadways totaling 8 lanes. The two center roadways are sunken into what had been the singel. To add insult to injury, one of the roadways is still named Catharijneskade, as if it was still a quay along the waterway. (Work began in 2010 to restore the waterway through this path, reconnecting the singel.)

As we did in Dordrecht, one of our first visits (I was going to write "first steps" but there were 465 of them!) was to the top of the Dom church tower, to see the layout of the city. This is the highest point in the city center, at 112.5 meters (the observation level is at 95 meters, still plenty high enough.) The tower stands alone, as the nave of St Martin's Cathedral was destroyed by an unusual tornado in 1674; the remainder of the church is 40-some meters away across the Domplein square.

We could see our mooring on the western edge of the Museumkwartier, the museum quarter. It is a "quarter" in name only, actually it fills the southern half of the island within the singel; the central city "downtown" is the northern half. The Dom tower marks the line between these halves and is located centrally east-west, so our view of the city was a complete circle. It extended out to the suburbs and even to the fields beyond, but our main purpose was to look down on the grid of streets so that we would know where we are as we walk around.

The central city is ringed by the Buitengracht, the star-fort singel; the line of trees can be followed from the tower view. The name means "outer canal" and refers to the entire ring around the city; it was built for defense in the 12th century. There were four poorts (gates): Weerd (north), Wittevrouwen (east), Tolsteeg (south) and Catharijnes (west). (The gates and ramparts were removed in the 19th century.) These names helped orient us as we walked around because they are used extensively in each quarter.

Directly under us, on the northwestern side of the tower, is the Vismarkt (fish market) and Stadhuis (city hall) bridges. These are both broad plazas rather than bridges, the boats passing beneath them on the Oudegracht are essentially in a tunnel. This is especially true under the Stadhuisbrug, where the tunnel curves slightly. The Stadhuis plaza teemed with people walking briskly in all directions, while the Vismarkt plaza was set with cafe tables from two or three restaurants.

On the western side of the Stadhuis plaza I saw the bookshop where I purchased my Dutch-English dictionary a few years earlier. Boekhandel Selexyz Broese is one of the largest general and scientific bookshops in the Netherlands. The public library of Utrecht is in the next building to the west; judging by the roof area that I could see, the bookstore is about four times as large!

Turning our view southward, we looked from north to south along the length of the Odegracht, the sunken canal that runs straight through the city. Several blocks deep on both sides of the canal are long rows of townhouses, so narrow that they resemble matchboxes with gable roofs.

To the southeast are museums, university buildings and city parks. The northeast is a jumble of curving streets, an area of residential apartment buildings. Someone in our group of sightseers pointed out that, looking to the northeast horizon, you can see that that the earth is, in fact, round!

Another local visitor took us to the four sides of the tower to see the kerkenkruis, a cross in the plan view of the city formed by five of its churches. This one in Utrecht is the most famous in the Netherlands. We were at the center of the cross; Pieterskerk is at the top (east), Sint-Gertrudiskathedraal at the bottom (west), on the arms are Sint-Catharinakathedraal (south) and Janskerhof, St John's Church, (north).

We descended from the tower and walked to the Oudegracht, then north along the Vismarkt quay, window-shopping at a coffee/tea shop, antiquarian bookshop, interior design studio, antiques shop and about a dozen cafes and bars. Oh, and the bicycles! Hundreds of them leaning against the railing at the edge of the canal, or tucked into the rows of bike stands. We found a good table on the north quay where we could enjoy a cup of coffee while watching boats come out from under the Stadhuis plaza.

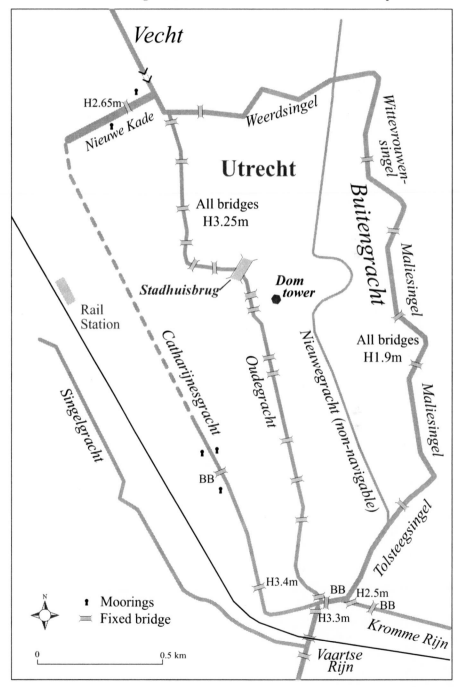

Cruising the Canals & Rivers of the Netherlands

We then headed north ourselves, along the Oudegracht, past more shops and cafes. We noticed a kayak/canoe rental and decided that would be the best way to see the canals through and around the city. Even though we would travel the Oudegracht on our own boat, we will be busy steering and watching for traffic; in a canoe we can take our time and poke around.

As we crossed a wooden-deck bridge over the Weerdsingel Oostzijde we could see ahead the Weerdsluis and on the left Weerdsingel Westzijde. This is the Nieuwe Haven, we relocated to a mooring here when our time ran out on the Catharijnesingel. It is another pleasant haven, not as sheltered as where we are now and also the base for public tour boats, so much busier. We walked along the quay to the west, office buildings and shops on our left and residences on our right, across the canal. In just two blocks the canal comes to an abrupt end, a victim of city planning in the 1960s. This is the junction with the Catharijneskade, the boulevard that took us back to the boat.

If the city's traffic engineer at the time had his way, the boulevard would continue around the central city, paving the canals and using the open spaces on the star-fort points for parking garages. After the populace saw what had been lost on the Catharijnesingel and Weerdsingel, the plan was aborted. These two blocks of the Weerdsingel were dug up and reopened in 2001; the Catharijnesingel is due to reopened by 2017, restoring the full perimeter to navigable canals.

The Buitengracht is now a city park, the "pearl" of Utrecht. It stretches over 5 km around all but the northern and northwestern perimeter of the old city. Although a narrow park, it feels like a large green area. We walked it early the next morning, starting out to the south from our mooring and circling counter-clockwise. We stayed on the inside of the canals so that we could pass by the public buildings and parks now installed in the star points.

The first was at Sterrenburg, where we had made a sharp right turn on the canal when we first entered the Catharijnesingel. At the time we couldn't see through the trees, now we can see the remainders of a bastion from the original fortifications. Then, at the Tolsteegpoort bridge we saw a pub that we had patronized on a previous trip, the Ledig Erf, and decided to return there later.

Off the city streets and onto a dirt pathway, we passed by the studio of the Dutch sculptor Pieter d'Hont at the Manenburg star point. Across the canal, along the Tolsteegsingel, is one of the long-term mooring areas used by local boaters; most are small open boats, 7 meters or less.

The next point is Sonnenborgh; a museum & observatory is located on top of an ancient bulwark. Dating from 1853, the observatory is more than just a museum; there are guided tours of the building and the bulwark, which dates from 1552, or visitors can have a look through the telescopes of the observatory.

Lepelenburg is next, an open park area where dogs are prohibited (Boo! But I suppose this is necessary to assure that people can stretch out on the grass or set up a picnic lunch undisturbed.)

The Lucasbolwerk is filled by a large modern building, the City Theatre. Stadsschouwburg Utrecht is the prominent theatre in the Central Netherlands. Annually, over 550 performances and activities are held in two auditoriums and at other locations inside and outside the theatre, varying from modern dance to musicals, and from modern theatre to romantic operas. The city theatre also enables numerous Utrecht festivals such as Springdance, Festival a/d Werf, Tweetakt and the Dutch Film Festival.

The Wolvenplein is a sharp point with high fortifications, however these are the thick brick walls of a prison. The huge building fills the point, there is no longer a path along the water; in fact there hadn't been a path since we passed the Wittevrouwenbrug and we wouldn't find parkland again on the northeastern and northern canals. We are still shaded by tall old trees, but we are walking on the paved quay and city streets. The bank of the canal across from the prison is another mooring area for local boats. A potential clever way to escape, perhaps?

Here we find the Nieuwegracht and decide to follow that non-navigable canal back to the southern end of the city. It is narrow; brick walls extend down into the water. The buildings are primarily residential, some are charming but most are easily ignored. The canal makes a loop to the east around the Domplein, becoming even more narrow and in some places completely covered by pavement. South of the loop the cut through the city widens, so that now there is a strip of land, planted with trees, on both sides of the canal, with access to the basement level of the buildings. This section is much more pleasant than the northern streets. We arrived back on the Buitengracht at Sonnenbourgh. Following the city streets this time, we came to the city's largest museum. The Centraal Museum was created in 1838, the oldest municipal museum in the Netherlands.

We weren't ready to deal with a visit, so we walked on and soon found an Albert Heijn supermarket, where we restocked on some needed supplies for the boat, which was now just a short distance ahead. In the last block before our mooring we wandered through some of the Zeven Steegjes, the "Seven Lanes" of row houses built long ago for the city's poor. There are 166 dwellings; the streets Korte Rozendaal, Lange Rozendaal, Kockstraat, Brouwerstraat, Boogstraat, Moutstraat, Suikerstraat and Fockstraat preserve the character of a popular neighborhood.

Lunch onboard, then an afternoon for Carol and I to each go about our own shopping excursion. She went looking for an art supply store (I'm sure she can find a few other shops of interest!) My purpose was to find a helpful clerk at a cellphone shop who could help me select and set up a 3G account for wireless internet access.

Cruising the Canals & Rivers of the Netherlands

We have two computers onboard. Carol uses an Apple iBook (laptop), while I have brought my venerable Mac Mini, a small "desktop" computer which is actually a 6" square box, 2" high. I have installed it on a shelf under the helm station, with power from the boat's batteries via an inverter (all of our electronics are suitable for 220 volts.) Currently I have a small monitor attached to the instrument panel; later I intend to add a second, larger monitor for entertainment and web surfing. Both of these computers have been accessing the internet through wifi connections, where available; now I had obtained a "dongle", a small antenna that fits into a USB socket and connects to the 3G wireless signal. This is expected to allow a connection in rural areas, although still not completely throughout the country.

I visited the retail stores of Vodaphone, TMobile, several brands that I hadn't hard of and even a thumping-loud place called the MediaMarkt (not recommended.) I don't want to say which one I picked, not because I am wary of an endorsement, it is because the industry changes so quickly. The company and the plan that I selected may be far from the best by the time that this book is read. Suffice it to say that the Mac Mini is now able to connect to the 3G network and that it also serves Carol's laptop via an Apple Airport wifi network (protected by a password.) We will use this system only when we can't find a wifi signal nearby.

I spent some time in Antiquariaat, located at Voorstraat 55. This used-books store has a regularly changing supply of English-language books that take up the front left corner of the store. It's a friendly shop and it looks like they have some more interesting - and probably more expensive - rare books in the back.

Carol has found the art supplies that she had been wanting. After enjoying spacious studios at home in the USA, she has adapted her work and her storage methods to suit the space available; obviously this is very limited on the boat. Sometimes she sets up on the dinette table, other times spreading out a bit in the salon. Currently most of her work is done with a digital camera and computer, not requiring a studio.

Johnnie is welcome at the Ledig Erf; "Ook je hond ist welkom..." He always enjoys a pub or restaurant visit, lying quietly at our feet while watching the other patrons, human and canine. Ledig Erf is a beer pub, offering a few insignificant snacks and some great soups. The main attraction is the selection of 12 draught beers and another 50 brands in bottle. It is a haunt of the students in the surrounding university area, for both the drinks and the chess board at each table. Outside, tables are set directly over the Oudegracht tunnel. Inside, the decor is 1900s dark-wood pub style. It's a lot of fun, without being a raucous party bar.   www.ledigerf.nl

The following day, Sunday, was our museum day, when Johnnie guards the boat and we can stroll through places where dogs are not welcome or are a distraction. We decided to "Go Dutch" and travel by bicycle. First stop: the Centraal Museum is a true labyrinth! Mainly situated in a former medieval monastery, it consists of a number of buildings around a large courtyard. It provides the opportunity to explore the old city history and view the paintings of Dutch artists.

Of special interest to us, Utrecht is the city where furniture maker and architect Gerrit Rietveld (1888-1964) lived and worked all his life. The Centraal Museum manages the largest Rietveld collection in the world, including the Rietveld Schröderhuis. We inquired about tours of the house; advance reservations are recommended, as each tour is limited to ten persons, but we were lucky that there was space for us on a tour that same day. After viewing the displays at the museum, we broke our self-imposed rule of staying inside the Buitengracht as we cycled east for two kilometers on city streets to see the Rietveld house.

It is very different than all of those on the residential blocks that we rode past, no sign was needed to tell us we are there! The exterior of the house is white, a series of rectangular boxes and panels, with black window frames and railings, highlighted by red, blue and yellow vertical features. The furniture mostly consists of horizontal and vertical lines, again with panels of red, blue and black. As I have previously written, the traditional Dutch architecture charms us, but it is the modern design that excites us.

For lunch we picked up some carry-out food and took it to a nice-looking tree in the Wilhelminapark. There were lots of choices for lunch in the blocks east of the park, some that were elegant and looked tasty but were quite expensive. We settled on sandwiches from Lunchroom De Smurf.

We rode back past a large building near the Maliesingel: the Nederlands Spoorwegmuseum, the Dutch Railway Museum, housed in an abandoned railway station. This is probably a very interesting place, but not for us. Close to the Centraal Museum is the Universiteitsmuseum Utrecht, the science and natural history museum of Utrecht University.

Another possibility is the National Museum van Speelklok tot Pierement; it has a collection of automatically-playing musical instruments, most of which still work. Among the instruments on display are music boxes, musical clocks, pianolas, barrel organs (including the typically Dutch large street organs) and a turret clock with carillon.

Instead we returned to the boat, put away our bikes and just relaxed for the afternoon. Later we walked Johnnie and ourselves along the southern half of the Oudegracht, at canal level and at the higher street level. We started at the Gaardbrug; north of that bridge there is no vehicular traffic, south of there streets line the canal on both sides (at "street level") but more importantly there are sidewalks at water level (about ten feet below street level) on both sides. Steps lead down from the street at intervals.

Cruising the Canals & Rivers of the Netherlands

What we found there are mostly basement entrance to the houses above, but some are residences built under the street. There are small windows only at the front, facing the canal. The homes are under a brick-arch ceiling. One of them was for rent and we were invited to go inside; a single line of rooms led back into the earth, each under the arched ceiling. First the dining room, near the front windows (a dining table outside, on the quay, offered alfresco dining.) Then the living room, and further back a bedroom and bathroom side-by-side. It was very well finished and furnished, but we decided that we could never tolerate the cave-like lifestyle.

However, we found some wonderful houses here in the Museum Quarter. On the last block before the Tolsteegsingel, the canal curves to the west; the east-side street continues straight, leaving an island between street and canal for a long block of houses which have been built right down to water level. These are handsome homes, with "normal" large windows and doors on the quay, just as they would be on a street. These are very elegant homes, and I am sure quite expensive. The simplicity of design, with the charming details in the shutters and main entrance, along with all the beautiful flowers always makes me pause and imagine what they're like inside.

Monday morning we prepared to move to the Nieuwe Haven, via the Oudegracht that we had walked the night before. The relatively low stone-arch bridges will scare off some boaters, as the height is 3.25 meters at the top of the arch. We can clear easily at 2.45 meters, but I understand how some taller boats will do damage to the corners of their wheelhouse in the curving Stadhuisbrug tunnel.

We traveled along slowly, avoiding the occasional private boat or work barge tied at the quay or motoring in the other direction. One of these was the beer barge, tied in front of the basement storage room for a bar, unloading cases and barrels of beer with a crane. Another barge appeared to be there long-term, used as storage and workshop for a building renovation project. And of course the glass-topped tour boats took their share of the waterway, as its most important user!

Other than enjoying the sights, it was a short and uneventful trip. We nosed into our assigned space, unfortunately one with no side piers. I would have preferred to put the stern on the dock, but we have a dinghy on davits at the stern. The boat has a suitable gangplank but we did have to climb over the bow rail; Carol preferred to do that when no one was watching!

For the next three days we stayed there, watching the boats on the canal and in the nearby lock, walking the business and residential streets at the north end of the city and patronizing the cafes and shops (as well as getting a haircut for each of us, Johnnie included.) One day the three of us did our canoe cruise of the Buitengracht, circling the canals clockwise. It was then, on the Maliesingel, that I spotted the jade-green and white canoe-stern motorcruiser Argo and fell in love. To this day I get a pang when I am going through my photo files and it comes up. It is similar to my current boat, Orion, but far more handsome, I hate to say.

On Tuesday I went off alone by bicycle, east along the north side of the singel, to the Veemarkthallen. The name translates as "cattle market halls" but I went there to see the Utrecht Car Market. Held every Tuesday, it is one of the largest car markets in Europe. I had no serious plan to buy a car, but after renting cars many times in Europe, I had often thought of buying a small hatchback. On this day I walked the aisles of about two thousand offerings. This is certainly the place to shop, but I did not investigate the legal requirements for non-EU residents. automarktutrecht.eu/en/home/

The Vredenburg market plaza is just three blocks south of the Nieuwe Haven; a large general market is held there on Wednesdays and Saturdays. We stocked up just before we left Utrecht, especially on fruits and vegetables, as we intended to find an isolated mooring for a few days of solitude and relaxation.

Our time limit had expired at this mooring, so we entered the Vecht, which begins at the Nieuwe Haven, for a much-anticipated slow cruise on that beautiful river. We headed north to the village of Oud Zuilen.

Vecht river

The Vecht, often called the most beautiful river in Europe and certainly the most beautiful in the Netherlands, flows north from Utrecht to the IJsselmeer at Muiden, a total distance of 40 km. It offers a leisure cruise paralleling the Amsterdam-Rijnkanaal, which is a highway for commercial barges.

There are three connections between them, at Weesp, Nigtevecht and Maarssen. All of these are through locks which normally stay open and are used only at times of flood. Small boats can pass from the Vecht under the Amsterdam-Rijnkanaal at Nieuwersluis or Breukelen to travel into the smaller waterways of the Heart of Holland.

"Vecht" translates (using online translation services) as "Fight". It's only a guess, but it is possible that the name dates from the time in the Middle Ages when the river was the front line of defense for Amsterdam. I have also found that the name derives from the Roman "Fectio", the name of a fort located here. What is definitely true is that the name has nothing at all to do with "fighting" the river.

It is a slow, calm stream with no sharp curves. There are no locks along the river, only those at each end (Utrecht and Muiden) and on the sides for access to lakes and canals. In fact the water in the Ijsselmeer is normally higher than that of the Vecht at the lock in Muiden, therefore the flow is reversed and may flow "upstream". Only in the case of very heavy rain will the water flow to the mouth of the river.

Cruising the Canals & Rivers of the Netherlands

At Nigtevecht, water from Utrecht is 'dumped' into the Amsterdam-Rijnkanaal; the lock here normally stays open. The water that comes into the river from Muiden gives the necessary counter pressure at this spot. Dutch officials say that it is too expensive to bring back the flow direction entirely to the original state, since the levees along the Vecht would have to be increased. According to others, the amount of water is controlled adequately via locks so that surprises are practically excluded.

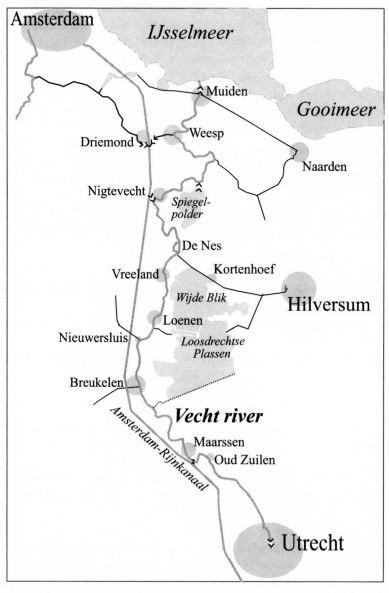

It is instructive to take a look at the chart to see the direction that the locks are pointing. At a real lock the gates point in a V toward the upstream direction; the symbols on the charts show this. At Utrecht the chart shows the gates of the Weerdsluis "holding back" the flow from the Kromme Rijn and Vaartse Rijn, which is as would be expected. But then at the other end of the river, supposedly the mouth of the river, the locks at Muiden point into the IJsselmmeer, "holding back" that water as well. The locks serving the streams and lakes alongside the Vecht point towards the river, keeping the higher water level in that waterway.

Oud-Zuilen

Our first stop on the Vecht was at the tiny village of Oud-Zuilen, just 5km north from Utrecht. We had to wait just a short while as the Plompbrug opened for us, then we tied up on the grassy west bank at free moorings (no services.) We couldn't see it from the water because of dense woodlands south of the village, but we knew that this is where Slot Zuylen (Castle) is situated.The most famous resident of the castle was Belle van Zuylen (Isabelle de Charrière), well-known writer and feminist. Slot Zuylen opened its doors to visitors about 50 years ago; we will be among those visitors soon. www.slotzuylen.nl

But for this night we dined on the terrace at the Belle Restaurant, of course named for the Belle of the castle. The location and view couldn't be better. Their terrace is about a three minute walk from our mooring, back over the bridge to the east side and directly on the quay, next to a large brick manor house. The house and yard is formal but enlivened by a row of red, yellow and white pansies along the low wrought-iron fence.

From our table we could look to our right, past a very nice Luxemotor barge moored at its *ligplaats* (mooring place) at the foot of the bridge. The bridge has a white steel lifting structure, simple but handsome, and often photographed. Across the river, near the bridge, there is a small park under some very large willow trees and then a bright green wetland in front; ducks paddled about in the river. To our left, down the quay, is a short row of small brick houses with beautiful flower and vegetable gardens. It's hard to imagine a more peaceful and charming setting, just what we needed after a few days in a busy city.

The restaurant is rustic and relaxed. Perhaps too relaxed, for the operation is fairly loose. The tables could be cleaner and the service a bit quicker, but when the waitress did arrive she served us competently. We both had a pike filet with parsley risotto and asparagus. The asparagus was perfect, not cooked enough for most people but just right for our taste. restaurantbelle.nl

After dinner we walked the streets of the village. As usual in the small Dutch towns, the houses of either red or white brick were very well maintained and surrounded by shrubs and flower beds. The river is very narrow here; the chart shows the bridge width to be 9 meters and I would guess that the river through the village is less than 20 meters across.

In the morning we walked past the restaurant and about 500 meters east to the castle, for a tour of the interior and the grounds. There is a moat, but not in the star pattern; this was not a castle that needed a defense structure. The staff served us our mid-morning coffee; there were no other visitors so we had a strong feeling of proprietorship.

We left the village traveling slowly so that we could enjoy the pleasant scenery. As the river curved to the left around a dense forest we watched, on the other side, a few gardeners at work in the largest community gardens that we have yet seen. It covered several hundred meters along the river and went back at least as far. The gardening sheds, fences and trellises were covered by vines, giving a jungle appearance.

The river looped back to the southwest then again turned north, now with the Amsterdam-Rijnkanaal right alongside us for a brief time. The Maarsen lock connects the river to the canal; it stays open except in flood. Bridge clearance through the lock is 3.75m. This lock is useful for boaters wanting to travel the Vecht but avoid Utrecht.

Maarssen

Maarssen is a much bigger town, with lots of shops and restaurants, from Greek dishes to the very elegant De Nonnerie. The Akropolis is right on the river, we had tied up just a few steps away, and I can't resist a good Giro sandwich, so that is where we had our lunch.   akropolismaarssen.nl

We walked around a few streets after lunch but we were eager to get on to Breukelen, a more interesting town. Just north of Maarssen we passed a magnificent estate on the right bank; I had noticed this property while previewing our route on Google Earth when we were in Utrecht and saw that it has its own one-hole golf course in the back yard, complete with sand traps and water hazards.

Across from the mansion there were some lagoons, left over from sand extraction. These always look inviting and I would like to go in and anchor, but I am always concerned about the depth and also about legal rights, they are probably private property.

Breukelen

Breukelen is sandwiched between the Vecht and the Amsterdam-Rijnkanaal. The 0.7km-long (and very narrow) Dannegracht/Kerkvaart cuts across the middle of town to connect the waterways. Small boats can use this route to the Vinkeveense and Nieuwkoopse lakes and on to Woerden; the recommended draft is 0.7m and the width is only 2.8m.

The ANWB Wateralmanak lists several boatyards and jachthavens at Breukelen, however these are all on the Loosdrechtse Plassen, a group of lakes off the river to the east. We stayed overnight (the maximum allowance) at the town quay on the left bank. Again, it was free but no services.

We had our dinner onboard but on a bicycle ride through town we saw Chinese, Indian, Vietnamese, Greek, Middle Eastern, Italian and French restaurants, along with others offering standard Dutch menus. This is quite a lot of choices for a small town, it is probably a popular weekend outing from the large cities. Perhaps it is also because the former Nyenrode castle is the home for international students at Nyenrode Business Universiteit.

Our bike ride took us to the east side of the river to view the many mansions spaced along that bank, as well as a couple that we could see on the west. As soon as we rode across the bridge we saw the moated Gunterstein mansion, the others are north from the bridge. I was especially looking for a house that had been profiled in NY Times article some years earlier, a modern design as opposed to the 18th century houses predominant here. I never found it, as many of the houses are obscured by trees. I think that one purpose of that article was to show the differences between this Breukelen and its namesake: Brooklyn, New York.

My 1845 map of the Netherlands shows a split in the river at the next town, Nieuwersluis. The right-hand fork is the same path as the current Vecht river to Muiden. The left-hand fork takes a twisting route into the center of Amsterdam; it is labeled on the map as "Amstel R." That route is available to boats such as ours, we could take a short canal named Nieuwe Wetering to a direct crossing of the Amsterdam-Rijnkanaal and then follow what is now named the Angstel river to join the Amstel at Ouderkerk. This will be on my list for a future excursion, through one of the largest agricultural zones of Holland.

Loosdrechtse Plassen

We left Breukelen and passed Nieuwersluis on the Vecht, then used the Mijndense lock to enter Loosdrechtse Plassen. The lock and canal has recently been renovated; the concrete work and gates look almost new. It lowers boats from the Vecht to the level of the lakes. The lock itself is unusual, in that it is a 50m-long curve, a tight one; from the west gate you cannot see the east gate because of the curve. After the lock, the waterway passes by a large development of waterfront homes; the area is named Recreatiecentrum Mijnden. Part of this new construction, at the lake side, is Jachthaven Mijnden, a full-service marina with 350 slips. We stopped there to use their wastewater disposal service, before continuing into the lake.

Aside from using the pumpout service, I have been wanting to boat on this lake ever since my early visits to the Netherlands. During my boat search I walked the docks of boat brokers at Oud Loosdrecht including

Wolfrat. www.wolfrat.nl Now I cruised around the lake and past those same docks, then returned to the river at Loenen. It was Saturday and the lake was busy.

The lake is shallow and using the correct chart is important. The paper ANWB chart used by travelers on the Vecht is labeled I-Vechtplassen; it shows the Loosdrechtse Plassen, but not in sufficient detail. For that, obtain chart P/R Vinkeveense & Loosdrecht Plassen, which shows depths throughout the lake and also shows all of the havens and boatyards. As I wrote earlier, I use the electronic version of these charts, from Stentec, on my computer; the detailed chart version appears by simply double-clicking on the image of the lake.

I counted the havens and boatyards shown on the chart around the shore of the lakes: 37, and I may have missed one or two. On our cruise through the lakes I did not count the number of boats that were moored or cruising, if I had I am sure it would be over one thousand. This is a busy place, as I had expected, and so we didn't moor here, even though some of the small islands did appear inviting. They have that "desert island" appeal, in fact one is named Robinson Crusoe island. We stopped briefly at Markus Pos island for lunch onboard and a dog walk, then found the entrance to the Muyeveldse Vaart channel, not an easy task. We had been advised during our marina stop to use this channel because another cut, which appears to be an obvious route on the chart, has sections as shallow as 0.5 meter.

We did find the channel without trouble; on the way into the lake I had made a point of looking back and noticing the layout of the narrow strips of land. Two boats ahead of us were already in the lock. As soon as we entered the gates closed behind us and we were quickly through, the rise being less than 1 meter. The line of boats moored on the west bank of the Vecht at Loenen began right across from the lock, in front of a large manor house; we turned north and found an available space beyond a bridge, closer to the town. The bridge had opened for the three boats, synchronized with the lock operation.

Loenen

The town mooring quay lies next to a large plowed field; there is a path along the river bank but it ends where the riverside houses have their private yards right to the water, so we had to turn in and walk the main street, Dorpstraat, paralleling the river. We walked about a kilometer north, to the De Hoop windmill. Returning, we saw several restaurants. We could choose from Tante Koosje, De Proeverij, Brasserie Het Amsterdammertje and De Eterij. The menu at the last one seemed most suited to our tastes and budget, so we went there later in the evening. Fresh handmade pasta with veal strips, mushrooms, spinach and grand padano cheese was excellent, as was the service and the ambience. www.de-eterij.nl

We have noticed more than the usual number of fine restaurants in these towns along the Vecht, a result of the pleasant views and the easy access from larger cities. This is a popular region, and not just for boaters. Some of these are far too elegant and expensive for us but there is usually a range of choices. The only exception was at the tiny village of Oud Zuilen, which has but one choice, luckily we were happy with that one.

My plan for the next day was to cruise through Vreeland, De Nes and Nigtevecht enroute to the Spiegelpolder, where we would anchor at one of the islands for a day or two of rest. I was expecting this lake to be more peaceful than the Loosdrecht Plassen. I did have to make a plan; the distance on the river is 14 km and then the lock into the lake operates only twice a day, between 10:00-11:00 and 17:30-20:00 h. The morning opening is too early, so we will take our time and arrive for the evening hours. Once we pass the lock we can go directly to the string of islands on the southeastern corner. We would arrive there on Sunday night, expecting that weekend visitors will have left.

So there was no need to leave Loenen early in the morning. We used the time for a 5km bicycle ride, crossing the bridge near our mooring then cycling north on a narrow lane. We enjoyed the view of some more elegant homes on the east side of the river but the real purpose was to see the woonboten permanently moored on both sides of the river between Loenen and Vreeland. We will of course see them from the water, but we were curious to see the land side.

It did turn out to be very interesting, these homes have parking, storage sheds and well-gardened front yards. It resembles any housing development of "box" style homes, except that the boxes are floating. There were dozens of homes in this group; the basic design is simple but the materials and design details make them varied and very attractive.

Our turnaround point was in the center of Vreeland, where we stopped for coffee and pastry, as well as some bread for the future. On our return through Loenen we stopped for some more shopping, to be ready for eating onboard for two or three days.

Vreeland

We departed Loenen just before noon. We did not stop the boat at Vreeland but motored along slowly, which was our desire but it was also enforced by waiting for two bridges to open. No problem, this is a beautiful town and we enjoyed the sights. This is one of many towns in the Netherlands where we would be happy to live. The town provides a grass riverbank mooring, if we hadn't already picked up our bread we could have tied up there and walked back to the bakery. But then we might have seen a "house for sale" sign and been tempted! The view back to the south on the river can't be beat: beautiful flowerbeds, trees hanging their long green limbs over the water, handsome small boats (*sloepen*) tied at their owner's docks, white houses with red tile roofs, all topped by the tall spire of the church.

North of Vreeland we passed by the windmill De Rietgors and then noticed a 38 meter cargo barge, converted into a houseboat, permanently moored on the west bank. We haven't seen many of these, most of the houseboats are constructed for that purpose, using lumber and land-based home construction materials. The barge offers more interior space than most of them; a 38x5 meter barge offers almost 190 square meters of floor space on one level. That is similar to a villa, not just the average home.

At the entrance of the Hilversum canal the old river takes a loop to the west, named De Nes, and the channel continues straight. More houseboats have taken advantage of this quiet place away from river traffic. I suppose that the loop does resemble a nose, quite a long one.

A series of sweeping turns through farm fields brought us to Nigtevecht. If we had wanted to go quickly to Amsterdam we could just go straight on, through a lock which stays open, onto the Amsterdam-Rijnkanaal. We didn't, of course, so we followed another series of curves past the town and out into open, flat countryside. Shortly we arrived at the lock into the Spiegelpolder and tied up at the wachtsteiger to awaiting the opening hours. This is also on a loop of the river, about 300 degrees of a circle. The inside of the loop is now a lagoon, again most likely from sand extraction.

Promptly at 17:30 we were the first into the lock; it went quickly and we were soon headed down the 2km-long lake. We ran slowly down the southeastern side of the lake along a string of narrow islands, looking for an anchorage. A surprising sight in the narrow cut between two islands was the sudden appearance of four men rowing a broad-beamed boat. Each man pulled an oar, two rows of two men seated side-by-side in classic galley-slave style; probably members of a rowing club in training for an upcoming race.

We selected our desert island and anchored on the open-water side. A sandy strip on the mainland is not far away behind the island; on the next morning we used the dinghy to get there for a day at the beach. As the crow flies we were 10 miles from the center of Amsterdam, but the city seemed a thousand miles away.

Waterway	From	To	KM	Hours
Merwedekanaal	Vreeswijk	Utrecht	7.0	1.5
Vaartse Rijn	Utrecht	Utrecht	2.2	0.3
Oudegracht	Utrecht	Utrecht	1.6	0.5
Vecht	Utrecht	Muiden	40.0	6.8

Vecht to Amstel

The rest stop did turn out to be at our own little "desert island". If it has a name I couldn't find it. We stayed there Monday and Tuesday, it seems that is a good time to be there alone; it's largely a weekend recreation site. There were boats active on the lake and at the boatyard on the western shore, about 1km away, but none came down to our corner in the southeast.

According to the chart we are actually in the Blijkpolder, the southern half of the lake; the northern half is the Spiegelpolder. Spiegel means "mirror" and that was the status of the water, as smooth as glass. Each day we rowed the dinghy over to our private beach. While we stretched out on a blanket, Johnnie sniffed out the surroundings and reported back: two dachshunds, a cocker spaniel and a mixed breed had been there before him.

Onboard the boat, I took a few hours in the afternoon to spread out a paper chart on the salon table to plan our next route. (Yes, there is a good use for paper charts, they display a large area in a broad view; the computer screen is best for seeing the details.) The charts showed the many waterways, the canals, rivers and lakes within the Randstad, the circle of the largest cities in the Netherlands: Amsterdam, Utrecht, Rotterdam, Den Haag, Leiden and Haarlem.

I did some trial-and-error planning using the table of waterway dimensions that I had previously researched for the EuroCanals Guides. There are a few places that I would like to go that we can't do in this boat because of shallow depths and/or low bridges.

Eventually I worked out a plan for circling through the "Heart of Holland". This will necessarily take us back through the city of Rotterdam; I would prefer a suitable waterway shortcut through the wetlands from Gouda to Delft, but none exists. I thought that I had found a marginal but possible route via the Rotte river but then I saw that one short section has a depth of 0.7m and height of 2.4m (our boat is D1.15m, H2.45m.)

So it will be necessary to pass through Rotterdam again. From Gouda to Delft the distance is 35km and there are two locks. The river travel, 26km, will be at least at 10 km/hr (downstream) and the canal from Rotterdam to Delft will be at 6 km/hr. Allowing 15 minutes for each lock, the total travel time will be 4.6 hours. That is certainly do-able, we can expect to arrive at Delft in mid-afternoon. After Delft we will travel up the western side of Holland, through Leiden and Haarlem, before looping back to Amsterdam.

We will not stop at Amsterdam at the beginning of this circle, even though we will touch the southern city limit. It is because this time I want to enter the city from the southwest, before mooring in the city center. I selected our first destination to be Ouderkerk on the Amstel river, about a 4-hour cruise from the island. Then we will go south to Woerden, a town on my star fort list that I had visited previously, then on to Gouda. This route will take us to some of the best-known tourist stops in Holland and along some interesting waterways.

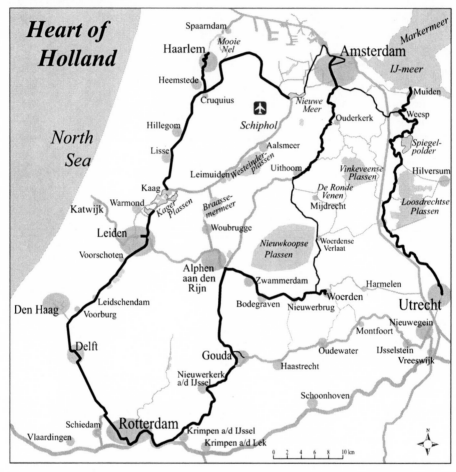

The lock at the top of the lake doesn't operate until 10AM so we took our time casting off. There were a few other boats gathered at the lock but all went through quickly. We followed the other boats northbound but dropped behind as we passed Fort bij Uitermeer (the fort by Uitermeer) which is part of the Waterlinie that defended Amsterdam. We didn't stop but we did have a good view of the cylindrical tower and the bunkers. There is a canal leading east from here, the 's Gravelandse Vaart, which small boats can use to the town of Naarden (D1.0m H1.2m). We saw a possible mooring quay a few hundred meters further along the river but we were reluctant to stop so soon, for even a short visit to the fort.

Heart of Holland

Five kilometers north, as we could see on the chart, we expected the two windmills De Eendragt and De Vriendschap on the west bank followed by the docks of WSV De Vecht in Weesp. Our stop here was a necessary one; we used the vuilwaterstation (wastewater station). www.wsvdevecht.nl (This haven might be useful for other needs; I used Google Translate to read their web page and found that one of the services provided is: "Police: Once the port area allows you to end the police"???)

From there we moved to the town docks just north of the bascule bridge, for a short stay. The dock is on a canal cut through the heart of the star fort. The singel and four star points remain on the east and south. The WSV De Vecht is located on one of these points and another club, WV De Zeemeermin uses the southeastern singel, on the south side of a low fixed bridge. The other parts of the singel have been filled in and built over, with just a narrow drainage ditch remaining.

But in this case I was less interested in the star fort than in the cylindrical fortress on the Ossenmarkt island (ox market, no longer in existence.) Its design is almost exactly the same as the one we visited at Asperen, on the river Linge. That is not surprising because they were both built in the same era, to anchor the ends of the Waterlinie, the water defense line for Holland. There is much more history to be learned about all of the fortresses, but at least now I have an idea of how and why the line existed.

Parallel to the main canal where we are docked, Weesp has its own Oudegracht, passing through the town as the one did at Utrecht. The gracht here is not navigable, it is filled with beautiful water lilies. Baskets and urns of flowers provided by the municipal government overflow with purple and white pansies. The walk along the Oudegracht was a very pleasant one. If we were to have a full meal here, we probably would have selected the CuliCafe. www.culicafe.nl Instead we found a small grocery store and took some supplies back to the boat.

On the way we passed the shop of De Sloepenmakelaar, a broker of small wooden boats which they find in Sweden. This was of interest to us because our first years of traveling on the lakes and canals of the USA were on an 18ft wooden boat, a Lyman. The brief visit renewed my thoughts of replacing our plastic dinghy, which is rather well-worn, with a handsome wooden boat. Maybe later. www.desloepenmakelaar.nl

There is a lock at Weesp and another at the exit of the canal, the Smal Weesp, onto the Amsterdam-Rijnkanaal, but both normally remain open. The three bridges in Weesp open on demand; *bruggeld* (bridge toll) of €2.50 is collected at the Zwaantjebrug, the middle bridge. On the north bank of the canal is yet another windmill, this one ('t Haantje) has a residence attached. A short distance later there is an interesting structure located in a circular lagoon at the western end of the Smal Weesp: a circular residential building, sweeping through about 270°, lines the edge of the lagoon. It appears as if the open section of the circle had been cut away and relocated 100 meters away. It is a very strange sight.

Next we crossed the Amsterdam-Rijnkanaal into a stays-open lock, and a bridge to be lifted, at Driemond. We waited a few minutes before crossing, as two huge barges were passing southbound side-by-side while two more were coming up northbound; then we followed the recommended procedure of turning to our right, with traffic, for 100 meters then across the canal and finally back to the Driemond lock. A U-crossing, rather than straight across.

The waterway was now the Weesper Trekvaart, leading to the Amstel river at the southern edge of Amsterdam. I usually think of a trekvaart as a narrow waterway that passes through open countryside; this one is that for the first 3km west from the lock but on the western half of its length the curves of the eastern half turn into a series of arrow-straight canal lines.

We were third in a line of motorcruisers following an unladen barge; it looked very ungainly because it sat so high in the water and took up much of the width of the waterway. We just followed, watching the sights on both sides. To be honest, they weren't very interesting, a long line of low suburban residences and occasional industrial zones. This waterway will get you there, but after the Vecht it is quite dull and utilitarian.

That feeling changed quickly when we reached the Amstel river. We could have turned right on that river and been in central Amsterdam within ten minutes. Instead we followed my plan and turned south; the river almost immediately became a smooth, wide path curving across the flat fields of Holland. Dikes hold the river higher than the surrounding land; the dikes are not much higher than river level so the view is wide open in all directions and well above the fields. Sheep and cows spread out over the land. There are trees and brush on the banks but they are scattered, only the first kilometer at Amsterdam can be described as "tree-lined", because of a large park on the western side.

The Amstel is a significant river but it can't be included with the Great Rivers, even if it is the namesake for Amsterdam. For one thing, it is only 29 kilometers long. It doesn't start hundreds of kilometers away in the Swiss alps or in France; it starts at the junction of the Drecht river and the Aarkanaal, a man-made waterway cut to connect the Amstel with the Oude Rijn and the Gouwe river. For most of its length it averages about 60 meters wide and slowly widens as it approaches Amsterdam to 100 meters, which it maintains right into the heart of the city. It ends there, splitting into several canals which flow into the IJ river.

There is a slow current to the north but we could easily cruise against it at 8 km/hr, good for sightseeing. Still, we couldn't quite keep up with a large group of bicyclists on the west bank road. The area beyond them is heavily wooded but then we can sometimes see the pathways of the park.

After the park ended we came to a well-known restaurant with a dock welcoming boaters, the Kleine Kalfje. Even on a weekday the riverside terrace and the outside tables along the roadway were just about filled with those having a lingering luncheon. Off to the west we could see one aircraft after another descending into Schiphol airport.

Two very nice Luxemotor liveaboard barges looked to be permanently moored in front of some large modern homes, an upscale suburb of Amsterdam. Swinging around a sharp curve and some esses, we came up on about a dozen rowing shells in practice; singles, pairs and eight-man crews. I was so busy watching out for the shells and their coaches' boats that I never did see the clubhouse and dock, about which I was curious. (I later learned that it was far behind us, not far south of the junction of the Weesper Trekvaart; three adjacent basins on the east bank are the homes of two rowing clubs and a rowing school.) I have rowed recreationally and went to a university where the crew was more revered than the football team (Cornell), but I didn't row at school, being approximately one-third smaller than the average oarsman.

No sooner had we passed the last of the shells when we saw the Wester-Amstel mansion, as the name indicates on the west bank of the Amstel. It is one of the three remaining places of sixty who once graced that shore. The grounds include modern sculptures. A visit might be of interest to us, but even from the water we can see an icon-sign "No Dogs" so we probably won't take the trouble to walk back to it from our destination.

We encountered more rowing shells as far south as Ouderkerk; skippers need to be alert in this part of the river, between Amsterdam and Ouderkerk, even though there is a lot of sightseeing to be done. After we docked I chatted with a local gentleman who told me that there are rowing races every year in March which bring out hundreds of rowing shells and thousands of participants. The races are on the 8km stretch between Ouderkerk and Amsterdam; they start in over 20 different categories, at short intervals, with the result that there are frequent overtaking actions on the winding river. Sounds a lot more exciting than the well-matched races in straight channels that I had seen years before.

Ouderkerk

I had already made a plan to stay overnight at a west-bank quay in front of a row of restaurants, across the river from the village of Ouderkerk. The chart showed that quay about 200m south of a highway bridge; it is a BB bridge but we could clear under the span, so we did so slowly and pulled over to the quay. As expected there was a good choice of restaurants and a great view over the river to the old church, most likely the one that the town is named for. The town is said to be two centuries older than Amsterdam.

Cruising the Canals & Rivers of the Netherlands

This is a popular outing for Amsterdammers, arriving by car, motorcycle, boat and bicycle. Terraces on the river offer open-air dining, with dining rooms inside across the roadway. Of the various restaurants, Loetje aan de Amstel was our choice. loetjeaandeamstel.nl

It was still early, however, so we walked over the highway bridge, stopping to watch some more shells pass underneath; we must have seen at least two dozen altogether. We walked through the village as far as the bridge over the small river which comes in from the southeast, the Bullewijk. There we found the Bakker Out bakery, at just the right time for a mid-afternoon coffee and pastry. "Sinds 1897", says the sign over the doorway. I was clever enough to take a sack of good things for tomorrow's mid-morning coffee, when we will be out in "the middle of nowhere".

Later we learned that the cemetery alongside the Bullewijk, which we could see a part of from the bakery, is the Beth Haim, the oldest Jewish cemetery in the Netherlands, dating from 1614. But now I am not so sure about the "old church" as we walked past two others, St Urban's (Catholic) and the Amstelkerk (Protestant). On the way back to the Amstel bridge, in fact at #2 Brugstraat, we stocked up on nuts, olives and fruit at Hekelaar Mediterranean delicatessen.

The brief view that we had of the Bullewijk was very inviting, and looked even more inviting on the chart; a small river that curves like a snake, leading to other, smaller, rivers that curve even more like a snake. We were now getting into the Groene Hart, the Green Heart of Holland.

VVV, the tourist bureau, describes this region as the low ground, lakes and rivers circled by the cities of Amsterdam, Hilversum, Utrecht, Rotterdam, Den Haag, Leiden and Haarlem. The lakes were created by peat extraction; now pieces of nature are returning to the ancient peatlands. In the region are characteristic Old Holland towns and villages, situated on canals and rivers, including Woerden, Bodegraven, Gouda and Delft. The VVV recommends routes for seeing this land and water up close by walking, bicycling, canoeing or roller-skating.

We were of course traveling on a cruising boat, quite large relative to the smaller, low draft/low height *sloepen* used by the local boaters, such as the handsome boat shown at right. The potential waterways that we might take are very limited. So I made a careful check of the chart (ANWB Waterkaart Groene

Hart) and decided that we would continue southwest on the Amstel river to Uithoorn and then turn south on the Kromme Mijdrecht toward Woerden, stopping overnight in the open countryside.

I would have liked to take a side excursion starting on the Bullewijk, but had to put aside each of the three options onward from that river. First, because of my interest in rivers, I would like to travel up the branch of the Rhine represented by the Bullewijk and the Angstel rivers. I can work out a route to do that, but we would only end up in Breukelen, where we have already been. Also, depths as little as 0.8m will prevent us from using the major part of the Angstel, defeating the basic purpose.

We could easily reach the Vinkeveense Plassen, and we might do that in the future, but it is too similar to the Loosdrecht Plassen and the Spiegelpolder, both of which we had enjoyed just days earlier.

I seriously considered a day's trip on the Waver and Winkel rivers, on a loop which would return us to the Amstel. The draft is sufficient (just barely) and the bridges all open; the chart notes that the bridges are *Zelfbediening*, self-opening. That doesn't mean that they open themselves, it means that we will have to get off the boat to open the bridges. That doesn't concern me at first, as we have opened many bridges in France. But I spoke with a local boater moored at our dock and he explained that these bridges are, in some cases, homemade by the farmers and used by them daily to access their fields and barns. I would need to enlist the help of someone locally to help in the opening; they may not be available or may not be too happy about a tourist interrupting their workday. So I abandoned the idea, we will stick to the main waterway, the Amstel.

We set off southward at about 08:00. Just around the first curve we passed another fine restaurant, the Jagershuis; its terrace, set up with white tables, white chairs and white umbrellas, looked very inviting. The west bank is the main road, and most, if not all, of the restaurants are located on that side of the Amstel.

The high bridge (H5.9m) of the A9 autoroute passed overhead, then we entered the only straightening cut on the river, a short one that has formed Amsteleiland inside the original curve. For several kilometers we cruised through pleasant scenery. Green fields stretched as far back as we could see, cut by long lines of narrow irrigation ditches perpendicular to the path of the river. On the river banks are scattered homes and farms, and some large greenhouse plantations. Always there are small boats tied up among the riverbank grasses and covered by canvas. Small groups of trees add to the scene but don't block the view.

A wooden terrace extending out over the water announced the presence of Eetcafe De Zwarte Kat. And at the village of Nes aan den Amstel the quay and waterside tables of Cafe Restaurant De Vergulde Zon and Cantina Del Corazon offer two more dining choices.

Soon after, the river Oude Waver joined from the east. This is where we would have returned to the Amstel had I decided that we could make that excursion. On the spur of the moment I turned into this river and followed it for a half-kilometer to a mooring place marked on the chart. Rather than stay at that spot overnight, as I had hoped, we will stop here for our coffee break and for a short walk.

The attraction here is Fort Nessersluis, another part of the Waterlinie that defended Amsterdam. At first glance the fort appeared to be a low grass-topped hill, which of course would be very unusual in this part of Holland. We walked back along the bank of the river and could see the moat surrounding the fort and the line of stone walls with windows and doors facing us. The fort is open for visitors at certain times but not when we were there; that wasn't too disappointing to me because I am mainly interested in the existence of these forts and their geographical location, not the interior of the rooms. The forts form a 360° ring around Amsterdam; those that I have been finding extend from the IJsselmeer near Muiden to Weesp, Uitermeer, Hinderdam, Nigtevecht, Abcoude and three on the Waver river, including the one in front of me today. For more information on these forts see: www.stelling-amsterdam.nl

We left the Oude Waver, aiming for the Kromme Mijdrecht river; *kromme* means "twisting" and the Amstel itself is very kromme in the section between Ouderkerk and Uithoorn, especially so in the two kilometers north of Uithoorn, where there are nine curves, some of them very sharp. But "very sharp" doesn't mean much to a boat of our size when the river remains at least 50 meters wide, and there is almost no traffic from large barges. It's just a matter of staying to the right side of center and keeping a good watch forward for approaching boats. I did say that there are "almost no barges" but we did encounter one, a long and very low fully-laden fuel barge, of which at first only the wheelhouse was visible over the low ground inside a curve. He took the middle of the channel through the curve, forcing us to change our line but still with plenty of room.

Uithoorn is the largest city on the Amstel, other than Amsterdam. It has three or four more waterfront dining locations, as always on the west side, and two more forts in the Waterlinie, both not visible from the river.

South of Uithoorn is the junction with the Kromme Mijdrecht, flowing up from the south. We left the Amstel here and slowed down a bit, both literally and figuratively. Traffic is rare and the boats are usually smaller than ours. Since our coffee stop we have been tracing the western edge of De Ronde Venen.

The "Round the Fens" (bogs) area was created by peat production and subsequent reclamation. It is roughly a circle, centered on a U-shaped canal connecting Mijdrecht and the Vinkeveense Plassen. Surrounding this area are the rivers Kromme Mijdrecht, Amstel, Waver, Winkel, Angstel and

Aa. The peat production parcels were laid out in a radial pattern from the central canal. Hundreds of irrigation and drainage ditches radiate from the ring of rivers.

Woerdense Verlaat

We cruised south on the Kromme Mijdrecht to a spot just north of the village of Woerdense Verlaaat, where we moored on the Amstelkade, across the water from a windmill, and did some exploring of the nearby fens. There was a Y-shaped dock, one wing for us and the other unused. Later we would be able to watch the sun set behind the sails of the windmill. But first we found a lane leading to the open fields where we walked Johnnie on one of the rows of earth between the ditches; the parallel lanes and ditches repeat over and over on both sides.

A flock of sheep milled about, grazing and ignoring us. Near the beginning of our walk we passed through a corral with gates on both ends; we guessed that this is for handling the sheep. Both gates were open, so we weren't disrupting anything.

After returning Johnnie to the boat, we set off on a bicycle ride. We were not as much in the natural area as the chart had led me to believe; there are homes along the roads and an industrial compound served by barges. But we took a dirt lane near the windmill and followed it along one of the earthen ridges. This brought us to an area of trees and brush, far enough away from the homes to give a good feeling of nature around us. This has spoiled us, so before we returned to the boat we rode a short distance down the waterway, where we came to the end of the homes and we could see another mooring out in the open country. That's where we decided to spend the night.

We first passed through a lock in Woerdense Verlaat. Now we are in the part of Holland where the locks and bridges are operated by local authorities; tolls will be more common. First we asked for a bridge opening; *geen bruggeld* (no bridge toll), then around a 90° corner we entered the lock and paid *sluisgeld* of €1.50.

From the lock the canal ran dead-straight for 1.7km to our mooring, located in the short leg between two more 90° corners; not a good spot if there was much traffic, but we expected none. We tied up on the wooden dock and had a look around the open countryside. No windmill here, but we did enjoy seeing the five local boats moored in a side-channel, protected by a wooded spit of land: two converted barges, two Dutch cruisers and a small motorboat. This was more to our liking. We could see a number of farmhouses and barns, but there was no car traffic as there was at our first mooring. Mostly we look out on acres and acres of green fields, spotted with geese, sheep and cattle, and just a few trees here and there.

After the straight canal and sharp-edged corners, the waterway becomes the natural river Grecht. This was a good location to start from in the morning, as we can be in Woerden in about an hour. My plan was to spend two or three hours there and then move on to Gouda by evening. The latter segment should take 4 to 5 hours, so I want to be away from Woerden by 11:00. I planned to get us underway immediately when we woke up, with Carol fixing breakfast while we crossed the fields. That would put us at the quay in Woerden just after 09:00. There I wanted to view the star fort by walking the singel. No fortifications remain but we could have a look at Woerden Castle.

Woerden

This town is a significant bottleneck for some good potential cruising. A quick look at the chart shows an 11km waterway running straight west from the center of Utrecht to Woerden, then on to Leiden; this is the path of one of the original branches of the Rhine: the Leidse Rijn and the Oude Rijn. It is easy to jump at the chance to make this trip, until a careful look at the chart shows a series of fixed bridges with height from 2.0 to 2.6 meters, then a final blow at Woerden is the fixed bridge of 1.7 meters height. Only very low boats can travel this beautiful waterway. It is partly because of these limitations that we traveled a route 78 kilometers longer to get to this point.

We did get an early start as planned and didn't see another boat, car or even a person on the green path of the Grecht until we arrived at the northwestern outskirts of Woerden. There we had to slow to a crawl as we watched a mother and two children using a self-operated ferry to cross the canal. A square, flat platform, just large enough for maybe ten people to stand, is pulled across on a cable, probably by an electric winch. It didn't take long, the canal here is just over twice as wide as our boat.

The ferry is adjacent to the marina of WSV De Greft, where we would be looking for a slip if our stay was to be overnight. This is a full-facilities marina right at the edge of the built-up area, about 1 kilometer from the town center. That 1km on the Oude Rijn is bordered on both sides by a surprising number of industrial buildings, but once we passed through the BB bridge and into the star-fort singel we saw only a traditional and historic Dutch town. Visitors moorings on the singel are limited, the docks and quays are filled by local boats. But with the help of the harbormaster we found space at the town quay, after assuring him that we would be gone well before noon. Near us on the quay was a large Dutch sailing barge, looking as if the crew might raise the sails at any time and simply sail away. No one was aboard, but I'm sure it is a long-term resident at that mooring.

We set off down the quay to follow the singel. In two blocks we looked into the town center to view the windmill De Windhond. It was unusual in that it wasn't right on the water, often they are situated in the star point. It was also unusual that it sat atop a mound of earth, so that it towered over that part of the town. We learned that it turns for tourists on summer

Wednesdays, unfortunately this was a Friday. The VVV tourist office is beside the mill, so we gathered some local information, including the fact that the mill stands on a Molenberg, originally a fortress that was a part of the ramparts. The mill is still in use for milling corn. The miller lives in the base of the structure.

There is much history to be seen in Woerden. The VVV gave us a list of 49 national monuments, from the castle to a "Whitewashed little building". The castle is a very impressive block of brick, with low cylindrical towers on each of the four corners; it was built in 1404. It originally was surrounded by a moat, in these modern days two arms of the moat have been filled-in and paved for a parking lot.

The Oostsingel led us from the castle to a residential area. The typical Dutch brick houses enjoy a view of the park and the water, of course with ducks paddling about. One of the proud homeowners has installed on the brick front wall, in steel script letters, "Bella Vista". We continued along the north and came back to the town haven and the quay where we had tied up. Coffee and bread from Paninoteca and some groceries from an adjacent market, as well as some cash from the ABN-AMRO geldautomaat (ATM), readied us to get back underway.

Oude Rijn

The Oude Rijn west from Woerden is a pleasant cruise. The river curves slowly through the agricultural heart of Holland. Scattered homes line the riverbanks, most of them with gardens. We loved watching them as we passed by, wondering if we would be happy living there; most of the time we thought we would! The occasional group of industrial buildings seem out of place here, but they are unobtrusive and quickly left behind.

We had driven this route previously, during our first quick visit to the country. I recall that Nieuwerbrug was a quiet and charming small village, strung along the river. This time we enjoyed the view from the river rather than from a car window; many of the homes presented their good side and their flowerboxes to the river. We paid our bridge toll for the opening and continued without stopping; I noticed that here the cars must pay a 50-cent bridge toll as well, although pedestrians can cross for free. The car toll is probably meant to discourage traffic, as this is a river and pedestrian-oriented village.

Bodegraven is a larger town, a regional services and shopping center for the farm economy. Its main feature of interest is the windmill located at a turn in the river; it can be seen for some distance in either direction. I had looked at a Te Koop boat here, at a long quay for local boats on the western side of town.

We stopped here briefly because we decided that we needed more towels, laundry facilities being a little hard to find. If I can figure out the space question I will see if I can install a clothes washer onboard. That would have to operate on shore power, or a generator, which we don't have (yet.) Carol did find a dry goods store not far from the short-term quay and was very happy with the design and quality of the towels that she bought.

We didn't linger because I wanted to get settled in at Gouda as early as possible. The next town we came to on the Oude Rijn, Zwammerdam, is the entry point to more lakes and a large natural area in the Nieuwekoopse Plassen. This is a zone that requires a permit from local authorities and much of it forbidden to use by motorboats, so it is out of bounds for us.

The small city of Alphen aan den Rijn spreads out on both sides of the Oude Rijn west of the Aarkanaal intersection, but we are turning south there and so we just nick the corner of the city. The waterway coming up from Gouda is the Gouwe, a canalized river. The banks are hardened by concrete or wooden walls, the river itself is not as pretty as the one we have just left.

Gouwe

We rather suddenly returned to city/suburban life as soon as we made the turn south. First there was a busy road bridge, with enough clearance that we didn't need an opening; I was glad for that because it seemed that traffic would back up for miles if forced to stop. Then we found the railroad bridge already open. This is an unusual bridge, the span over the canal rotates over a support in the center of the waterway; boat traffic passes by on either side of the rotated section of rail.

Then another first for this cruise as we sail over autoroute traffic on the Alphen Aqueduct. A four-lane superhighway dips under our canal. We can't see directly down on the cars and trucks, of course, but it gives an eerie feeling as we glide over them.

Heart of Holland

As quickly as we entered this area of busy modern life we left it again, for now we are in the Boskoop. The name means "Trees For Sale". For much further than we can see on either side, tree plantations and greenhouses fill every inch of the land.

There are three *hefbrug* on this canal; on this type of bridge the entire span travels straight up, lifted by cables on tall towers, one on each bank. (Most bridges in the Netherlands are the "bascule bridge" type, where the span is hinged at one end or it is split in the middle and each end is hinged.) I suppose that they are used on the Gouwe because the canal is relatively wide and even a span hinged at both ends would be too long to lift. The cable towers are steel-girder construction, resembling an oil drilling rig, and are a strange sight in this otherwise horizontal landscape. The result is ugly and rather jarring.

We were able to pass under the first hefbrug at Alphen but at the next two the chart shows a clearance of 2.45m, close to our height. We might have been tempted to see if we could squeak under but don't get the opportunity as the bridge spans lift before we get there for the barge that is traveling just in front of us.

The approach to Gouda begins with another aqueduct over an eight-lane highway, the A12, then a bascule bridge. That bridge may help to prove my theory about the length of the span to be lifted; the Coenecoopbrug is a bascule bridge, hinged on the east bank and lifted by a mechanism underneath that structure. But the opening section spans only one-half of the water width; a concrete pier in the center of the canal supports the non-opening western half. We didn't see this bridge in action, as the clearance of 4.3m was sufficient for both the barge and us to pass under. Two more rail bridges are higher yet. The first lifts by mysterious means, because we didn't see it operate; the second is obviously a hefbrug but is much better looking. Tall concrete columns at each of the four corners are connected at the top by horizontal cylinders, forming a rectangle high in the sky; the rail span is lifted inside this box. This is a massive structure which dispels any fears that the mechanism isn't up to the task. Unfortunately we don't see this one lift either.

Gouda

Just south of this spectacular bridge is the left turn onto the Nieuwe Gouwe, toward the center of Gouda and its network of city canals. We passed up a possible dock at the yacht club WV Gouda and headed for the Kattensingel on the north of the central city, in a residential area but just a short walk from the tourist section. A nearby quay on the Turfsingel offers a pumpout station.

It was Friday afternoon when we arrive, just missing the weekly cheese market on Thursday, one of the main attractions of Gouda. But we did want to see the market plaza and Johnnie was more than ready for his walk, so we followed the Hoge Gouwe canal to the market. This promenade is shady and good for walking, but it is entirely paved and not decorated with flower urns as in many of the cities that we have visited. Where there might have been park strips of grass or flowers, there are cars parked. The canal is theoretically available for mooring but it is little used, and I can see why. There are several low bridges that must be opened and it eventually comes to a dead-end, so boats must turn around and come back by the same, not very pleasant, route. I am glad that we didn't bother with this canal just because it is closer to the center of town.

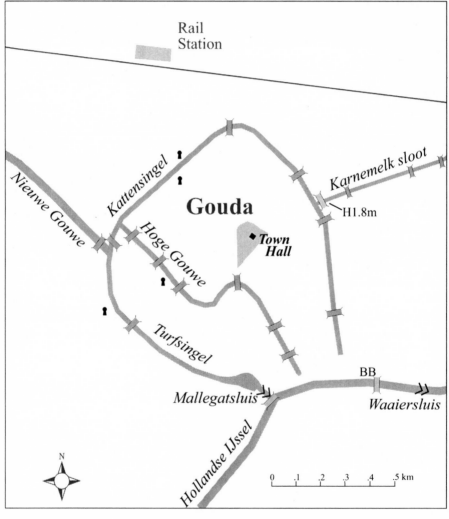

Near the market, flower boxes appeared on the railing of the promenade (a gesture to tourists?) We entered the market through the narrow end of a funnel-shaped street, which opened out in front of us into the wide plaza. The plaza is a V, with us at the the bottom. It seems to be the restaurant and tavern zone, I could stand in one spot and count more than a dozen, along both sides of the street. At the open end of the V there are another dozen, each with their tables set up on the edge of the plaza. I think that we accidentally found the best way to enter the market plaza, to see it open up as we walked in.

In the middle of all this stands a tall, highly ornate step-gable building, the old city hall; it is the one most often seen in the tourist-guide photos, with stacks of the orange "wheels" of Gouda cheese laid out in front of it. Actually this is the back side of city hall; the Waag (weigh house) is at the other end of the cheese display, but city hall gets in the photo because it is ornate and handsome while the weigh house is ugly (at least in my opinion.)

The left leg of the V is Hoogstraat, which takes us back to the singel and to the mooring. It is the classic "High Street", lined by shops and restaurants. Gouda is well-known as a tourist destination and there are certainly enough dining spots to take care of thousands of visitors each day. I don't know where the tour buses are parked but they must be around somewhere.

We had been given a tip by another boater that The Old Inn is a good place for dinner. During our walk we found it and liked the location, on a small canal near Hoogstraat, a little way off of the heavily-beaten track but only two blocks from our mooring. We returned that evening for an excellent pork dinner. The next day would be our museum and history day.

Along with cheese, Gouda is known for pottery. First for clay pipes, then later the production of decorative pottery became successful. The hand-painted products from the period 1898 to 1930, with characteristic floral decorations, are very popular. Museum Gouda exhibits the key Gouda pottery factories: Plateelbakkerij South Holland, Goedewaagen Ivora, Zenith, Regina and Flora. The museum is alongside St Janskerk, a large church (longest in the Netherlands, at 122 meters) famous for its seventy multi-panel stained glass windows, now on the UNESCO Heritage list. We visited both sites on Saturday morning.

For the afternoon Carol returned to the museum for a more thorough look at the pottery, while I took off by bicycle 2km up the Goejanverwelledijk, a bike and walking path along the dike on the west side of the Hollandse IJssel river, to inspect the *Waaiersluis* (translates as "fan lock"). I went alone because Carol loves boating, but her interest in locks is limited to whether the gates swing open, like doors, or drop down from above, like a guillotine. The former style is much preferred, although we will pass under the latter type as we leave Gouda. My own interest is justified not only by my college degree in mechanical engineering but also by the model of an operating lock which I built for an eighth-grade science fair (it worked well mechanically but leaked water all over the display table.)

Cruising the Canals & Rivers of the Netherlands

The Waaiersluis divides the tidal section of the Hollandse IJssel, heavily used by large ships and barges, from the upstream section that flows from Nieuwegein to Gouda. Above the Waaiersluis there are no more locks; the river is natural and is used only by pleasure boaters. In fact, bridges do not open in the off-season, November through March. The upper section of the river is not affected by the action of the tides.

The purpose of my excursion to the lock was to watch it in operation, if possible. We had already passed through such a lock, the Wilhelminasluis on the Andelse Maas. At the time I had failed to notice the fan doors, although I do recall wondering whether the water level is always higher in the Waal, or can it be higher on the Maas side? Apparently it can be, requiring the use of this special type of lock, one that will hold back higher water levels from either side.

It turned out that my visit was somewhat disappointing, as the lock did operate for some small cruisers headed down to Gouda but the operation appeared normal, the higher water was upstream as usual. I was able to get a look at some of the mechanism and finally could understand how it works. It is simply a structure of two lock gates fixed at 90 degrees to each other; one is 20% larger than the other. This extra area allows water pressure to be directed by pipes and valves so as to hold the gate closed regardless of which side has the higher water level. Engineers call this an "elegant" solution.

On Sunday morning we walked down the Turfsingel to view a full quay of beautiful classic barges, some converted as live-aboards, others restored to their original working status. We passed the molen De Roode Leeuw and then saw the equally-tall masts of the barges. Ironically these symbols of history are matched on the other side of the canal by the chimneys and piping stacks of a modern petrochemical plant. It's best to try to ignore the western side of the canal and just enjoy the traditional Dutch barges and buildings on the east side. At the southern end of the singel is a small haven for the barges and the nearby barge-history museum.

The town of Gouda is officially trying to attract more barges of this type, for permanent residence and also for the biennial Gouda Havenstad, a three-day gathering of over 100 such vessels. The celebration was held in June of 2008 and 2010, hopefully it will be continued. We were sorry to be here at the wrong time.

Hollandse IJssel

Early on Monday we left Gouda, passing through the Mallegatsluis. This is a standard style of lock except for the single gate which rose above us, and dripped on us as we went under and out onto the Hollandse IJssel river, southwest toward Rotterdam.

Heart of Holland

Regarding IJ and Y usage, as in Hollandse IJssel and IJsselmeer: IJ is a combination vowel and not separate letters. Usually words starting with 'IJ' are alphabetized as the letter I, but IJ is sometimes alphabetically listed under Y, even when the vowel is within the name rather than at the start. An example in the ANWB Wateralmanak is the river "Zijl" alphabetized after "Zwolle", not after "Zierikzee" as one might expect. Also, Oude IJssel is alphabetized after Oudeschild and Oude Tonge. When a word starts with 'IJ' and is a name or is at the beginning of the sentence, both letters are always capitalized.

The tidal section of the Hollandse IJssel is wide, so the busy traffic that we encountered was not a problem, there was plenty of room for all. There is quite a bit of industry and several large towns on both sides, but also there are open stretches with a view over the fields or to plantations of trees. The river hasn't been straightened, so it was pleasant to steer along the curves; at Nieuwerkerk the path of the river abruptly turns from southwest to southeast, then slowly returns to southwest after a series of more curves.

Before long we arrived at Krimpen aan den IJssel. This lower part of the river could be considered one of the arms of the sea, even though it is over 30km to the coast; here the Dutch have installed a massive apparatus, called the *Algerakering*, to control the high waters coming from the sea during major storms. It consists of a storm surge barrier with a steel screen 80m wide and 11.5m high, hung between two lift towers. The towers and barrier are duplicated 120 meters further along the river. In the case of unusual circumstances, these screens would be let down into the water, onto thresholds which had been installed under the river. In the normal situation ships would be able to sail under the barriers and over the threshold. Alongside is a lock which allows passage by ships when the storm barriers have been lowered.

We could see the four 45m-tall towers from the *Hoogteschaal* (height scale), a marker about 1.5km before the barrier, which showed the clearance available under the screens. In all but rare circumstances a boat such as ours can stay in the main channel and pass under the structure. Which is not a comfortable thing to do, as each of the two "guillotines" weigh 60 tons. As we passed under I could see that the barrier screen is reinforced by a steel truss, making the piece look like a truss bridge turned on its side. Carol didn't see this, she preferred not to look up! To me the whole arrangement looked very industrial but the design is quite handsome.

After this adventure the day settled down to cruising on to Rotterdam on the river that we had seen a week or two earlier. By now cruising among busy traffic had become comfortable, so we enjoyed the sights to be seen from the river. This time we knew that we simply had to pass under the

Erasmusbrug, take note of the Veerhaven where we had stopped for two nights, then turn in at the Euromast to enter the Parkhaven and follow the canal to Delft.

Rotterdam

Again the dreaded lifting lock gates, but we are starting to get used to them; they haven't dropped on us yet, have they? We followed a barge through ten BB bridges as we crossed through the western half of Rotterdam, all but two of them high enough for both us and the barge to pass under without lifting. We were able to cruise along at about 4 km/hr, with just a brief wait at the lift bridges. Most of the view was filled by long blocks of brick apartment buildings, but we did enjoy a beautiful view of the Mevlana mosque and minaret, the latter resembling one of the rockets which sent men to the moon.

Just beyond was a road bridge and then a rail bridge, both of which lifted for us, then we were struck by the imposing sight of a huge white factory complex, with large signs stating "Van Nelle" on both the south and east roof of the buildings and also on a very nice looking visitor's dock. A long row of identical warehouses fronted on the canal. I had no idea what this place was, but later looked it up on Wikipedia and learned that it is a UNESCO World Heritage Site: "The former Van Nelle Factory on the Schie river is one of the most important historic industrial buildings in the Netherlands. It is a former factory now used as an office complex. The building was designed by architects Johannes Brinkman and Leendert van der Vlugt and built between 1927 and 1929. It is an example of Nieuwe Bouwen (modern architecture) in the Netherlands. In the 20th century it was a coffee and tea factory. Currently it houses a wide variety of new media and design companies."

Five identical haven-channels for industrial warehouses showed that we were still in a major shipping area as we arrived at the Spaansebrug, a bascule bridge that needed to be opened for us. I was glad that it did, as the lifting mechanism of this bridge is a sculptural design, very smooth and sleek curves, painted pale green. It would look right at home installed in a park, with no span to lift.

The next lifting bridge was the Hogebrug, a series of brick arches with one lifting span, of the traditional steel-beam design. Then all of a sudden we were in the countryside, as we turned east on the Schiedamse Schie and then north on the Delftse Schie. This was the same river, the Schie, that we had cruised on our earlier visit to Schiedam.

I had not been looking forward to this route through Rotterdam, fearing that it would be a drudge of locks, bridges and not much sightseeing; I was very wrong, this was an pleasant part of our cruise.

Heart of Holland

Now our attention was drawn by aircraft dropping low in front of us to land at Rotterdam airport; the end of the runway was just a few hundred meters to our right. From there it was a straight run of just over 7km to the quay at Delft.

Delft

The tourist office states "Delft is a town abounding in water." It's true, there are canals throughout the city, one of them used by permanent houseboats. But when you arrive in Delft on your own boat you cannot use these canals. You can bypass the old town center along its eastern side on the Rijn-Schiekanaal and/or you can stay at the only mooring place, Haven Zuid Kolk for 24 hours or less. I don't know how rigidly they enforce the time limit, but since we had arrived at about 13:30 we planned to leave right after lunch the next day.

The Zuid Kolk haven is at the southern end of the town, at a triangular enlargement of the canal intersection, part of the original singel surrounding the town. We arrived from the south on the Delftse Schie; the through route makes a 90-degree turn to the east, becoming the Delftse Vliet of Rijn-Schiekanaal, then two more turns bring it back onto the original path at the north end of town. The singel on the west side has been replaced by a street and rail lines. Local small boats are moored along the Buitenwatersloot, a very pretty canal to walk or visit by dinghy from the Zuid Kolk. It is lined by trees, shrubs and on both sides; waterlilies grow between the boats. Many of the boats and the houses are charming. We used this street for our dog walk early the next morning. The canals of the historical town centre are of course a good way to walk and see the sights, or you can go on a canal tour boat or step into the Canalhopper (water taxi).

As soon as we had settled in at the dock we set off on a walking tour. I wanted to see the Oostpoort (East Gate), built around 1400. It is a picturesque sight that I thought we should see from across the water; I was right, the wide view of the two tall cylindrical towers with a white drawbridge alongside made a great photo.

We got to the Oostpoort viewpoint by first walking south one block on our mooring quay, the Hooikade, then across a bridge over the Delftse Schie. There we found the Royal Delft porcelain factory on Rotterdamsweg; we didn't stop, but they do offer guided tours, demonstrations and a factory shop. www.royaldelft.com

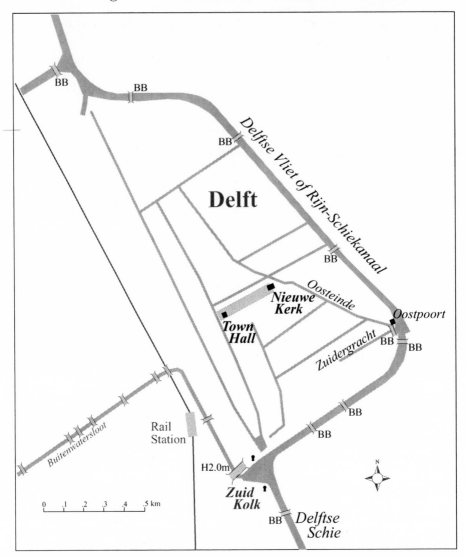

We crossed the canal again, to the Oostpoort, then behind the gate, along the Zuidergracht, walked the row of woonboten. The interesting designs of these floating houses and the well-landscaped quay make these an attractive way to live in the city. The Oosteinde canal quay, paved with bricks, led us right to the heart of the old city, at the back end of the Nieuwe Kerk; this canal also has lots of water lilies, it is a pleasant walking route. White-railinged footbridges cross the canal at frequent intervals.

The slender tower of the Nieuwe Kerk (New Church, 1381) shoots up almost 109 metres from its location on the Markt, opposite the town hall. The royal tomb in the church has long been the last resting place for the members of the Royal House. There are views to Den Haag and Rotterdam from the tower.

The many outdoor cafes on the Markt, the largest market square in the Netherlands, are a great place to enjoy the view of the town hall and the Nieuwe Kerk, but we moved on, to those on the lively Beestenmarkt square, two blocks to the south, because of the shade. This square is notable for its complete coverage by leafy trees and the many indoor and outdoor cafes which line all four sides. There seem to be many more eating and drinking places in Delft than in Gouda, even though they are similar towns of the same size.

In the evenings you can choose from a wide range of restaurants and cafés. From a small café to a restaurant with Michelin stars, from Italian cuisine to Greek, Spanish, French, Thai, Mexican, Indonesian, Chinese, African, Surinam or Dutch cuisine, there is always something to suit your taste. We chose the restaurant Spijshuis de Dis, on the eastern side of the Beestenmarkt.

The ambience and the menu drew us in; we wanted seafood and this restaurant offered Brakkemast, brackish-poached fish. We each enjoyed one of these dishes, as copied from the menu:

Brammer €19,75 White sea fish, salmon, large fresh water shrimp, mushrooms, carrots, fish sauce, cubes of bacon. Prepared in the oven. Served with a little glass of homemade Bocksinth.

Brakkemast €19,25 White sea fish, salmon, smoked mackerel, smoked ham, brie cheese, vegetables, fish sauce. Prepared in the oven.

www.spijshuisdedis.com

The next morning was dedicated to learning more about Vermeer. The painter Johannes Vermeer (1632-1675) lived and worked in Delft almost all of his life. We started at the Vermeer Center Delft, which is housed on the site of the former St. Lucas Guild, where Vermeer was Dean of the painters for many years. The museum gives a very thorough guide to his studio and his approach to painting, stressing his use of light.

They say the light in Holland is something very special. Vermeer placed most of his subjects inside the box of a room, but used the Dutch light coming in through a window to create highlights and shadows. His most famous landscape is "View of Delft", painted from the exact place that we were moored, on the Zuid Kolk. The view is not just as it was in 1660 but we could still see the spire of the same church above the tree line; we just had to use two fingers held horizontally to block off the row of white motorboats on the far quay, so that we could include the water in the view, as in the painting.

Later we followed the Vermeer Cube Walk that guided us past six Vermeer sites in the city. Vermeer painted all his masterpieces in Delft. Six different places in the city centre have rotating cubes with information about his life and his work. Each of the six cubes are related to a particular period in his life. This walk is a good way to see the city, as well as learn more about the Vermeer history.

After a simple lunch at a sidewalk cafe near the Oude Kerk (140 years older than the Nieuwe Kerk), where we could clearly see the two-meter lean of the church tower, we returned to the boat and headed north.

I had been told that the Rijn-Schiekanaal is very busy during the summer on Friday and Sunday afternoon & evening, as boaters from Rotterdam, Delft, Den Haag and the smaller cities travel to and from the Kaag lakes. We wanted to anchor out on the lakes ourselves, preferably when it isn't crowded, so our schedule worked out well: travel the canal on Tuesday night to Leidschendam, stay Wednesday night in Leiden, arrive at the lakes on Thursday for an overnight and leave Friday morning for Haarlem.

Leidschendam

After the left-right swing of the canal at the northern end of Delft we followed alongside a busy road and rail line, then under the wide bridge of an autoroute. We soon realized that we were in the suburbs of Den Haag, first Rijswijk, then Voorburg and Leidschendam. The last seemed to be the best place to stop overnight; we did have time for a brief visit into Den Haag, but for us the only reason to go there would be the Mauritshuis museum, and that would require a full day. The royal painting collection is one of the best in the world; it includes works by Rembrandt and Vermeer. I didn't check the schedules but most likely there are commuter rail and/or bus connections from Leidschendam into central Den Haag, so that might a good mooring for a future visit; the museum is just a few blocks from the central rail station.

At about 16:00 we tied up to bollards on the stone quay immediately south of the lock at Leidschendam and looked for our afternoon coffee. We found it right away, at "FastFood" which offered tables on the lock wall, decorated by a five-foot high cone of simulated French Fries. Not exactly charming, but the coffee was good and we enjoyed the small-town atmosphere.

Afterwards we walked Johnnie north along the canal, finding a fuel dock that we would use when we depart. No pumpout service here, but we were assured that we would find one at the Passantenhaven in Leiden. The view of *H.H.Petrus & Pauluskerk* (Saints Peter and Paul church) across the canal was impressive, an austere gray building highlighted by the row of typical Dutch boats moored in front.

We could see a large molen on the other side, north of the church, so we walked on. It was interesting because we first noticed stacks of lumber at one end of the long building under the windmill, then at the other end we could see a large log on a ramp leading into the building; voila, a windpowered sawmill! I am sure that it must be maintained now for historical reasons, but it is the only one of that type that we had seen. (Other windmills were used for milling corn or grain, or for pumping water.)

By the time we walked back to our mooring we were ready to sample the efforts of *IJssalon Fanieltje*, also located right at the lock. It was easy to find, another five-foot sculpture, this one of an ice cream cone. Carol found that the *Beautique Jacqueline* two doors away would have time to give her a manicure, so she went in while Johnnie and I went back for some boat maintenance (me working, him supervising.) We also decided that we could stock up on bread in the morning at *Bakkerij Remerswaal*. These merchants are very clever to congregate along the wall of a very busy lock. There are restaurants as well, but we ate dinner onboard. We enjoyed our stop here.

After locking-through quickly at 08:00, we topped off our diesel fuel and continued 13km north into Leiden, settled at the city docks and pumped-out by 11:00, despite having used the services of seven drawbridges. We were in a small convoy, so the bridges opened quickly in sequence.

Leiden

It was raining on and off as we docked at Leiden; that didn't bother us much, Carol and I enjoy a rainy day. Johnnie doesn't so he spent the day in bed at *Gemeente Leiden*, the city docks. There are 50 slips on the Oude Rijn, right inside the encircling singel. Leiden is a prime example of the star fort, the moats are intact and are immediately recognizable on the chart.

Leiden is a city of canals, floating cafes and many bridges. That's easy to say, as there are many towns and cities in Holland with the same description. But there are more here than in most, perhaps second only to Amsterdam, a much larger city; there are two dozen named canals and 88 bridges inside the singel ring. Most of the canals are lined by small boats and houseboats, too many to count. The boats have to be small, as many of the bridges are low and do not open. Those on the Oude Rijn, which passes west from the docks, as well as those on the Oude Vest across the center of the city, are 1.3 meters clearance.

This oldest branch of the Rhine river is little more than a city canal here. Historically, this waterway is what gave the area its importance, first as a Roman border, then during the Golden Age as a trade route. Nowadays, river traffic doesn't use this branch and the river just serves to fill the city's canals with water.

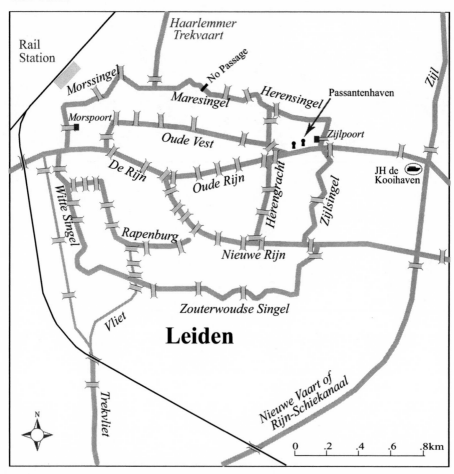

Our visit started at the Zijlpoort, one of the two remaining gates of the city. It is a very handsome brick structure, with very intricate white masonry and sculptures surrounding the gate openings, topped by a clock tower, cupola and weathervane. From the east side a brick-arch footbridge crosses the singel, with a drawbridge for boats.

Then we turned back to the west, into the city center. Lured by a beautiful converted barge tied up on the south quay of the Oude Vest, I led us down that route. It is a broad canal, more utilitarian than charming, but it took us through the old city to the Morspoort, on the western singel.

I thought that the Zijlpoort was an impressive sight, but the Morspoort outdoes it. It is located at a similar position on the western edge of the city, alongside the Rijn. The Morspoort is also a square brick building, domed and well decorated with stripes of white bricks. From the nearby footbridge there is a great view of the singel, covered with waterlilies, and the molen De Put.

We decided that we were ready for a tour-boat ride, letting the local expert show us the sights from the canals. At the kink on the Oude Vest we found the Beestenmarkt plaza, where we bought tickets and set off on the one-hour tour. The approximately 6.5km long outer canal ring of Leiden is still intact, although the old walls and bastions are now mainly greenery. There are parks and an old cemetery in the star points. The tour focuses on the canals within the city, so we didn't see the entire ring from the boat. We walked most of it later in the day, with special appreciation of the Witte Singel pathway around the botanical gardens and the Observatory, at the southwestern-most corner of the singel.

The area between the Oude Rijn and Nieuwe Rijn, south of the passantenhaven, is one of the most undisturbed bits of Leiden. The canals are narrow, the trees and flowers are plentiful and the houses are charming. This is a place to stroll around, not searching for the tourist sites, just enjoying the Dutch way of life. The light rain didn't bother us, in fact it made the scene more beautiful, putting sparkles on the flowers.

We followed the curve of the Nieuwe Rijn to the Burcht, a circular fortress atop an earthen mound. It is centrally located in the city, so a walk around its ramparts gave us a full view of the city. We walked back to our boat along a portion of the Oude Rijn that we had seen on the boat tour, but now we enjoyed more of the details of the architecture, as well as the dozens of local boats.

For dinner we decided on Donatello's, touted online as "Good pizza, if you enjoy a student atmosphere!" Having lived in college towns, and having been students ourselves many years ago, this sounded okay to us. And it was; the pizza was as good as some, better than most. Johnnie went with us, he enjoys the restaurant atmosphere and is always well-behaved there. The walk to and from the restaurant was along the Haarlemmerstraat, the pedestrianized main shopping street, which was somewhat of an adventure in itself; lots of window-shopping, and gawking at other shoppers.

Kaager Plassen

It is only three kilometers from Leiden to the first of the Kaag lakes. We were lucky to have bright sunshine on the day that we toured the lakes. We have a special attachment here, as we stayed for several days at a hotel on

Kaageiland (Kaag Island) and used it as a base for our first driving tour around Holland, visiting many of the towns and cities that I have written about in this book. Our hotel was the Hotel Orion; I didn't remember that when I picked that name for our boat, but I was happy when I saw it again on this visit.

We wanted to come back here by boat because on our first visit we only had a car and watched the leisure boaters out on the lake with envy. The lake had been busy with motorboats, large sailboats and several small-sailboat regattas. It was quieter on this day, so we spent the time just cruising all of the bays and cuts, stopping for a while to swim and sun at the only sandy beach, on the southwestern corner near Warmond. That town was a place where I had roamed the docks looking at boats during that early visit.

One of the channels near Warmond is dotted with woonboten, but in this case none of them had road access. Probably most are holiday homes, reached by boat. The permanent residents in the neighborhood are sheep, grazing the fields of the many islands. All of the land hereabouts is polderized, or reclaimed; the old maps show a lake many times larger, with no islands. Some of the windmills remain, that were used to pump water from the polder. The land inside the polders is criss-crossed by a grid of hundreds of small ditches.

The village of Kaag is totally devoted to sailing on the lake. It's a pleasant place to walk around and see the cottages, but mostly there are docks and more docks, along with restaurants, bars and a few services. When you arrive at the island by car, you cross via a small ferry and then drive by the huge buildings of the De Vries Lentsch shipyard, where very large Feadship and other small ships are built. We always have missed seeing one in the water, but photos in the nearby Restaurant Tante Kee show them dominating the skyline of the low island. The first shipbuilding was begun here in 1877. I don't understand how they can sail away, as the depth of the canal is only 2.5m. (We didn't dine at the Tante Kee on this trip, but we can highly recommend it from our previous visit.) tantekee.nl

The lake is big enough to get a little choppy, so for our overnight mooring we selected a spot inside a hook of land on an island, which itself is protected by another island. It is on the Balgerij, a narrow cut at the north end of the lake; it gave us quick access to the canal to Haarlem or Amsterdam, Ringvaart van de Haarlemmermeerpolder.

Ringvaart to Haarlem

Within five minutes of getting underway on Friday morning we were westbound on the Ringvaart (it is the only Ringvaart, "ring canal", so it is not necessary to use the full name.) This is a 60km waterway, roughly oval, with Kaag at the southwestern tip, Amsterdam at the northeastern and Haarlem at the northwestern. The full name is descriptive, for it encircles the

Heart of Holland

Haarlemmermeerpolder; in other words, the polder of Haarlem lake. Polders are defined as land reclaimed from the sea, a lake or marshland. When the polder lies below sea level, as this one does, the water must be pumped out and into the canals. This was first accomplished here by the use of steam engines, a unique event in that time, because until then this had been done mainly by windmills. The Haarlemmermeerpolder became dry land in 1852. The land is used for agriculture and a few towns but a large part of it now consists of the runways and terminals of Schiphol airport.

The ferry from Kageiland to Buitenkaag was busy with commuter traffic, so we slowed to wait. Then I noticed the chandlery v.d. Wansem Service Center; I had been thinking of adding some new mooring and locking lines so I took advantage of this opportunity and quickly pulled over to the quay. By the time I finished, the ferry had made several more passes to keep Carol and Johnnie entertained. One of the things that Carol noticed while waiting was in the windows of the apartment above the store: each of the windows had, along with some small flowerpots, a large table lamp centered in each window. This seems to be *de rigeur* Dutch style.

Back on our route north to Haarlem, we soon passed through Lisse. This is the closest town to the world-famous Keukenhof Gardens, open March through May with spectacular displays of the famous Dutch tulips and other flowers. We had a wonderful day there on our earlier trip, so we didn't stop this time. Moorings on the west bank here, south of the drawbridge, are a short bicycle ride from the entrance. www.keukenhof.com

Haarlem

The bridge at Cruquius, 16 kilometers from Kaag, is the landmark to be ready to turn left onto the river Spaarne, a few hundred meters east of the bridge. We will go into Haarlem for an overnight visit, then return back to the Ringvaart to travel east to Amsterdam.

While the Ringvaart is a man-made canal, with straight, hard banks and uniform width, the Spaarne is a true river. Current is not significant but the twisting path and the irregular shoreline make the sightseeing more pleasant. For the first kilometer green fields come right to the water on the west side. The east side is a continuous line of moored boats and houseboats, always an intriguing sight for us. The city begins as we pass under a bridge and encounter two 8-man rowing shells in a practice race; I had noticed on the chart the dock of the KRZV Het Spaarne, the local "royal rowing & sailing club"; we soon came to it, a very large and nice looking building and docks. I longed to be a member!

The homes on both sides of this part of the river are very nice, some traditional Dutch and others modern style, all with spacious gardens. On the east side we saw a large tennis club, with many courts. My late friend Leo would call this sort of living "high-zoot".

Cruising the Canals & Rivers of the Netherlands

We waited while a few other boats gathered, then two drawbridges on busy streets opened together, allowing our convoy to pass, bringing us in to the city center. Here the residences are apartment buildings and townhouses, but still there is a long line of woonboten moored on the east bank, and a few houseboats and liveaboard barges on the west side.

The river makes two consecutive S-turns as it cuts through the center of the city. We waited for two more drawbridges, then were able to go under the closed footbridge *Gravestenenbrug*. There we saw our intended mooring quay on the right bank and noticed the nearby shower building, the former bridgekeeper's quarters. Strangely, the small brick building is the base for what might be a large sculpture of the winged foot of Mercury. We continued on, for the time being, to the northern edge of the city in search of the *Havenkantoor*, the office of the city moorings; a fee was due for the use of the waterway and for overnight mooring.

The ANWB Wateralmanak #2 advises that the Havenkantoor is north of the Prinsenbrug; it is shown on the chart, but not precisely. It was easy to find, however; it is a long blue box building set on pilings right in the river. We paid our fees, €7.93 for *doorvaart* (passage) and €9.58 for *overnachting* (overnight mooring). They gave us access tokens for the shower and we filled our water tank from a free hose; a pumpout station is also located on their quay.

Only a short section of the Haarlem star fort singel remains, a line of six points across the north of the city, now maintained as a park. It happened to be just behind the Havenkantoor, so with their permission we left the boat at the quay and took a walk along the paths of the singel. The north side is a peaceful place, a suitable location for the museum that we noticed there, Het Dolhuys, the museum of psychiatry. The south side of the park is the rail line and the station, where thousands of commuters' bicycles are stacked tightly.

We returned to the Gravestenenbrug and tied up. Although the quay is along a street, it wasn't very busy with cars and the location near the footbridge gave us good access to the heart of the city, on the west side. The market square, the church and many restaurants and shops were only two blocks away.

We toured that area and decided that we liked it, although this is generally a city to live in, not a tourist destination. It is the capital of Noord Holland province (rather than Amsterdam, as one might think.) One advantage of living here would be that the city is only a few kilometers behind the sand dunes of Zandvoort, one of the most popular beaches in Holland.

The Grote Kerk van St. Bavo dominates the market square; inside is one of the most stunning church organs in Holland, a Muller that was constructed in 1738. It's over 90 ft. high and has more than 5000 pipes. Both Handel and Mozart played it, the latter when he was only 10.

Heart of Holland

We found three of the canals which cut across the loops of the S-curves of the Spaarne; these serve as moorings for local boats. The canals and the streets alongside are not nearly as charming as those in Leiden, Delft and Gouda. Even though there are occasional trees, there are only parked cars where there might be flowerboxes and cast-iron lampposts.

For dinner we wanted American-style meat; on the market square we had passed the steakhouse Wilma & Albert, so we returned for steak and barbecue. The decor was a little overdone but it set the right tone for a hearty dinner. The food was pretty good, allowing for the fact that Haarlem is not Texas! wilma-alberts.nl

Ringvaart to Amsterdam

We were southbound on the river early the next morning, although not as early as I had wanted; the bridges do not operate until 09:00. We hadn't found much reason to remain in Haarlem longer and I was eager to get back to the Ringvaart early. I had a particular mooring in mind for that day, Saturday, staying there overnight. I expected that the waterway would be thronged with boats and I wanted to get to the mooring first.

It took just over an hour to reach the *Molenplas* (Mill Lake), a small lagoon off the northern side of the canal, named for the windmill at its entrance. The depth was marginal for us, however, so we tied-up at a wooden dock on the south side of the canal, facing the windmill, with the Haarlemmermeerpolder at our back.

We were here because I wanted to experience a typical day out on the water for the Dutch boaters. I could watch an all-day parade of boats, we could have lunch at the waterfront restaurant on the lake (by dinghy) www.molenplas.nl we could walk along the dike of the polder and I could tour the Cruquis Museum. Carol could have afternoon tea at the *Theehuis Cruquis*. A well-planned day of leisure! If I were a golfer, I could have included a round at the 27-hole complex of courses behind the dock.

The Cruquis Museum is one of the three original pumping stations used to dry out the polder. The neo-Gothic building is itself very handsome but the real interest is the engine that was installed there in 1849. It is the world's largest and best preserved steam engine, a Cornish-built engine with a cylinder diameter of 3.66 meters. This machine drives eight arms connected to pistons which lift water from the polder level up to the canal level. At each stroke of the steam engine, 64,000 liters of water are brought up five meters from the drainage canals of the polder, then through locks into the Ringvaart. The building faces directly onto this end of the Spaarne river; water is discharged to the north, toward the river. The engine is no longer operated by steam, electric motors move the arms as a showpiece. www.museumdecruquius.nl

Cruising the Canals & Rivers of the Netherlands

Our day went as planned, except we added a cycling tour along the dike, past the land side of another row of woonboten, to the fort at Vijfhuizen and then on to the Groene Weelde park. The name translates as "Green Wealth", an accurate choice as it contains many acres of planted shrubs and trees, a green wonderland. There is an earthen pyramid with views from the top as far as Amsterdam, Haarlem and the dunes at the North Sea. We were there near sunset, so the latter view was a thrill. I had stopped at the Molenplas just on a whim, but it was one of our best days in Holland.

Again I wanted an early start, to get going on the route to Amsterdam before it became too crowded. Unfortunately the Vijfhuizerbrug doesn't operate until 10:00, so we had to bide our time. I did move to the bridge to be ready, where we watched the Sunday morning cycling teams whoosh by on the dike road, their multi-colored uniforms making a streak of light.

The Ringvaart turns north here, rather than directly east to Amsterdam. It makes a loop that "breaks out" of the roughly oval canal path, then turns south again near Amsterdam, following the outline of the Haarlem lake as shown on an 1849 map. This extra space allowed a long runway to be installed in the polder, part of Schiphol airport; I don't think that this was included in the mid-19th century planning.

One of the arms of the lake passed to the north here, paralleling the Spaarne river. It is now called the Liede river, available for cruising by small boats (less than 1m height.) This is a very beautiful natural area leading to the Mooie Nel, a lake northeast of Haarlem; it's a popular recreational area, but inaccessible from the Ringvaart for us. There is a line of three forts along the Liede, part of the Amsterdam defense ring. The Ringvaart makes a short detour around *Fort aan de Liede*, but nothing can be seen through the trees.

Five kilometers further east I discovered a new Dutch word: *Zwaaikom*. It is marked on the ANWB chart but I had to look it up, although then it was immediately obvious. It is a turning basin, a wide spot on the canal to allow the turning of barges which are longer than the canal is wide. This one opens into a short dead-end waterway on the north, yet another location for houseboats. The nearby town is Halfweg, "halfway" between Haarlem and Amsterdam.

Here the canal turns south, actually even about five degrees west of south, as it approaches Lynden. This is the site of another of the original pumping stations for the polder. The building is almost an exact copy of the one at Cruquius and is maintained as a historical monument, however the pumping equipment has been removed and the work is done by electric pumps in a low modern structure nearby.

The fields of tulips surrounding Schiphol are matched by the blue and white of the overpowering sky. You see it immediately on landing at Schiphol airport and on the train into Amsterdam. Traveling on a boat, you can experience it every day. Everything has so much bright color; the colors look richer than they do in other countries.

We continued east from Lynden another five kilometers and entered the Nieuwe Meer, a lake at the southwestern city limit of Amsterdam. From here the Ringvaart swings back to the southwest; if we hadn't selected the Nieuwe Meer route into the city, we would have had to return all the way south to Alphen aan den Rijn, returning north past Uithoorn on the Amstel. That can be an enjoyable route, there are sights to be seen, including the spectacular arrival in the center of Amsterdam on the river Amstel. But it would have added several days to our trip. From the Nieuwe Meer we were only about two hours from our destination at Amsterdam's Sixhaven Marina; as planned, we arrived there just after 15:00.

Waterway	From	To	KM	Hours
Smal Weesp	Weesp	Amsterdam-Rijnkanaal	2.0	0.3
Weesper Trekvaart	Amsterdam-Rijnkanaal	Amstel river	9.0	1.3
Amstel	Amsterdam	Uithoorn	19.0	2.4
Grecht/ Woerdense Verlaat	Uithoorn	Woerden	21.0	3.5
Oude Rijn	Woerden	Alphen a/d Rijn	12.0	1.5
Gouwe	Alphen a/d Rijn	Gouda	14.0	2.0
Hollandse IJssel	Gouda	Nieuwe Maas	17.0	2.3
Nieuwe Maas	Hollandse IJssel	Rotterdam	9.0	1.0
Delftse Schie	Rotterdam	Delft	9.0	1.5
Rijn-Schiekanaal	Delft	Leiden	25.0	4.3
Zijl	Leiden	Kaager Plassen	10.0	1.5
Ringvaart	Kaager Plassen	Cruquius	18.0	2.5
Spaarne	Cruquius	Haarlem	5.0	0.8
Ringvaart	Cruquius	Nieuwe Meer	20.0	2.5
Schinkel of Kostverlorenvaart	Nieuwe Meer	Noordzeekanaal Sixhaven Marina	9.5	2.0

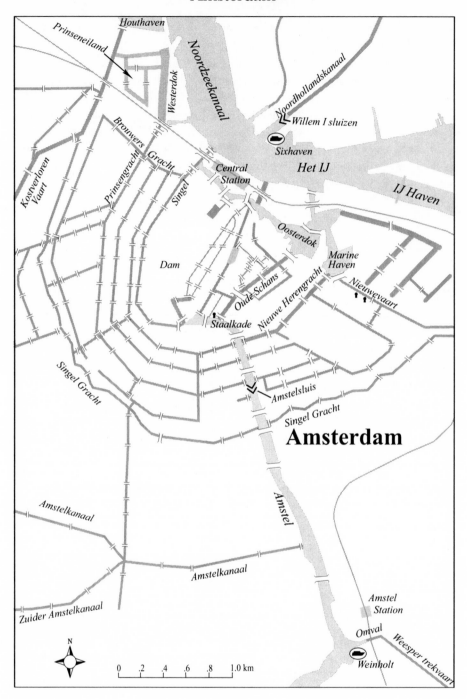

(Note: The map on this page, as elsewhere in this book, shows only waterways, not streets. For walking I use "Streetwise Amsterdam", a plastic pocket map. www.streetwisemaps.com)

Amsterdam

To enter Amsterdam from its southwest corner I wanted to use the Amstelkanaal, a 3km-long canal which passes directly east across the southern edge of the city, joining the Amstel very near where we had entered it two weeks earlier, when we came in from the Vecht on the Weespertrekvaart. But we could not go that way, it and the other canal rings from the west side of the city have bridges with height restrictions of 2.1m to 2.4m. Instead we used the "Standmaste" route to pass along the western edge of Amsterdam, to the Noordzeekanaal.

The Standmaste route allows sailboats or tall motor boats to travel across the Netherlands from Zeeland to Delfzil, at the far northeastern corner of the country, without the need to lower their mast or other parts of the superstructure. Although there are a great many bridges to pass through, they are all opening bridges; the route avoids all fixed bridges.

At Amsterdam the route begins at the Nieuwe Meer and follows the canals Kostverlorenvaart and Kattensloot to the Houthaven (The initial section of the route is named Schinkel of Kostverlorenvaart, meaning "shank".) However, there are rail and highway bridges on this route that are not opened during the day; passage for tall boats is made in a convoy, at night. The passage is about 8km long and requires 1.5 to 2 hours. Bridges on the south end at the A10 autoroute open eight times between the hours of 23:56 and 05:53. The rail bridge on the north end opens four times between 02:20 and 04:34. Convoys are organized to pass in either direction, with the bridges opening in sequence; city fees are must be paid.

This is the same route that we have to take, fortunately for us we could do it in the daytime because we have plenty of clearance under those bridges, although there will be nine low-clearance BB bridges through the west side of the city that will open on demand. I didn't expect that we would do this alone; as it happened, we left the lake along with about a dozen cruisers similar to ours, as well as a couple of mast-down sailboats. All of us merged into a line and moved slowly through what looked like a tunnel, 7.0m high, under the first A10 autoroute bridge, then a bit of sky overhead, then two rail bridges and another A10 bridge.

At the end of the bridges all of the boats moved smoothly to their places in the *Nieuwe Meersluis* lock; at 120m long and 12m wide, the lock could accommodate more than twenty boats of our size. The operation went very quickly, after we had all paid our "port dues" to the city of Amsterdam, €0.80 per meter of boat length for 3 days stay (€9.60 total.)

As we left the lock, we were surprised to see a whole village of woonboten; on seven long finger-piers, 5 or 6 houseboats were tied on either side of each pier. That totals about 70 or 80 houseboats, not counting the others moored in the normal manner, parallel along the banks. Just north of this houseboat village is the connection to the Amstelkanaal, which passes around the Olympic Stadium (from the 1928 Summer Olympics, I had to look that up.) Too bad we can't go that way, the bridges are just a bit too low.

Soon the canal narrowed and went arrow-straight through the city; it felt as if we were driving on a boulevard, as the water level is only slightly below street level, so cars were passing right alongside. There were slight waits at some bridges, but most of them opened in sequence for our convoy; the bridgekeepers had done this before. Some of the boats, lower than ours in height, dropped off to take one of the side canals.

We went all the way through with six remaining boats. When we reached the wide waterway of Het IJ (The Water) our group split up, some going west, others straight across into another canal. We followed a single cruiser to the right, eastbound. In fact it was also headed for the Sixhaven, so we tailed along, passed by the entrance to the Noordhollandskanaal and turned into the marina entrance with no trouble, at 15:10. We soon went for our walk and found the Florapark, then returned for dinner onboard.

Sixhaven is not the most refined of marinas but it is in the most convenient position for those wanting to visit Amsterdam. The nearby Florapark is one reason that we selected Sixhaven; it is a tree-shaded park laid out for 2km along the west bank of the Noordhollandskanaal, a perfect place to walk Johnnie (and ourselves), just a few blocks away. The primary reason for Sixhaven's popularity is its location, immediately across the IJ river from Amsterdam Central Station. Within a five minute walk from the marina there is a free foot ferry that operates continuously to take pedestrians across from the marina to the station and back again. From the station all of Amsterdam is easy to visit: walking or cycling is the very best way of 'seeing' the city up close, but trams are available and a canal cruise is a must in such a city of canals. www.sixhaven.nl

We had visited Amsterdam previously, and knew the highlights: canal tour-boat cruise with commentary, the Ryksmuseum, Van Gogh Museum, Flower Market, Modern Art Museum, traditional cafes good for basic food and their atmosphere, and certainly coffee or a beer at pavement cafes for 'people watching'.

It is a complex and varied city, so planning is necessary. Buy the guide book from the VVV office immediately across the road from the station entrance. Also get tickets from the VVV for a canal tour boat – it's not to be missed, especially at night. You can buy 'I Amsterdam' pass which entitles you to entrance to several sights and museums. www.iamsterdam.com

Aside from cars and people, the two overwhelmingly prevalent sights in Amsterdam are bicycles and boats; they are simply everywhere along the canals, and the canals are everywhere. Some of the boats are rafted three wide; most are small, low motorboats, some of them are of a graceful wooden traditional style, others are well-used plastic dinghies. But the impressive boats are the many barges, most of them former working barges converted as live-aboards. These are the ones that make Amsterdam a famous place for canal-walking and boat-watching.

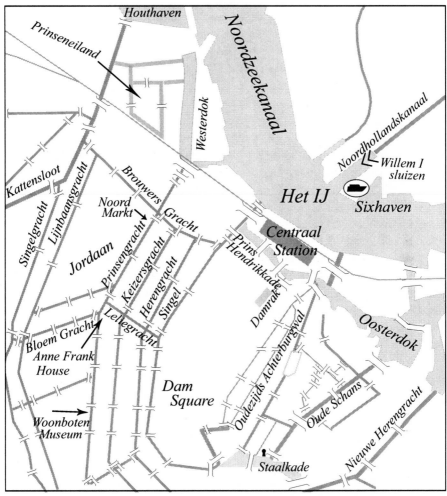

We set off on Monday morning to the NoordMarkt (09:00 - 13:00) for some fresh vegetables and fruits. The market square (in this case it's a triangle) is at the Noorderkerk, a handsome octagonal brick church. It is on the Brouwers Gracht at the Prinsengracht, in the Jordaan quarter, three blocks west from Centraal Station.

To get to this quarter, we came out of Centraal Station on the west end, by the Hotel Ibis, crossed to the Prins Hendrikkade and followed this broad, busy street west one block to the Singel. Then we walked south on the Singel. Of the many open-air cafes, we liked one situated on the wall of a picturesque old lock gate, at the intersection of the Singel and the Brouwers

Cruising the Canals & Rivers of the Netherlands

Gracht, the northeastern corner of many blocks of prime viewing of houses, canals and boats. But it was crowded so we continued west on the Brouwers Gracht to reach the Prinsengracht and had a coffee and pastry at Café Thijssen, a popular bar at night but also fine for a quiet morning coffee.

The Prinsengracht is a prime canal, it is the one used by the Museum Boat Line, a popular canal tour/transportation service. On the east side is the Anne Frank House, near the Westerkerk. Moored on the Prinsengracht, three blocks south of the Anne Frank House, is the Woonboten Museum, a live-aboard barge opened for public viewing. houseboatmuseum.nl

This is a canal that we could cruise on our own boat, but the heavy tour boat traffic would make it uncomfortable and we would need to have the bridges opened, disrupting both street and canal traffic. These are busy waters and the tour boat skippers can be quite rude if they're held up - they will always try to claim priority over "leisure boaters".

Making our way back to Sixhaven, we stopped for a rest and a drink at Biercafe 't Arendsnest on the Herengracht at Herenstraat, a bar that serves a variety of special Dutch beers. It is housed in a small canal house with a relaxed atmosphere. In front of the cafe, on the canal, is a small terrace overlooking the Herengracht; the canal was quiet, only a few boats passed by.

Laden with fruits and vegetables, we returned to the boat for a few hours, then crossed again into the city for the evening. This time we walked straight out from the station, along the Damrak to Dam Square. This is "Tourist Central", the tour-boat harbor and tour bus stop. It certainly doesn't look like it now, but this was probably the dock from which Carol's ancestor, a Mr. Teller, departed in 1609 as a crewman with Henry Hudson and eventually sailed up the Hudson River in America. The Teller family remained there, 30 miles north of Manhattan, where Carol grew up, on the west shore of the Hudson. She had always wanted to visit this spot in Amsterdam, unfortunately it is not possible to envision how it was 450 years ago.

Dam Square is the very center of Amsterdam; around 1270 a dam was constructed in this spot in the river Amstel. Dam Square was once the central marketplace of Amsterdam. The Royal Palace is located here; it was built 350 years ago as Amsterdam's City Hall, then taken over in 1808 by Louis Napoleon and later by the current royal family. HRH Queen Beatrix does not live here; she does entertain her VIP guests in this palace.

As an American, a country just over 200 years old, I am always interested in the European use of "Old" and "New". We saw a good example near the Dam square: *Oude Nieuwstraat*, Old New Street; I wondered how many centuries have passed since it was deemed "new" and then "old". We walked east on Damstraat until it became Oude Hoogstraat; it's our opinion that this "Old Highstreet" is now the "New Junkstreet", with every kind of trashy shop imaginable. We didn't walk far, we turned back towards Central

Station on a canal that we couldn't resist because of its name, the "Oudezijds Achterburgwal" (Google Translate just gives up on that!) The scene immediately changed from shops to residences, a quiet neighborhood just around the corner from busy modern life, with pedestrian-only streets. As we got further north we found many tasteful clothing and design shops, as well as some pleasant cafes. To get to the station we then passed through the red-light district, a sight every tourist should experience! The peace and relative quiet back at Sixhaven was a welcome refuge.

It is possible to cruise the canals inside the city of Amsterdam on your own boat. It will be much easier if the height of your boat is less than 2.40m. The ANWB charts have bridge measurements for all but the most central bridges, and there are lots of boat shops in Amsterdam which have maps called the "Vaargids" which is a better guide to the city's waters. You should also try and find out which canals are blocked as there's always building activity going on somewhere. A very useful website is offered by the city of Amsterdam: vaarkaart.bba.amsterdam.nl It is an interactive map which shows the details of all bridges and locks; news of blockages are updated daily.

I had gone online when we were at Haarlem to book a rental 6-person boat for a brief canal cruise. I wanted to cruise some of the canals on our own but the fixed bridges on most of the Amsterdam canals are too low for our cruiser and I didn't want to cross the IJ river in our tiny and not very seaworthy dinghy. So I booked a reservation for an electric "Open boat Zelfstandig te varen" at www.rentaboatamsterdam.com This would cost €100; I had hoped to find some friends at Sixhaven who might be interested and willing to share the cost. As it turned out, we met two British couples at the marina who had similar thoughts but hadn't yet made a reservation; Bob & Susan and Ian & Jacquie were happy to join us and pay their share.

Our reservation was for Tuesday morning 10:00 to 12:00, so we all set out on foot at 08:00 to the ferry and then across the Jordaan section to the rental dock on the Nassaukade, the west-side quay of the Singelgracht. We did some sightseeing of the houses along the canals enroute but still had time for coffee at a street cafe before our cruise time. The payment and checkout was quick; it is a tiller-steered boat with forward and reverse, that's about all we needed to know.

I knew from the online reviews of rentaboatamsterdam that the electric boat is very slow and so I had plotted a route that would let us see some scenic canals within our 2-hour limit, without wandering too far astray. We started out north on the Singelgracht to the Brouwers Gracht, then east across the busy Prinsengracht, then south on Herengracht. These are all prime canals to view the typical Amsterdam sights: rows of tall townhouses, continuous lines of moored boats, tree-shaded streets on the quay along both sides. We took our time, sometimes coasting along slowly as we savored the details of the bricks, shutters, gables and sculptures on the houses After two long blocks on Herengracht we turned right into the Leliegracht, a smaller cross-link between the north-south canals. The brick-arch bridges on the Leliegracht were even more beautiful than the more utilitarian bridges on the main canals, which we had thought looked very charming.

The Leliegracht dead-ends at the Prinsengracht, which is very busy with tour boats. We joined in with the traffic going south, luckily we had only one short block to go because we weren't fast enough to please the tour boat skipper behind us. We saw the throng of people either waiting to enter the Anne Frank House or to gawk up at it; this was our cue to turn west into the Bloem Gracht, turning back toward the rental base. A work barge was rebuilding the north quay, but we had enough room to pass by safely. The chart didn't show it but we found a narrow, dark passage under the wide Marnixstraat which brought us right to the Singelgracht, just 200 meters south of the base; we arrived slightly early, but we were satisfied with a very enjoyable tour. My recommendation: use the electric boat, just don't try to go too far.

We had lunch with our friends at Vennington cafe on Prinsenstraat, lured by the sandwich descriptions on their menu blackboard (and by the Brit-sounding name, one of our group had heard of it.) Inside we found we could have fruit shakes to go with the sandwich, a good informal lunch in a cosy cafe.

Then Carol and I set off alone for a walk around Prinseneiland, a "funky" residential are quite a bit different from the formal townhouses. To get there we walked west on the Brouwersgracht, turned north on the Binnen Oranjestraat until we had passed through a tunnel under the elevated highways and rail lines, where the name of the street changed to Grote Bickersstraat. There we turned left through a small park to get to the Bickersgracht waterway and the Minnemoersstraat (did you get all of that? you can follow our walk on a strreet map.) This is where the good part starts; lots of greenery, small boats, barges, houseboats, row-houses that are not as imposing and formal as the ones on the inner canals. These islands are the homes of middle-class people, a very comfortable neighborhood of family residences. North of the bridge over the Bickergracht we were awed by the jumble of boats and boat pieces: old commercial barges, some of them sinking, newer tour boats and launches, sailboats, rowboats, loose masts and rudders.

Then on to Prinseneiland, with its blocks of converted brick commercial buildings and warehouses, very nicely modernized. It is lovely old area which doesn't see many tourists. We walked around the perimeter of the island and off from the west side, over the Sloterdijkerbrug, a handsome double drawbridge, with graceful white arches over a footbridge path. Back under the elevated roads and east to Central Station for the ferry ride back to Sixhaven.

Amsterdam

I laid out the charts to make a plan on how we would depart from Amsterdam. First some history: Sixhaven is on the IJ river; in the 19th century there was no connection west to the North Sea; Het IJ flowed from the former Haarlemmer Meer and other lakes northwest of Amsterdam into the Zuider Zee (southern sea.) Between 1865 and 1876 a canal was dug through the coastal dunes, opening the Noordzeekanaal from the North Sea to Amsterdam. That route continues east as Het IJ and then Afgesloten IJ (locked IJ) into the IJsselmeer, through the huge and very busy Oranjesluizen lock complex. We could leave by that route, crossing the IJ Meer to Muiden. But we had a little more to see in the city, as well as on the Amstel and on the northern section of the Vecht, which we had missed a few weeks earlier. So I needed to select a route through the center of Amsterdam.

The city of Amsterdam recommends six *Doorvaart* (passage) routes, to aid travelers in planning how to get through the maze of canals in their boat. Our own entry was along route A, the Kostverlorenvaart, which bypasses the central city. We will eventually leave on the Amstel river; we can get to the river from Sixhaven on a choice of two *Doorvaart* routes, B1-Oude Schans or B2-Nieuwe Herengracht. At first I decided on the Oude Schans route because we could pass under all bridges without requiring an opening and it leads directly to the Staalkade, a city mooring quay where we could stop for a few hours before continuing out of the city on the Amstel. But then we decided that we would stay another two days and considered other moorings in the city.

We settled on the *Overnachtingsplaats* on the Nieuwevaart, a little further to the east of the Staalkade. 3X24 hours moorings are available with payment of the city daily haven fee, however with no services. The location allowed us to investigate the Plantage area; we were lured to the area by this description on the website www.deplantageamsterdam.nl

"Welcome to the Plantage, an oasis in Amsterdam's inner city. Amid its verdant streets the Plantage offers a rich assortment of culture, history, nature and science. The Plantage is one of Amsterdam's most varied neighbourhoods. Where else would you find a zoo, several museums, a botanical garden and a science centre all within walking distance?" How could we resist?

Early on Wednesday morning we checked out of Sixhaven and crossed through the busy traffic on Het IJ to Oosterdok. We managed to stay clear of ferry boats full of commuters and barges full of who-knows-what. On the south side of the river we passed under three bridges, with adequate clearance to not require opening, then docked near the Oosterdokdraaibrug to update our 3-day *havengeld* sticker. We had a good view from there of Nemo, the huge green hull-shaped building that rises above the entrance to the IJ road tunnel; it holds Amsterdam's comprehensive science center, and certainly gave us an unmistakeable landmark to find Marine Haven on its east side. Moored along there are around twenty beautifully restored river barges.

Cruising the Canals & Rivers of the Netherlands

Located on the southeastern shore of Marine Haven, Netherlands Maritime Museum holds the largest collection of boats in the world. Unfortunately it was closed for renovation, so we couldn't visit, but we did take a slow pass by the museum's three-masted Eastindia-man sailing ship *Amsterdam* moored temporarily alongside Nemo. This is a true "tall ship", not only the masts are tall but the hull itself rose high above our little boat. The poop deck must be 15-20 meters above the water. The volume inside the bulging hull shape is unimaginable; it looks to be about the size of a 747 airliner, or maybe the new huge Airbus. www.scheepvaartmuseum.nl

The square *Scheepvaartmuseum* building is also an impressive sight from the water, four stories high and as big around as a city block. We cruised around its front and side to enter the Nieuwevaart, easily locating the unattended city moorings. There was one small cruiser already there, leaving plenty of space for us. The neighborhood is one of apartment blocks, not as beautiful as the Jordaan and Prinseneiland areas but clean and quiet.

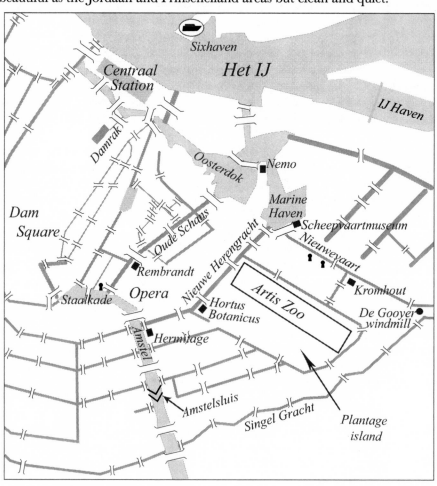

Amsterdam

A three-block walk and a bridge took us to Plantage island. As the name suggests, it is an unusual green zone inside the city. The Plantage lies just to the east of Amsterdam's city center but differs strikingly from the rest of the inner city. It has canals but they are not the draw that they were in the Jordaan area. There are just a few commercial shopping streets and squares with cafés.

Much of the island is filled by the Artis Zoo. We walked right to it, as soon as we had crossed over the Nijlpaardenbrug footbridge we saw the dome of the planetarium building and then the zoo entrance, its elegant iron gates topped by two gold eagles.

Artis is a unique spot, where animal noises and children's voices melt together under the canopy of trees. We were thrilled first by passing along Parrot Alley, then by a group of Japanese Macaques; they quickly took us from Amsterdam to an exotic place. The feeling continued as we crossed the bridge over a pond with pelicans and on to the lemurs. That was just the beginning; we hadn't been in a zoo for years, but we enjoyed this one greatly. We spent the rest of the day there, no problem with finding good coffee and an excellent lunch.

Right across the street from the zoo entrance is the Sabrine Snackbar, offering some great looking breads. We bought two loaves to have for our dinner, along with sausages from the street market bought on our first day here. While we were enjoying these, sitting in the *kuip* (the cockpit, the open deck at the stern) and enjoying the peaceful surroundings, I noticed that only an occasional small boat would pass by, so I decided that this would be a good place to use the dinghy. We could follow the quiet canals back to the zoo area, putting along as we wished.

We turned east from our mooring and passed through the open *keersluis* (flood gate). As we turned into a short cross-canal I was pleasantly surprised to find the Werf 't Kromhout workshops. I had read of Kromhout diesel engines, used in barges, small ships and yachts (as well as trucks and buses) many decades ago. The canal hosted a small group of classic working barges and Dutch motorboats, which tipped me off to look around and find out why. They were moored at the small, still working, Van Amerongen shipyard; the Kromhout shops and engine collection are in the next two buildings. The shops are now a museum, sometimes called Machinekamer (Engine Room), but its official full name is Museum Shipyard "'t Kromhout".

This was a lucky find, I wasn't aware that such a place was so close to our mooring; I walked there later and found that I could visit the museum, but unfortunately not on this trip because it is only open on Tuesdays, 10:00 to 15:00, and this was Wednesday; I had just missed the opportunity.

The bascule bridge on the Hoogtekadijk nearby was made long ago, of riveted steel; the massive supporting columns reminded me of the legs of the Eiffel Tower. The single bridge span was lifted by two huge riveted-steel quarter-circle plates with a ring gear along their edge. I would have liked to have seen this bridge in operation, but the clearance was adequate for us and the other small-boat traffic and so it is not often opened.

Our mini-tour cruise circled the island of the zoo and the botanical garden; we ventured out to the Amstel, then returned back along the same route rather than mix it up with the dinner-tour boats. It was just getting to be dusk, a pleasant time for sightseeing, so when we arrived near our mooring I took us the other way, to the east, to see the old windmill De Gooyer. It looks very out of place in this modern section of Amsterdam, other than the Kromhout works it is the only old structure anywhere nearby. The mill is very tall (26.6 meters, I learned later); a wooden octagon sits on a stone foundation, then the actual mill is another wooden octagon on top of that base. When it was built the mill was on the edge of the city, now it is surrounded by streets and apartment buildings. Since our little boat floated about two meters below the top of the quay, the mill seemed even taller. At its base is a brick building, the IJ Brewery, a brew pub. Around the corner is the Singel Gracht, the zig-zag outer canal ring around the entire city; that would be a good route for a future evening cruise (small boat required, height 2.16m.)

We set out on foot again the next morning to see more of the Plantage district. We learned that it has many Jewish connections; the Dutch Resistance Museum and the Holocaust Memorial are located here. Once, thousands of Jewish families lived here; there were Jewish shops and theaters, and Jewish children paraded through Artis with their mothers on Sundays. All these things came to a sudden horrific end with World War II. The Hollandsche Schouwburg (Dutch theatre) symbolizes that end. It was the prison where the Jewish population was detained before being deported to the concentration camps.

On the western end of the Plantage Middenlaan, the main east-west boulevard, we found the Hortus Botanicus Amsterdam, one of the oldest botanic gardens in the world. The garden and greenhouses house more than 4,000 species. The Hortus is the home of ponds with exotic water lilies, heated greenhouses with palm trees and butterflies, rustling bamboo and flowering trees. The Orangery, located in the middle of this living museum, was our lunch choice, on one of the most beautiful terraces in Amsterdam. dehortus.nl

Immediately west of the Hortus is the Nieuwe Herengracht, which would be our route to the Amstel river and then out of the city. We lingered on the bridge for a while to watch the traffic beneath and to see what the passage might be like. Busy with tour boats and private cruisers, but manageable. We were then on our way off the island to visit the Hermitage Museum and the Rembrandt House, walking south along the canal. After all of the canals that we had seen lined with boats and barges, this one looked unusual because, being a passage route, no mooring is permitted.

Amsterdam

The works of art exhibited in the Hermitage Amsterdam are all on loan from the bountiful collection of well over three million objects in the 'parent museum' State Museum Hermitage St. Petersburg, Russia. The Hermitage is located two blocks west from the Hortus, on Nieuwe Herengracht at its junction with the Amstel.

From there we walked along the Amstel across the front of the opera house to the Oude Schans and across it to the Staalkade, noting that all visitors moorings were filled on that day. Another block further and we came to the "end" of the Amstel river, where it splits into three canals and passes north to the IJ. The classic old Doelen Hotel is a beautiful sight here, a red brick building with white masonry around each of the many windows and sculptures of two Dutch soldiers guarding the clock tower.

North on the Kloveniersburgwal then east on the canal Raamgracht brought us to the Waterlooplein Flea Market and the Rembrandt House. The Raamgracht and its intersecting canal the Groenburgwal are a hidden gem in the city center, lined with some elegant live-aboard barges and a very beautiful stone-arch bridge.

The picturesque Rembrandt house with its magnificent oak door and four stories of green shutters (which show red on the back side when opened) covering the windows stands on Jodenbreestraat. Gold numbers high up among the bricks states "1606". This is where Rembrandt van Rijn lived and worked for almost twenty years, painting such famous works as the Night Watch. By the early twentieth century, Rembrandt's house had fallen into disrepair; major restoration was needed to save it. In 1998, a new, modern adjoining museum wing was added. The interior and furnishings of the original house have been recreated in style of Rembrandt's day.

We took a quick walk through the flea market tents, not finding anything that we couldn't live without. It's primarily a market of clothing and housewares. We were soon back at the Nieuwe Herengracht again, where we detoured through the quiet Wertheim Park for a respite from the streets that we had just walked, avoiding cars, trams bicycles and pedestrians. We hurried back to the boat, for these two days were not suitable for a dog, Johnnie had remained aboard. I took him for a well-deserved walk along the canal opposite our mooring, where the trees and the shade are plentiful. It gave me a chance to walk down the canal so that I could see the Kromhout Museum across the water; the two steel arches on the front of the side-by-side workshops were a wonderful sight from an earlier time.

For our final evening in Amsterdam, we walked one block from our mooring to the IJ Brewery. They don't serve full meals but we enjoyed their draft beer and delicious snacks, including Trappist cheese, salami, smoked raw beef sausage, and meatballs in a gravy made with their beer. A great way to finish our visit to this diverse city. www.brouwerijhetij.nl

A very quick and easy way for us to leave from this mooring would have been to just follow the Nieuwevaart straight east for two kilometers to the Amsterdam-Rijnkanaal, but I wanted to go across the center of the canal ring on the Amstel river. So we left to the west from our mooring and turned left on the Nieuwe Herengracht. There are six bridges and one lock on that canal; I had checked the *Bruggen & Sluizen* schedule and found that they operate from 06:00 to 07:00 and again from 09:00 to 16:30. So we didn't rush, planning to be ready after 09:00. At the Marine Haven I lingered just a bit as two tour boats and a cruiser came along and I convoyed behind them. We could have squeaked under all of the bridges except the last, the Walter Suskindbrug at the Amstel junction, but the other cruiser was taller and so they were all opened for him and we followed. (Tour boats are low enough to pass under all of the bridges; if they weren't all street traffic would be gridlocked, as there are many tour boats and they move constantly.) The bridges on the Amstel are high enough and the Amstelsluis is usually open, so we cruised comfortably up the river, turning east at the edge of the city onto the Weesper Trekvaart.

Amsterdam to Naarden

Our next destination would be the star fort that got me started, Naarden. It is one of the best-preserved bastions in the Netherlands and is the only fortification in Europe that has unique double walls and moats. It is one of the *Waterlinie* fortress ring around Amsterdam, on the northeastern end of that defense line, with just the inland sea on its north.

Although it has been located at the southern end of the Zuider Zee for more than 1,000 years, Naarden has never been a port and is even now accessible only by very small boats. The normal way to visit Naarden by cruising boat is from the Gooimeer, one of the lakes that form the waterway between Flevoland and the mainland. Jachthaven Naarden is less than 10km to the east from the mouth of the Vecht at Muiden and less than 20km across the IJmeer from Sixhaven marina, Amsterdam. Coming from the north, Friesland or Overijssel, it is at the southern end of the Randmeren.

I always try to avoid going back along a road or a waterway that we had just traveled, and we could have taken a shorter, more direct route but this time I decided to reverse our path of two weeks earlier, back to the Vecht river via the Weespertrekvaart. We had cruised the Vecht from Utrecht to Weesp, a distance of 38 kilometers, now we could complete the last five km to Muiden and into the IJmeer sea, then east to the Gooimeer.

There was another option to consider, an inland route; our boat Orion can go there, but just barely. The Naardertrekvaart leads east from Muiden, however it is size-restricted (boats 12m x 4m x 1.1m) and is effectively a dead-end, boaters must return to Muiden on the same canal; there are fixed bridges beyond Naarden with clearance as low as 1.1m. Also, there are no overnight moorings available. The town had plans to build a *passantenhaven* for about ten boats, on the outer moat, but it was denied by other government authorities. A possible solution is still under consideration, to extend an arm of the moat to a direct connection with the Gooimeer. There is currently a navigable moat which reaches to within 100 meters of the lake, but the connection is blocked by the A1 motorway. Making an access through that highway will be difficult, expensive and probably highly unpopular with commuters from the east.

After a lengthy review of the charts, road maps and Google Earth, I came up with a third way to approach the town: we would go 3km south from Weesp on the Vecht to a free mooring near Fort bij Uitermeer. From there we could go by bicycle around the Naardermeer and enter Naarden from the south. I measured it to be about 8 kilometers each way from the mooring, along farm roads and bike lanes, an easy ride. We decided to do it.

We were influenced by a statement in a cruising guidebook "the huge yacht harbour" (at Naarden) and also by a friend's comment on his blog "There is a really huge marina close by." After just spending a week in a "really huge city" we were certainly ready to tie up somewhere quiet, among open fields and reedy lagoons, with a fresh-air breeze and good sunset views. Plus "free" versus €1.50 per meter per night seemed like a good idea. And it was, we enjoyed two pleasant nights there.

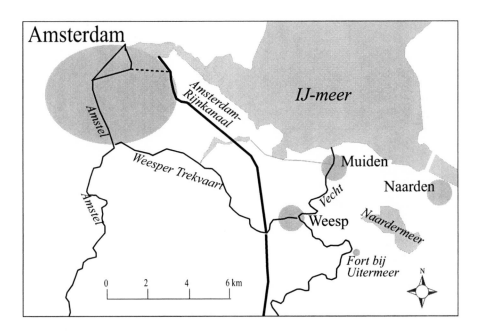

Zuider Zee, from an 1845 map:

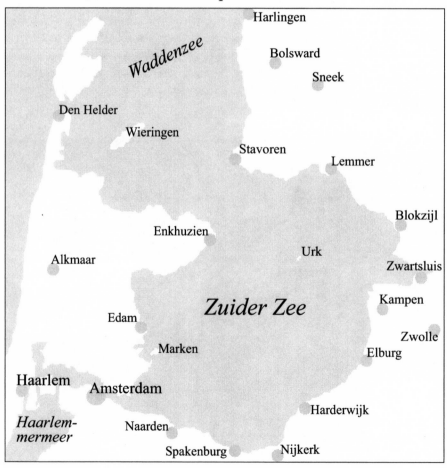

Zuider Zee - IJsselmeer

Before we go there, however, some comments about the geography and history of this region. Soon we will be traveling on the waters that sixty years ago was known as the Zuider Zee (Southern Sea). Today these waters are divided into the IJsselmeer, Markermeer and IJmeer, and much of the area has been polderized into usable land.

What is a polder? In the 14th and 15th centuries windmills came into use to pump water from low-lying lands, creating the first polders. Polders are defined as land reclaimed from the sea, a lake or marshland. Some polders are above sea level and surplus water is returned to the sea through locks. When the polder lies below sea level, as many do, the water must be pumped into the canals. This is now accomplished by a combination of traditional windmills, modern sleek windmills and diesel or electric motor-driven pumps.

IJsselmeer, on the current map:

Cruising the Canals & Rivers of the Netherlands

The IJsselmeer is the largest freshwater lake in the Netherlands. It was formed in 1932 by the completion of the Afsluitdijk from Den Oever to Makkum, separating the Zuider Zee from the Waddenzee. Notice the fishing ports of Blokzijl, Zwartsluis, Elburg and Hardewijk, now isolated from the sea, and Urk, no longer an island, now on the mainland.

The Wieringermeer polder filled shallows to connect the island of Wieringen to the mainland prior to the completion of the Afsluitdijk in 1932. Noordoostpolder was drained during World War II, while the big new island of Flevoland was created in the 1950s. Flevoland polder was created in the 1950s. The causeway Houtridijk from Enkhuizen to Lelystad (1967) further divided the lake into IJsselmeer on the north and Markermeer on the south. The latter is named for Marken island or, more correctly, Zuidelijk IJsselmeer (Southern IJsselmeer). A subdivision of the Markermeer is named the IJmeer. The term IJsselmeer is commonly used to designate the entire inland sea.

Naarden

In just two hours after leaving our mooring in Amsterdam we were back in Weesp, sitting at a waterfront table at 't Gat van Weesp for our usual mid-morning coffee. From there it was back to the pumpout station, then on to our planned mooring, 3km south on the Vecht. The concrete quay on the east bank of the Vecht was open, so we claimed it. We walked though the tiny village nearby, to the Fort bij Uitermeer. Activities at the fort are underway to make it more of a cultural attraction, but for now we just walked around and looked it over. I was especially interested in the very old lock and bascule bridge over the canal 's Gravelandse Vaart; the lock has double sets of gates on each end, so that high water can be controlled from either direction and the lifting bridge is made of cast iron with some delicate scroll decorations. I found that the lock and bridge date from 1878. The original lockkeeper's house is now a very handsome private residence.

The river and the views invited relaxation, so we sat out the afternoon, barbecued sausages for dinner onboard and enjoyed the sunset over the river and the moonrise over the fields. In the morning we would be off by bicycle.

The Naardermeer is one of the most beautiful nature reserves in the Netherlands; it consists of a freshwater lake surrounded by marshland. It is home to thousands of bird species, deer, small mammals and fish. Access is restricted, but we could see birds occasionally in the fields as we rode along the narrow farm lanes. The scattered farmhouses boasted some beautiful gardens. Sheep were everywhere, along with handsome black horses. We circled the northern arc of the preserve and arrived at Naarden in just over an hour of leisurely pedaling, including a brief excursion on the Meerkade lane for a view of the lake.

We entered the fort on the impressively-named Burgemeester van Wettumweg, crossing the outer moat on a bascule bridge. At this point the water looked like a curving natural river, lined by willow trees and not very fort-like. But as we arrived at the inner moat we knew that this was clearly a fort, across the water the long star-point walls rose five meters straight up from the water, made of concrete and stone. On top of the walls rose several layers of grass berms. The Dutch flag and a church steeple, along with tall tress, completed the scene. I don't think I would have wanted to try to attack!

Our first step on arrival was more pedaling, as we followed the bicycle path around the outer moat, twelve star points, almost 2km around. As we rode we counted six very sharp points of the stone wall, as well as six more star points on islands that seemed to float in the inner moat. I hadn't realized that serious rowing was so prevalent in Holland, again we saw six or seven two-man rowing shells, using the outer moat.

The walls around the town are intact but the gates have been removed and now the entrance through the walls is lined by two sturdy maple trees on each side of the road, at this time of year making the dense cover of a small tunnel. I realized later that the entrance from the jachthaven side is much more open; I'm glad now that we came in the way we did, through the "back door".

We continued to ride, this time circling the town on the inside of the walls, and came across Restaurant De Turfloods near the end of the circuit; we decided that their terrace tables on the Nieuwe Haven would be a great place for lunch. The menu is pricey at night and reservations are usually necessary but a salad and bread lunch was both elegant and reasonably priced. deturfloods.nl

After lunch a walk across Marktstraat to the Grote Kerk showed us what we had been told, that the shopping in Naarden is seriously upscale. We did a lot of window shopping but managed to avoid buying a complete new wardrobe for the fall. The first shop we saw set the tone, named "Dressed to Kill".

As a fan of the star forts I couldn't miss the Nederlands Vesting Museum, the fortress museum, located in the southernmost star point. The original interior spaces of the bastion have been preserved here. The director of the museum describes the town: "The fortified town of Naarden nowadays is a lush green pearl in a hectic world, with beautiful houses, rugged barracks and overgrown ramparts. But it used to be one of the Netherlands most elaborate defense works, defending the rich province of Holland and its trading city of Amsterdam from invaders coming from the east."

The museum rents space in the bastions, for private parties and receptions; they offer "bomb free" meetings in a bomb shelter. You can patrol the moat in the museum's army-green boat, or follow a gunner along the ramparts. A great opportunity to play soldier! vestingmuseum.nl

Muiden

My interest in Naarden satisfied, we cycled back to the Vecht mooring on a southerly route around the lake, following the Karnemelksloot and 's Gravelandse Vaart canals across the open fields. The open-air riding in the late afternoon was very pleasant. Dinner onboard, then another glowing sunset; this will be a difficult spot to leave.

But we did, traveling on the Vecht through Weesp and on to Muiden. It is Sunday morning, so I expected that we would be part of a fleet of boats heading out onto the IJmeer and I was right.

Zuider Zee - IJsselmeer

The chart showed a 330° reverse left turn at the eastern side of Weesp; it was good that I knew to expect it, as I was busy watching the row of quite elegant houseboats on the south bank and the two large boatyards on the north bank, De Bruyn and De Leeuw. I had seen De Leeuw's Whaleboat line at a boat show so it drew my interest as we passed by. The turn in the river opens widely, so there was no problem as we all followed in a line.

The next attention-grabber was a huge three-masted white sailing barge, at least 40m long. It looked to be permanently moored there, or at least in for long-term service by one of the boatyards or other marine services. Another sharp turn in the river, this time to the right, brought us in close along another row of houseboats; several of the residents, having their breakfast on the docks, greeted us and wished us a good day on the water (I assume that's what they said!)

Soon we passed under the busy A1 motorway bridge and immediately slowed for boat traffic ahead, all looking to get quickly through one of the two locks, right in the middle of the town of Muiden. Since everybody was heading to the IJmeer it wasn't difficult but it did require some give-and-take until we secured onto a bollard and relaxed. But the skipper and crew need to look sharp here, the cafe terraces alongside the locks were filled with spectators on this busy morning.

There are three locks lined across the river in Muiden; two are used regularly and I assume that the third is primarily used to control flow into and out of the Vecht. The locks are well fitted with bollards, both on top of the lock walls and set into the walls. In addition there are horizontal lines slung along the walls, for the use of small boats lying between bollards. The rise or fall of water in the lock is usually small, it varies with the canal level and the lake level. As I had seen in other situations like this, there are double sets of gates at each end of the locks, their use depending on which water is at the higher level.

Looking toward the lake from the lock, we could see the Muiderslot castle, located at the mouth of the river. It's an impressive sight, one of the better known castles in the Netherlands, and has been featured in many television shows set in the Middle Ages. It is a tall square of bricks with a cylindrical tower and cone-shaped turret on each corner.

We didn't stop in Muiden, it was too busy a place for us on this day. We followed a long line of boats out into the inland sea. The sight of this many sailboats was unusual for us, we hadn't been among so many since our days on Pamlico Sound, North Carolina. But of course this is the perfect place for them; the IJmeer and Markermeer enjoy quite a bit of wind and offer open spaces for sailing.

Not wishing a bad day for the sailors, I was glad that we had a day that wasn't too windy; the shallow waters in this corner of the sea can make for an uncomfortably choppy ride. We didn't have far to go, only 6.5km of open water, and navigation was no problem because we had chatted with a local cruiser while in the lock. He was also cruising into the Gooimeer and suggested that we follow him to avoid the crowd. He led us on a sharp right turn immediately upon clearing the jetty, along a marked channel inside three barrier islands. This made for a very smooth ride for most of the distance, then when we did leave the shelter of the islands we turned southeast, putting the wind straight on our stern. In about ten minutes we had gone under the rail and motorway bridges (clearance13m) and into the calm string of lakes called the "Randmeren".

Waterway	From	To	KM	Hours
Weesper Trekvaart	Amsterdam	Amsterdam-Rijnkanaal	9.0	1.25
Smal Weesp	Amsterdam-Rijnkanaal	Vecht	2.0	0.25
Vecht	Weesp	Muiden/IJmeer	5.0	1.00
IJmeer/Gooimeer	Muiden	Naarden	10.0	1.50

Randmeren - Flevoland

The nine lakes of the Randmeren (border lakes) did not exist until Flevoland was created; a channel was needed for the drained water, and the result was a series of excellent recreational lakes. The unbroken chain (just two locks) provides an inland route for boaters traveling between Noord/Zuid Holland and Friesland/Overijssel. The open waters of the IJsselmeer can be daunting for some skippers and, technically, an upgraded license is required.

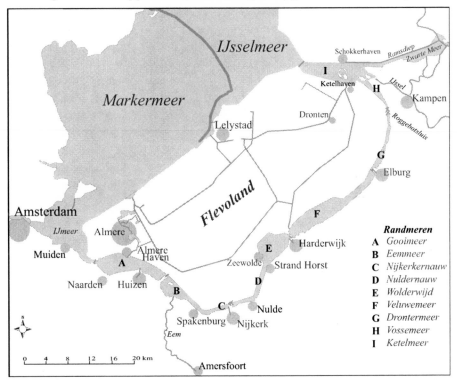

We entered the Gooimeer at about 11:00; I had intended to cruise the channel along the north shore into the Eemmeer, destination Spakenburg. But as we passed Dode Hond (dead dog!) island I had another idea. We tied up at a quay on the south side of the island, had our lunch on the grass and, while I consulted the charts, Carol walked the edge of the nature preserve on the island. (The dead dog was long gone, that story started when the island was used as part of the polder project; the dog belonging to one of the workers on the island died there, a natural death, and was buried there. The name stuck.)

I decided to change our destination to be Amersfoort, at the upper end of the river Eem, 18km from the Eemmeer. There is a new visitor's mooring at Amersfoort, reportedly offering excellent facilities, which we could reach by 17:00 or earlier. And if we did get delayed or weary, I counted seven free mooring quays and two jachthaven stretched out along the route. The lure was a twisting, narrow river through the fields, a few small towns and an interesting city at the end. We decided to spend Sunday night at Amersfoort.

Eem river

As soon as we had entered the mouth of the river we noticed the first free mooring quay; this would be a good place to stop when traveling on the Randmeren, if the skipper wanted something other than a marina or town quay, such as one that is quiet and free. About 2km up the river is the village of Eemdijk, with another mooring quay. The village looked to be both a farming and an upscale bedroom community, a new development of nearly identical homes which looked strange in the midst of pastures. A small ferry crossed the river just in front of us, with cars, bikes and hikers onboard.

We cruised along slowly, enjoying the views of well-kept farms, green pastures with sheep and horses, and the occasional patch of woods. One of the sharper turns in the river had been cut to make the channel straight, creating a side channel filled with small boats. We were accompanied by dozens of Sunday-afternoon cyclists riding the road paralleling the river.

The peaceful spell was broken for a while by the appearance of a sand and gravel operation, then a series of boatyards and the docks of boat clubs and finally the bridge of the A1 motorway. The large suburban town of Baarn, stretched along both the highway and the river, doesn't offer a quay; it's just as well, it didn't seem to have any interest for tourists like us. There is a mooring quay on a tiny island just a short distance farther on the river.

A *fietsboot*, ferry boat for cyclists, transports bikes and riders to and from points along the river. The cycle path crosses on a bridge over the river, at 3.0m clearance we could pass under and watch a long string of serious cyclists, in their team uniforms, whizz across over us. As long-time Tour De France fans, we enjoyed the experience and the sound of the tires. Just after that we again encountered rowing shells, two 8-man crews; we pulled to the bank to give them space on the narrow river.

Amersfoort

Soon we arrived in the industrial outskirts of the city, somewhat shielded by dense trees on the banks but stark modern office buildings rose above the treetops. More rowing shells, one and two-man, skittered along in front of us. The banks began to lined with houseboats, barges, cruisers and small boats, with jachthavens and boat clubs tucked in behind narrow openings. We continued in through industry on the west bank and apartment blocks on the east bank, to the passantenhaven on the east bank at a very wide rail bridge. The facilities proved to be excellent, at a low rate and with a pumpout station. Not the quiet location that we might have hoped for, but okay for one night. There were five or six trains per hour overhead until midnight, then a couple during the night and a full schedule starting again at 06:00. Amersfoort is a central crossroads for trains to and from all of eastern and northern Netherlands. Good news if you want to travel by rail, bad news if you want silence at night. The central station is a short walk from the dock.

It was also a short walk to the spectacular Koppelpoort, built directly over the intersection of the inner and outer moats. It was a good place to start our dog walk; from there we walked east on the Plantsoen Noord, a pleasant stretch of parks alongside the outer moat that could take us halfway around the city if we wished. We weren't ready for that so we turned back after inspecting a very old cemetery, through the windows in a ancient double wooden door; a high brick wall with ivy protected the graveyard from visitors like us.

Amersfoort has a medieval core with moats and ramparts, but it is not a star fort. In fact, on the map it resembles a heart. The historic town center is exceptionally well preserved, with picturesque canals and houses and a street layout that has remained the same for centuries..

Unfortunately our unplanned arrival brought us here on a day other than those of the various street markets, which include a flower market and a fish market (both on Friday.) From the dock we walked up the east bank of the Eem, right through the gate under the medieval shield in the photo. That led us to the inner moat and a canal, the Kortegracht/Langegracht, that strikes south through the center of the heart. The houses along this canal were as charming and beautiful as any we have yet seen in a Dutch city. It took us to Langestraat, the main shopping street.

Cruising the Canals & Rivers of the Netherlands

A few blocks east we came to the church, the market square and cafes. Many of the shops followed the tradition of closing on Monday. We even had some difficulty finding a place to get coffee, eventually buying from a walk-up stand. We picked out a cafe that looked good for lunch, although it opened at noon rather than the usual (on other days) 10:00. Restaurant In den "Kleinen" Hap did serve us an excellent lunch after we had strolled the shopping streets. www.kruispuntamersfoort.nl

We didn't know in advance that this was the birthplace of Piet Mondriaan, one of our favorite artists; the Mondriaan House Museum for Constructive and Concrete Art is now a museum with some of his works. But guess what? Not open on Monday! This find was important enough to us to convince us to stay over.

But not at the rail bridge. We packed up and traveled back out into the countryside, mooring at a free quay adjacent to the cycling bridge. There we gave Johnnie some more exercise, then set off on our bikes to try out the cycling paths for ourselves. That was a good move; we rode a long circuit on narrow lanes shaded by young trees, on a beautiful afternoon. We always enjoy seeing the Dutch farms and in fact stopped to chat with one farmer, on his own bicycle, who gave us a tour of his modern barns and equipment. We spent a quiet evening and night on the river, with a few cruisers and commercial barges passing by before sunset, then nothing but the sounds of a flock of sheep.

The morning light was a perfect display of "Dutch Light". It was beautiful because of the softness and closeness of atmosphere and sky, while the land all around us had no vertical dimension, just a flat table of various shades of green. There is a low horizon and a large panoramic sky in many Dutch paintings, as there is in the countryside of Holland.

We weren't far from the IJsselmeer; at the center of the country, it is a major reason for this special light. It has been called the eye of Holland. In other parts of the country the reflections don't just come from the IJsselmeer, they come from the North Sea, which is just a few kilometers off to the west of Heart of Holland, and the Waddenzee, which rims Friesland.

Our delayed visit to the Mondriaan House brought us back to our very enjoyable tour of the Rietveld-Schroder house in Utrecht, designed on the same geometric themes as Mondriaan's art. The museum is at the far southern end of the central canal, so we used our bicycles and returned on the outside of the inner moat, passing a long row of neighborhood shops. We still had no street market available, but we did find a small grocery which allowed us to gather some fresh provisions and pick up some sandwiches to go for our lunch.

Spakenburg

In early afternoon we were northbound, to return to the Eemmeer for the short cruise east to Spakenburg. When the Dutch closed off the Zuider Zee with dikes, they essentially put small fishing villages out of business. It was either find something else to do or die. Small villages like Spakenburg found their salvation in tourism. On view are the typical fishing boats of the area, called "botters", lying in the harbor or on the slipways in a museum boatyard. Local culture and history is celebrated in events throughout the summer, when women wear traditional clothes.

The harbormaster directed us to a space on the entrance channel west quay, convenient to the town center via the Oude Haven but also convenient to the strand. A concrete path right on the edge of the Eemmeer took us a few hundred meters west to a small, smooth sandy beach, with a green lawn behind it. We had a plunge in the water then stretched out on the grass. What a life!

Near the havenkantoor (office of the harbormaster) we saw the bicycle ferry, a retired fishing boat; apparently cyclists can leave from here and ferry to the Eem river for their excursion. That wasn't the only interesting boat, the quay was lined with wooden and iron-hulled barges, wooden sailboats and even an unrestored two-masted fishing sailboat.

We followed the arc of the Oude Haven quay until we came to the long row of botters, 8-12m wooden sailboats with flat bottom and a protruding keel, gaff rigged with jib and mizzen, sometimes six sails flying from the single mast. The hull design is very handsome, a peaked stem reaching high and a highly swept stern are a feast for the eyes. At the old shipyard we saw a new hull in the water, not yet painted or rigged; the beauty of its bare wood was a memorable sight.

For dinner, how could we not choose a fish restaurant? We wanted to eat at the Visrestaurant De Pieterman, which rates five stars in its online listing and gets rave reviews. depieterman.com But foiled again, they are open only Thursday-Sunday. Instead we found the old skippers house, 't Schippershuys, and had a satisfactory, if not great, fish dinner.

Southern Randmeren

Wednesday morning brought rain, steady but not heavy. This would be our longest daily run, 45km to Elburg. It is all open water except for one lock and a brief zig-zag past islands and a bridge at Harderwijk. The speed limit is 20 km/hr; we can't do that, our top speed is about 12 km/hr, but it means paying more attention to other boats. We were under way before 08:00, planning to be in Elburg by 13:00.

Despite the rain there were plenty of small motorboats on the water. Most of them seemed to be going our way for the first hour, but as we approached the Nijkerkersluis a broad fleet of boats came toward us. They had been concentrated in the lock and then "took off" and spread out, so that it seemed that a small navy was rapidly coming toward us across the entire waterway (which had narrowed here on the approach to the lock.) But of course all that I had to do was hold a steady course and the pack split around us, leaving us rocking a bit in a maze of wakes.

Since the lockkeeper had just recently released those boats, he kept the gates open and the green light on, so the dozen or so boats around us flowed together into a line, entering the lock and each finding a spot to secure their lines. As usual the rise was very small and we were soon out the other side.

The Gooimeer and the Eemmeer are both named *meer* (lake) and they do have the feel of a lake, even with a few islands. The next two sections of the Randmeren, the Nijkerkernauw and Nuldernauw, are different, more like a broad river than a lake. The word *nauw* means "close", in English we would call these waterways the "Narrows" (nauw even sounds like narrow.) The waterways are about 700 meters wide, from Spakenburg to Strand Horst. It is relative, of course, they are not all that narrow. A typical cruiser is about 3.5 meters wide, thus 200 of them could theoretically travel here side-by-side.

The separation between lakes first came at a bridge, then a lock; the change from the Nijkerkernauw to the Nuldernauw comes with no actual marker, but at the Jachthaven Nulde the heading swings from just a bit north of east to north-northeast. On the Nijkerkernauw there had been a few beaches (*strand*) on the Flevoland side and a brushy strip of land separating off a long, narrow parallel lagoon on the mainland side. After the turn at Nulde the beaches became bigger and more prevalent on the mainland, with lots of swimmers and sunbathers; this is obviously a popular recreational area. A stop at either Jachthaven Nulde or Jachthaven Strand Horst, on the mainland, would give access to these beaches, by bicycle or on foot.

Then comes the Wolderwijd, 4,000 meters wide and 4,000 meters long. The suffix sounds right if you remember to pronounce "ij" as "eye", thus "Wolder-wide". We followed channel markers straight across the Wolderwijd, which took us right to the Flevoland shore, where several islands block the northeastern end of the lake. The channel curved around these islands until we were headed almost due south, into the harbor of Harderwijk. We decided to go on in, to use a convenient fuel dock, even though we didn't intend to stay.

Harderwijk

Harderwijk was an important trading port on the Zuider Zee, but silting and the eventual making of the Flevoland polder has turned it into a popular stop on the inland Randmeren route. It is a beautifully preserved town, blending the old and new in a pleasant manner. The major tourist attraction is the Dophinarium, the largest sea-zoo in Europe. There are plentiful moorings in the centrally-located municipal Visserhaven or nearby marinas.

We motored in past the huge blue dome of the Dophinarium and took a short pass by the picturesque Visserhaven, where a molen sits above the harbor on a small mound, with a classic double-span drawbridge in front. On the way out the fuel dock was clear so we filled both our fuel and water tanks. We might have waited until Elburg, but it would have been embarrassing to run out of fuel a kilometer or so short.

We left the harbor and immediately turned northeast on the aqueduct, a relatively new passage over a highway, replacing a lock and drawbridge. On the way in we had noticed a highway bridge further north that we could easily pass under, however the chart warns *Doorvaart tussen Wolderwijd en Veluwemeer voor recreatie en chartervaart via het aquaduct* (Passage between Wolderwijd and Veluewemeer for recreational and charter boats via aqueduct.) Passage under the fixed bridge is reserved for barges. We noticed that not all small boats honor this advice, it may not be a formal rule.

North of Harderwijk the waterway names revert to ...*meer*, with the Veluwemeer, Drontermeer, Vossemeer and Ketelmeer. The Veluwemeer contains numerous small islands and shallows; the marked channel hugs the Flevoland shore and becomes quite narrow for the last few kilometers into Elburg. Here the lakes are again separated by a bridge, not surprisingly named the Elburgerbrug. There is plenty of clearance; the harbor entrance into Elburg is immediately north of the bridge.

Elburg

Elburg is a star fort town, this one with a rectangular moat and no star points. The original town is well preserved and offers a weekly street market, several nice restaurants and a full range of shopping. The extensive boating service community, spread along the 1km-long entrance channel, is focused on leisure vessels. Along with mechanical and hull services and chandleries, there is a substantial paint shop, Klaver Yachtpainting.

Elburg has its own fleet of botters, about a dozen are moored at the west end of the town dock. They differ from those at Spakenburg in the obvious lower peak at the stem and, I am told, less draft, both to deal with shallower water here on what was the eastern side of the Zuider Zee.

We arrived feeling like old friends, as we had been here several times before and had looked at several barges offered for sale by De Elburger Scheepsbemiddeling (ships brokerage.) On our first visit we not only met the Managing Director, Pieter De Jong, but also his wife and new baby, who were at the office that day; our morning coffee had been enjoyed in a family atmosphere. The brokerage office is in the middle of a long row of handsomely renovated buildings facing on the Binnenhaven. We said hello right away, but didn't stay as it appeared that a sales negotiation was in progress. www.esbship.nl

The harbormaster had assigned us a space outside the Binnenhaven but just a short walk from the waterfront and, over a cobbled footbridge, into the town. The bridge crosses the singel, in this case a single singel, one moat surrounds the town. We stretched our legs with a walk around the inside of the singel, an excellent place for a pleasant stroll. There are no fortifications or even a berm left from the original fortifications, just a gentle slope of grass and flowers leading up to the residences. Again we found an ancient cemetery in one corner of the rectangle, a very peaceful place because of the open fields across the water, occupied by a flock of sheep.

The streets inside the town center are pedestrian-oriented; although cars and delivery trucks are allowed, traffic is minimized by the large parking lots provided at the eastern entrance, outside the singel. We entered the center of town through the Vischpoort, the only remaining structure of the defensive walls, onto the pedestrian-only main shopping street. We had again missed the market day (Tuesday) but it didn't matter, as the street was lined with shops which had displays of shoes, clothing, housewares and groceries out in the open, in front of the shops. We fortified ourselves with ice cream cones from the IJssalon Casa Piccola as we walked past a long row of market offerings.

A narrow drainage canal runs transversely across the very regular street grid of the town. In fact this is the most perfectly-gridded Dutch town that I have seen, each block is the same size and all corners are square, very unusual for such an old town. There were plenty of choices for drinking and eating, from casual to elegant. We settled on the first one that we had seen, De Herberg, at the Binnenhaven on Havenkade, largely because we could sit outside and enjoy the view of the botters and activity in the harbor.

Northern Randmeren

We were back on the Randmeren the next morning, northbound on the Drontermeer. That lake perhaps should be called a "...nauw", as it is quite narrow. The channel is even more narrow, it hugs the Flevoland shore because the eastern side is irregular, with islands and shallows preventing navigation. In fact it feels much like a river, at a couple of points the shorelines are only 150 meters apart.

On the Randmeren, as at our Spiegelpolder and Vecht river moorings, the mist would come up in the morning and then burn off. The sky and the light constantly changed, with the geographical and meteorological conditions. In these places the light has a presence and volume; the light changes the landscape, and the landscape changes the light.

Randmeren

The northern end of the Drontermeer opened up some, but soon we were funneled into the Roggebotsluis, a very modern lock and drawbridge complex similar to that back at Nijkerk. These were obviously both built at the same time, both use the same futuristic style. There was only a short wait for more boats to enter, then we dropped about half a meter then continued on, into the Vossemeer.

Again the channel followed the west bank; the eastern side opened across a wide stretch of water dotted with small islands and grass, obviously very shallow. In less than an hour from the lock we crossed the Ketelmeer on its shallow eastern edge, following a marked channel but mostly watching other local boats for a safe route.

We had left the Randmeren when we passed through the *Balgstuw bij Ramspol*, a very unusual type of weir used as a floodgate. This one is the largest of its type in the world, used to protect villages to the east on Zwarte Water from northwesterly gales coming in off the IJselmeer. The weir is a rubber-cloth tube attached to structures on the banks and on a tiny island in the middle of the waterway. When the dam is needed a bellows fills the tube with water or air, creating a dam. The visible structures are designed with curved conical stainless steel shells as a roof, much like a lobster shell. The Dutch do the strangest things to manage water!

We followed a channel named the Ramsgeul east into the Zwarte Meer. Another hour of motoring across open water brought us to the intersection where we turned north, into northwest Overijssel province.

Waterway	From	To	KM	Hours
Gooimeer	Hollandsebrug	Stichtsebrug	14.0	1..2
Eemmeer	Stichtsebrug	Spakenburg	9.0	0..8
Eem river	Eemmeer	Amersfoort	18.0	3.0
Nijkerkernauw	Spakenburg	Nulde	9.0	0.8
Nuldernauw	Nulde	Strand Horst	10.0	1.5
Wolderwijd	Strand Horst	Harderwijk	15.0	1.3
Veluwemeer	Harderwijk	Elburg	19.0	1.6
Drontermeer	Elburg	Roggebotsluis	11.0	1.0
Vossemeer	Roggebotsluis	Ketelhaven	8.0	0.8
Ketelmeer	Ketelhaven	Zwanendiep	17.0	1.5

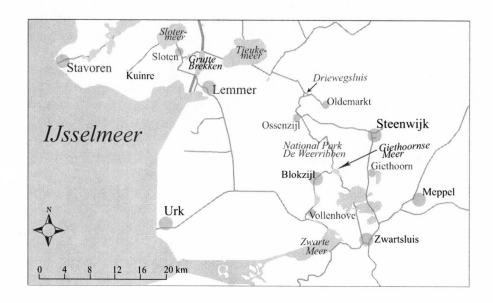

Vollenhove

The Kadoelerkeersluis awaited us, a massive structure of floodgates and road bridge. The passage through it remains open except during flooding, but the apparatus looked to me like a giant trash compactor that would squeeze our boat, and us, as we passed through. Of curse that didn't happen, the passage was uneventful and we were on a canal again. Soon we were at our destination, Vollenhove; we turned into the circular basin of Jachthaven Vollenhove and quickly found a space on one of the finger piers.

The main business street of Vollenhove was just a few steps from our dock; all of the restaurants are here, six or seven in a row. The necessary dog walk was accomplished by circling the very picturesque inner haven, a smaller circular basin with a small island at its center where small boats are docked. For dinner we returned to the Pizzeria Volante Da Piero.

Vollenhove was a Zuider Zee town before the polders; 16th century noblemen established their palaces here on the edge of the sea. After an early dinner we walked past some of the gardens remaining from that era, and through the forest of the Old Ruitenborgh manor.

On Friday morning we continued north, leaving the haven past the Royal Huisman shipyard, manufacturer of huge, sleek aluminum sailing yachts. It doesn't seem quite right to call these modern buildings a shipyard, there were no cranes, piles of blocking, miscellaneous boat pieces laying around; all work is done inside the sparkling clean workshops.

Blokzijl

In just over a half-hour we arrived at Blokzijl, a former seaport on the Zuider Zee, now well inland. Entering the haven through the original flood gates was like stepping back in time. Original 17th century buildings line the four quays of the haven; the spire of the Grote Kerk rises above the red tile roofs, straight ahead from the view at the canal.

I cruised slowly around the haven and saw a boat leaving the quay so we moved quickly and tied up for a walk along the waterfront and over to the lock on the main canal, which cuts right through the middle of the town. The lock is the source of much entertainment for the tourists, they lean on the railings right at the edge of the lock walls, so they are in intimate contact with boaters. A wooden pier extends well out into the haven as a wachtsteiger for waiting northbound boats; southbound boats wait at a quay on the west side of the narrow canal, immediately north of the lock.

During the summer months the haven is full of original sailing vessels along with modern cruising boats and larger tour boats. Looking at the map, perhaps I should have included this town as a star fort; it does have its points (pun intended!) But there are no fortifications and no encircling moat. The town is heavily touristic, filled with boating fans and others who have come to visit and to explore the history. If all moorings in the haven are taken or if you just want a more peaceful dock, there is a quay on the west bank of the canal 300 meters outside the floodgates.

We had our coffee at the Eetcafe Sluiszicht (lockview). A tour boat entered from the haven and almost filled the lock; the gates are listed as 7.0m minimum, so the boat must have had a beam of 6.99m! (The lock itself is 9.0m wide.) As it left the lock a southbound cruiser squeezed by, in a canal just barely ten meters wide. The fenders in between got a good workout; great fun for all of us watching.

We moved on, passing through the lock and the tight canal with no problems, then stopped on the north shore of the Giethoornse Meer for lunch onboard, out in the very quiet open countryside under clear blue skies. The canal took us north across wide open fields, with lots of swimming birds and lilypads, and occasional small forests on the banks.

De Weerribben National Park

We came to the Scheerebrug, marked on the chart as "Automatische brugbediening let op aanwijzingsborden" (Automatic bridge operation note nameplates.) The photoeye was mounted on a wooden piling set out in the water; I pulled alongside and read the instructions which basically said that the bridge would open automatically after sensing our boat, just be patient and watch the lights. And it did, with no bridgekeeper in the little glass house.

We were then cruising on the main street of the town of Wetering. It is two kilometers long, one house deep on each bank. North of the town are several very nice free moorings, with no facilities other than a swath of deep green grass, perfect for stretching out in the afternoon sun. We pressed on, counting on finding many more of the same.

The canal became a river with slight curves as we passed through the village of Kalenberg. It's a farming community but all of the farmers seem to have boats as well, the banks of the river are lined with them. Some of the simple but beautiful small houses have thatched roofs; we noticed one in particular which was topped by a short stake, with the profile of a steel lion mounting the stake, his tail curled in a full circle. Very impressive!

The passing view of villages create a real-life Dutch painting. The low horizon, the low perspective of many landscape paintings are unique and typically Dutch; the layout of the painting is suggested by the landscape.

It can be extremely crowded in summer, but we were early enough that our visit to De Weerribben National Park looked to be a good one. We staked our lines to the bank in the geographical center of the park, at the Kalenbergergracht corner. Here the canal makes a 90° turn to the east and an immediate 90° turn to the north. Except for the occasional passing boats, there was nothing to see or hear except nature. Further on ahead, at the little town of Ossenzijl, is the visitor's center for the park and several jachthavens with full facilities, but we prefer to be out on our own when we can.

Even here in the national park, lines of wind generators are prevalent, as they are at many places in the Netherlands. They didn't bother us, in fact we liked their slow rotation, especially when we could look along a row and see the unintended choreography of the blades, like a wave passing down the row.

We moved into town early the next morning for our usual pleasure, coffee at a terrace table where we can watch boating activity, in this case at a drawbridge across the very narrow canal in the center of Ossenzijl. The passantenhaven is north of the bridge, we moored there and walked back to the cafe, later noting the various canoe and kayak rentals available; we decided to pass it up this time.

Driewegsluis - Linde river

The Ossenzijlersloot north from the town soon intersected with the Linde river; we followed the river only 3km, to the Driewegsluis.

The "Three-way Lock" is a popular place for recreational boaters. The lock is at the middle of a triangular island, the cut forming two more islands. The perimeters of these islands are favorite mooring spots, in part because of a restaurant and snack bar on one of the islands. www.driewegsluis.nl

The Linde river marks the border with Friesland; as soon as we left the Driewegsluis we were in that new province.

Waterway	From	To	KM	Hours
Zwanendiep/ Kadoelermeer	Zwarte Meer	Vollenhove	6.0	0.6
Vollenhoverkanaal	Vollenhove	Blokzijl	5.0	0.5
Noorderdiep/Valse Trog	Blokzijl	Giethoornse Meer	3.0	0.3
Wetering	Giethoornse Meer	Grote Gat	5.5	0.8
Heuvengracht	Grote Gat	Kalenberg	1.4	0.2
Kalenbergergracht	Kalenberg	Ossenzijl	5.1	1.0
Ossenzijlersloot/Linde river	Ossenzijl	Driewegsluis	4.0	0.5
Jonkers of Helomavaart	Driewegsluis	Driesprong	7.5	1.0
Pier Christiaansloot	Driesprong	Tjeukermeer	5.0	0.6
Follegasloot	Tjeukermeer	Groote Brekken	5.0	0.6
Rijnsloot/Woudsloot	Groote Brekken	Sloten	4.0	0.5

Friesland Province

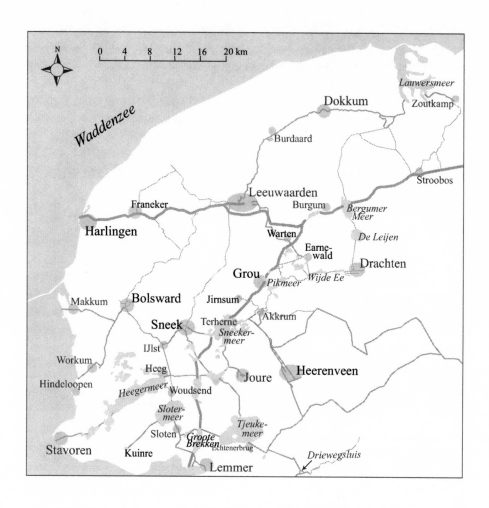

Tjeukemeer

Our first stop in Friesland was the star fort town of Sloten. From the Driewegsluis we followed a zig-zag route of canals and crossed three lakes, the Tjeukemeer, Groote Brekken and Brande Meer.

The Tjeukemeer is a significant lake, 4km x 7km; we went across the long leg, stopping in the middle to view the moorings at Marchjepolle island. In August there could be as many as one hundred boats moored here, even now there was about two dozen. I had thought of staying at the island overnight, but it was still early in the day and it looked too busy.

The next lake, Groote Brekken is long and narrow; our crossing from east to west was only 700 meters. The Prinses Margriet Kanaal crosses the lake north-south, so we were careful to watch for barge traffic, slowing down to steer behind a very large towboat pushing a series of huge barges. This canal is heavily used by commercial barges and by private boats traveling from the IJsselmeer to the North Sea at the far northwestern corner of Germany. Many of them will go on to the Kiel canal and pass through into the Baltic Sea.

Sloten

We proceeded on to Sloten, arriving at 14:50. We elected to tie up on one of the wooden docks along the canal, with no services, less than 1km walk into town, rather than in the huge Jachthaven Lemsterpoort.

Friesland is true boater's country; the residents have lived and worked by barge or small boat for hundreds of years and some remote farms can still be reached only by boat. A maze of canals and small channels connect dozens of meers, filled with boats of all types during the summer months. Dutch is a second language to many of the local people; the primary language is Frisian. In some places signs can be seen using both languages, such as: Sloten/Sleat.

Sloten is a star fort, enclosed by a diamond-shaped singel. (I call the shape of the town a diamond, the locals prefer to call it an onion, fat in the middle.) The haven is at the bottom point of the diamond. A very picturesque small canal runs north-south through the center of town, but visitors cannot moor there and height is restricted to 2 m by bridges.

The local people like to say "750 years old, less than 750 inhabitants!" It is a town of narrow alleys and cobbled streets, restored facades of merchant houses, guild rooms and historic houses. Our first sight on walking in from our dock was the molen De Kaai (The Quay.) It sits atop a high stone wall, the east bank quay of the central canal. We went there first, looking up in awe at the huge octagonal wooden structure. It is a grain mill, still operated on occasion.

From the molen we walked up the east quay of the canal, savoring the views of the old houses and of the small boats moored in the canal. At the north end of town we were shocked to see the grotesque presence of a very large, tall rectangular block of concrete and steel, a factory building. The company produces milk replacers for young cattle. I have no problem with industry, it is often seen throughout the Netherlands near old historic towns. What was strange here was that it is within the original singel, in fact it sits in a place where there were previously the walls of the fortified town. In Gouda, for instance, the refinery is on the outside of the singel; still rather obnoxious, but at least not destroying an entire corner of the historic town. I don't know local opinion, but there is mine!

Our return route was on a path along the western perimeter of the houses, looking out on a broad strip of grass and the waters of the singel. The day had been overcast and now a light rain started, so we hurried Johnnie back to the safety of the boat. Later we left him behind as we went back to the central canal to find a place for dinner. We liked the looks of Restaurant Het Bolwerk; they have terrace tables on the canal but we had an excellent dinner inside their warm and dry traditional tavern. www.restauranthetbolwerk.nl

Sloten is one of the historic "Friesland's Eleven Towns", along with two more that will would see on the next day, IJlst and Sneek. The 11 cities of Friesland encompass the history of the region, with old forts, castles, and ramparts still recognizable today. Stavoren was said to be founded as early as 313 BC, while Harlingen was founded in the 9th century by Vikings. Bolsward is a typical Frisian country town. Sloten is the smallest. The other towns are Franeker, Leeuwarden, Dokkum, Workum, and Hindeloopen.

Woudsend - Heeg - IJlst

The next day's destination would be the city of Sneek but we got an early start so that we could visit the towns of Woudsend and Heeg enroute. First we crossed the Slotermeer, maybe that is the onion they are talking about. Looking at it on the chart, it looks a lot more like an onion than the town does.

Woudsend and Heeg are probably the most thoroughly saturated towns in Friesland in terms of recreational boating. They are centrally located in the Friese meren, the largest area of lakes in the region; each town has canals pointing north, east, south and west for easy access to the nearby Slotermeer and Heegermeer or for visits to other towns. Both towns offer a large range of boating services, including the availability of day or weeklong charter of sailboats, modern or traditional.

At Woudsend a molen sawmill, De Jager, stands high above the town and the totally flat terrain, along with the tall square brick steeple of the church. We turned east on the Wellesloot for less than a kilometer, just far

142

enough to view the row of boatyards and other marine services; thirteen of them are named on the chart. Although there is a direct route to the north we then took the Woudsender Rakken, a twisting waterway (five 90° turns) leading to the Heegermeer. We nipped across the end of the lake, avoiding dozens of sailboats engaged in a race, schooling or just plain sailing around on a Sunday.

Heeg is certainly the sailboat center of Holland. There are hundreds of sailboats based here, both privately owned and for charter, by day or week. There are scores of one-design sailboats which compete in races on the Heegermeer. Fleets of *platbodem* traditional sailing barges are available for charter. Motor cruisers may feel a little out of place but are welcome at the Passantenhaven or one of several marinas and there is a Grand Banks dealer here to raise the motoring flag.

We did not stop at Heeg, or at IJlst, the town five kilometers north. As at Woudsend, this was a day for seeing the sights of these small towns from the water. We enjoyed the waterfront homes and the wide variety of boats and barges that are moored along the waterways.

Sneek

The past few decades have seen Sneek grow into perhaps the major boating town in all of the Netherlands. Because of its location among the lakes and the maze of waterways of Friesland, along with rail and major highway access (A7 from Amsterdam), the local government has encouraged business parks to be constructed at the eastern and southern sides of town. Along the Houkesloot all kinds of watersport companies have been brought together at Watersport Boulevard 't Ges; there is a great diversity among the forty companies represented. Another group of marinas, yacht brokers and yacht charter companies are grouped on the northeastern corner of town, known as De Domp, as well as along the Woudvaart at the south. Quayside moorings, with electricity, are offered in several places around the town canals. Water is available only at Oosterkade and the south side of De Kolk.

We were lucky to get a space on at De Kolk, across from the Sneeker Waterpoort, perhaps because the weekend boaters had gone back to work. It is a good location because the main shopping street is Grootzand, also the location of the Tuesday street market, just a short walk from the moorings.

Sneek is widely known as the home of Sneekweek, the largest inland sailing event in Europe. Races are sailed on the Sneekermeer in all international competition classes. Around the regatta are various activities; it has become a renowned festival week, beginning on the Friday before the first Saturday of August with a boat show with hundreds of boats and fireworks. Depending on your point of view, this is a great week to either be there or be out of town! www.sneek.nl

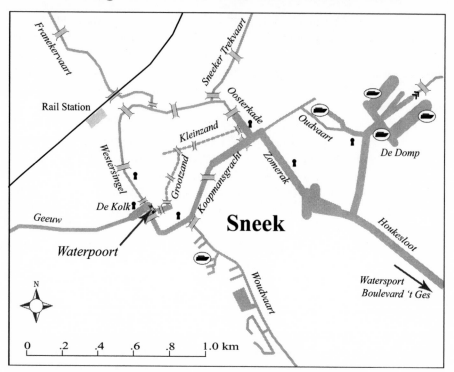

Sneek was a fortified city, but no more. The only remaining sights are the Waterpoort and the singel around the western and northern sides of the city center. The latter are not landscaped into a park, although it is still a nice walk to view the homes and the local boats.

We stayed at De Kolk two nights. Carol did some shopping and sightseeing while I visited many of the marine businesses (by bicycle.) Johnnie did the usual: eat, sleep and go for walks. Dinner on Sunday was tapas at Cook & NY, www.cookny.nl a modern restaurant on the Oosterkade next to the chandlery Simon Watersport. Monday night was at the more elegant (and more expensive) De Kastanje www.dekastanjesneek.nl

Tuesday morning we stocked up our provisions from the weekly market. then departed Sneek via the Sneekermeer. The Houkesloot is the canal out from the city, then it intersects the Prinses Margriet Kanaal, which has a substantial amount of commercial barge traffic. The canal crosses the lake on the western side along a well-marked channel, which keeps the busy sail and motor recreational boats separated from the through traffic.

Friesland Province

We did not linger on the Sneekermeer, although there are many islands and coves to explore on a cruise around the lake, as well as more than one hundred mooring choices, from full-service marinas to wooden pontoons with no services. There are other very busy boating areas in the Netherlands, but this certainly must be the center of boating activity for Friesland, if not the entire country.

There are many more boating services along the Prinses Margriet Kanaal, our route north for a few kilometers. At Terherne, on the north shore of the Sneekermeer, there are jachthavens, yacht charter and yacht brokerage. Three kilometers further on, the river De Boarn leads to the town of Jirnsum, again offering multiple services for yacht charter, sales and jachthavens. Then at Grou there are boatyards and boatbuilders which rival those at Sneek.

Grou

On my first tour of the Netherlands I had, by accident of timing, enjoyed an in-water boat show at Grou. That was in early May, but even then the town was full of visitors and the Pikmeer was full of boats, both sail and motor. The waterfront of Grou opens right onto the lake, joining town and lake activities much more than at Sneek. We stopped here for a walking tour through the small town and had lunch at an outside table of Theehuis Grou, where we could watch activities on the docks and the lake. hettheehuis.nl

From there we headed southeast on the Pikmeer and through the narrow pass of De Tijnje to the next lake, the Wijde of Peanster Ee. Our eventual destination was the Alde Feanen/Princenhof lakes region. Rather than taking the direct route on the Prinses Margriet Kanaal, we wanted to see the farms and countryside of the heart of Friesland by traveling the small lakes and the very small waterways connecting them.

We left the Peanster Ee on the river Ee, called by a different name each time it narrowed or opened into a pond. The first of these was the Jansloot; we passed through an open flood gate into the first small bay at a large farm complex, Goëngahuizen. We had seen one molen just as we entered the sloot, now there were two more near the farm. The landscape here is so flat and so open that these windmills stood out against the sky, strange and beautiful objects. These are poldermolen, meaning that they were used to pump water from the polder.

We cruised very slowly on the Goengahuistersloot, the narrow stream that curves across the fields. A strip of brush and low trees lined both sides of the waterway, with a grid of drainage canals separating the sheep pastures and hay fields. When the stream widened into a pond, the Modderige Bol, we decided to stop for the night.

Marrekrite

Our mooring, a short wooden dock, was one of the thousands created and maintained by the Marrekrite organization. www.marrekrite.nl To explain I will quote from their brochure:

"De Marrekrite is a partnership of 21 Frisian municipalities and the Province of Friesland (our participants) and was founded in 1957. The funding for De Marrekrite is raised by these participants according to a certain allocation formula. All boating enthusiasts may use De Marrekrite's moorings free of charge. Because De Marrekrite's moorings are unique and in high demand, a maximum of three days of mooring has been established to give as many boating enthusiasts as possible the chance to enjoy them! As a token of their appreciation, many boating enthusiasts buy our Marrekrite pennant. By doing so, they contribute directly to the maintenance of these mooring facilities. After all, a considerable percentage of the total budget goes to the maintenance and replacement of existing mooring sites. Our goal is to find a good balance between using Friesland's waters and surrounding land for recreation and conserving Friesland's scenic landscape and natural habitat."

Key figures:
• approx. 3500 free mooring sites
• approx. 550 mooring facilities at 280 locations
• 42 km of quay and sheet pile wall of which more than 5 km of landing stage and 1 km of sheet pile wall are made of recycled plastic
• 100 waste containers at 60 locations

We began to see the Marrekrite moorings as soon as we had entered Friesland, before we had even crossed the Tjeukemeer. I wrote earlier of Marchjepolle island; around that island there are ten Marrekrite moorings and one waste container.

The locations are marked on the ANWB charts. I use the Stentec electronic version of these charts; for a small extra payment I downloaded the Marrekrite database, which displays an icon for each location and a data window with details. The chart of Friesland is dotted with hundreds of these icons, especially in the isolated lakes, islands and streams to the east and northeast of Grou.

In the morning we continued to the east on the Goengahuistersloot. We came to a ferry crossing and tied up at the nearby dock to take advantage of an observation tower; at only three meters tall the term "tower" is a misnomer, but in this country that is enough to provide a broad view. We saw that the ferry is at the dead-end of a road; in winter months a moveable floating bridge continues the narrow lane across the river, serving the three farms on the north side, which are otherwise isolated from civilization. Because the waterway must be open for boats in the summer, the bridge is moved aside and a two-car ferry is used. We saw the bridge tied parallel along the north bank, in storage for the summer months.

Several more Marrekrite moorings were in use on the waterway now named the Grietmansrak, as we approached a recreational area. Jachthaven De Veenhoop offers a large marina, sailing school and campground on the south bank, followed by a row of eight more free moorings in the lake further east; on the north side is the Hotel-Restaurant Le Sicht. It is here that we turned north, on the Hooidamsloot, a short (1.6km) canal that took us into the Alde Feanen/ Princenhof National Park.

Alde Feanen - Princenhof

The "Old Fen" is approximately 25 sq km. Part of the national park is the lake area named Princenhof. The Alde Feanen is a versatile fenland with lakes, peat bogs, ditches, mires, reedbeds, marsh marigold meadows and swamps. In the field are more than 450 species of plants and more than one hundred bird species. There are nearly fifty marked mooring places, Marrekrite and other free docks, along with many suitable anchorages.

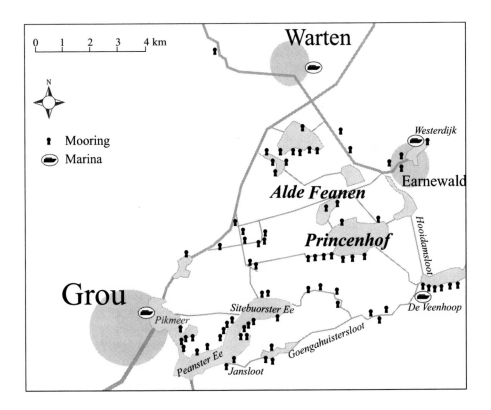

We spent a few hours visiting the different parts of Earnewald, the only developed area of the park and a large watersports center. We had a look around the two marinas and the rows of man-made islands and canals built for holiday homes, with water access to every house. There is a barge museum and several sailing schools, some have 20m sailing barges which take about 20 youngsters at a time, others have 7m open sailboats, which take an instructor and four or five others at a time. There is also a very large campground.

Frightened off by all of this, we moved out into the open waters of the Princenhof, for a while just drifting in a tiny bay where we could watch birds with our binoculars. We cruised around the islands and found an empty mooring quay alongside a tiny field of grass and an even tinier sandy beach. Perfect for giving Johnnie a place to roll on his back and for us to wade in the peaty brown water, familiar to me from my childhood in New Jersey USA, where we swam in what we called "cedar water" of abandoned bogs; our towels were always darkened by brown solids which stuck to our skin.

We settled there for dinner on the grass, and for overnight. The evening was made memorable by our hosts, a white ribbon of graceful swans, looking as though they were pushed along by the breeze rather than actually paddling.

The next day we moved to the northern section of the park, the Saiterpetten lake. From a mooring on the south shore we walked through and around one of the larger islands, enjoying the taller trees in several patches of woods. Some of the islands are farmed even though they are within the park.

In the afternoon we decided to go north into the pleasant small town of Warten. Barge traffic on the Prinses Margriet Kanaal brought us back into the real world, reinforced when we pulled into the very large Jachthaven Wartena for a pumpout. We didn't stay there, however, preferring the town quay and dinner at 't Skuthus "eten & drinken" establishment, which has been there since 1770, as a shipyard until recently. www.skuthus.nl

Leeuwarden

We were about ten kilometers from the center of Leeuwarden and a quick look at the chart appeared to show a route right across the city on the Nieuwe Kanaal. But on closer inspection I found that canal is not available for passage, despite showing the bridges as BB. We must pass around the city along its southern and western edges via the Van Harinxma Kanaal, which goes on westward to the port of Harlingen, then turn back sharply on the Harlingertrekvaart. We would eventually arrive at the Westerstadsgracht and the Noorderstadsgracht, the west side of the original singel of this star fort town.

The detour was well worth it, as we moored on the wide grassy bank on the inside of the moat, in a very picturesque setting named the

Noorderplantage. These are excellent moorings, with electricity, water and two shower/toilet/wastewater pumpout stations, one at each end of the moorings, accessed via a prepaid card. Boaters moored on the outside can cross the singel on a free foot ferry. The Prinsentuin park separates the quay from the historic city center. And what could be better than mooring on a star fort singel!

Leeuwarden is the major business center of northern Holland, it has the square modern office buildings and a huge shopping mall, Winkelcentrum Zaailand, to prove it. But what we came for were two museums.

Princessehof Ceramics Museum is located one block in from the Noorderplantage, on Grote Kerkstraat. The collection includes beautiful examples of historical and contemporary ceramics from Europe and Asia. It is housed in 18th-century palace of Mary Louise of Hesse-Kassel, princess of Orange-Nassau.

The Fries Museum is on Turfsingel, on the east side of the city center, almost at the Oostersingel; the Prinsentuin waterfront is a wonderful place to walk, but the remainder of the singel is not, so getting to this museum is an opportunity to wander through the old part of the city. There is no direct route, so we enjoyed a stroll on narrow cobbled streets and alleys and crossed the small interior canals, our general direction guided by occasional glimpses of a tall church spire near the museum.

Cruising the Canals & Rivers of the Netherlands

There are two parts of the Fries Museum; the main galleries display the history and culture of Friesland, including the story of Margaretha Zelle, the famed Mata Hari of World War I, born in Leeuwarden in 1876. The Verzets Museum Friesland is the Second World War Resistance Museum, displaying a chronological survey of the Frisian resistance.

For dinner, the closest restaurant was De Koperen Tuin, just steps away from our boat, but it seemed too elegant for the likes of us. We had walked by a couple of attractive pizzerias, but wanted something different. The other options ranged from Irish to Asian, but we hadn't had a good Mexican dinner since leaving our home in the southwestern USA, so the Yucatan restaurant drew us in. It was a good choice. yucatan.nl

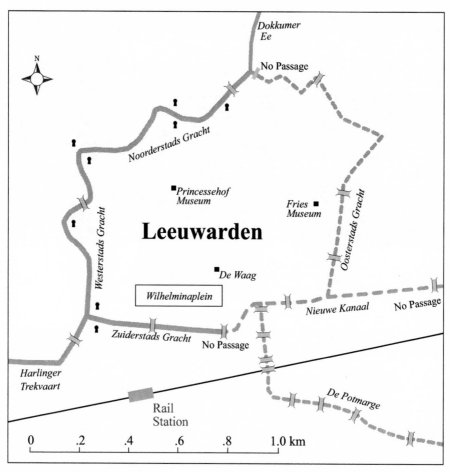

On Saturday morning we went for coffee at De Waag, the old weigh building, and picked up fresh fruits at vegetables at the street market on the Wilhelminaplein. Then we were northbound on the river Dokkumer Ee to first Burdaard, then Dokkum.

Burdaard

At the charming village of Burdaard we tied up in the center of the town for an onboard lunch, then a visit to Ruurd Wiersma Hûs Museum. A simple cottage from the turn of the century was the home of the artist until his death in 1980; he made his living room a large, colorful panorama. Walls, ceilings, furniture...nothing in the house escaped the brush of this passionate amateur painter. He also painted many biblical scenes. Wiersma's reputation was made when his stove exploded in 1965, leaving the living room covered in a thick layer of soot. On the advice of a house painter he covered the blackened room with white wallpaper, but the resulting large white area begged for color. So he bought paint brushes and pots and painted in five years his life's work "The Four Seasons".

Soon Wiersma was unstoppable and painted late into the night. Almost everything in the house fell victim to his craft: the bed, vases, bottles, the coal scoop, even his wooden shoes. His paintings are wonderful scenes of local life. Also on display are many objects used in such homes. The house sits directly on the north-side quay, the Mounewei. www.ruurdwiersma.nl

The river between Burdaard and Dokkum is almost a straight line, but the continual smooth curves add to the attractiveness of the farming country on both sides. I don't count sheep to go to sleep at night, but I am sure that if I had counted all that we had seen during this trip, it would be approaching a million, a good percentage of them here in Friesland. The farms are often thatched-roof low brick house with attached barn, surrounded by tall trees. Then we came to what always seems strange to me, an industrial zone on the outskirts of a very old fortified town. We passed by in just a few minutes and then we came face-to-face with a tall windmill.

Dokkum

Dokkum is a delightful town. It was a fortified star fort; the old town is completely surrounded by a singel with high raised banks. At six points around the outer banks of the town are the remains of what were cannon emplacements. On two of these have been built large windmills, Zeldenrust and De Hoop. We moored on the quay between the two molens. The available spaces filled up quickly with mast-up ocean-going sailboats.

The star shape is very regular and clearly-defined, so that on a late afternoon walk we could circle the town and view the entire structure. There are no walls or gates remaining, but the earthen banks and star points have been well maintained.

The river cuts east-west through the star, forming the main street. The quays, bridges, homes and shops along the canalized river are very handsome, it makes an especially enjoyable walk. We chatted with a local couple who told us that for value and taste we couldn't beat the buffet at "eetrij de Deurbraek". As it states on their website: "In a nostalgic monumental building on the waterfront." We did have good food and a good time. www.deurbraek.nl

The Dokkumer Ee river forms part of a through route, the Staande Mastroute, used by both yachts and motor cruisers as an inland waterways route, avoiding the open North Sea. A few ocean-going sailboats traveled along with us at times, especially noticeable here in the Frisian countryside. For some the route begins just 30km west on the Waddenzee, at Harlingen, but the entire route begins where we did, at Vlissingen, Zeeland. Many boats are bound for Lauwersoog on the north coast, as we are, others go on to Delzijl, the most northeasterly town in the Netherlands, to connect to the Kiel Canal. It provides an interesting sight of a vast variety of boats making their way out to the sea in the north.

We lingered on Sunday morning to let the through-traffic get ahead of us, then followed them to the Lauwersmeer. This is the northernmost lake in the Netherlands, a national park. I had noticed a Marrekrite mooring on a tiny island in the lake and decided that would be our destination.

East of Dokkum the river is the Dokkumer Grootdiep; this is one of my favorite rivers. It is calm, of uniform width, with no islands or obstructions, so it is much like a canal as far as steering the boat goes. But it is much more enjoyable than a straight-line canal. It twists across the wide-open landscape in sweeping curves. We were no sooner out of town before the first smooth loop to the south around a farmhouse set among the trees, and on the other side of the river a short wooden quay where a footpath led off along a wooded stream; we had just started, but wanted to stop already and walk that path. I made a mental note for a future trip.

Then we passed the bowling alleys, this tells us what the local people do during the dreary winter months, when the ice is not hard enough for skating. Another loop to the south and if we weren't careful we would have been heading out into the fields on a drainage canal. This pattern continued for two hours of pleasant cruising, curves on the river and canals connecting from both sides, some of them wide enough (but probably not deep enough) for navigation, although occasionally one will offer a dock off the main river.

As we waited for a bridge to open we were lucky enough to stopped at a field with magnificent black horses, a mare and her colt close to us, grazing on the high grass at the edge of the river. A paved path along the north bank was in use by hikers and cyclists, the latter leaving us behind as we enjoyed a slow sightseeing tour. We traveled just a bit faster than the hikers.

Eventually the river makes a long series of curves to the south and back again, a section too shallow for us. A straight cut connects the northern ends of the loop; at the eastern end of the cut is an important old lock, the Dokkumer Nieuwe Zijlen. It was actually "new" in 1729 when the lock and substantial dikes were completed to prevent the sea from flooding into Friesland; this is commemorated by monuments on the island nearby.

At the southern side of that island is the much newer lock and bridge that we would pass through. The channel into the old lock is blocked by a chain of yellow floats, but we stopped there for coffee at the quay in front of a square brick building with bright red awnings, which describes itself as an art cafe which "breathes the salty atmosphere of the ancient times". We did enjoy it as a unique place for a cup of coffee. I later tried to find a DVD of the movie "The Dream" which was filmed here, but no luck so far. www.dedream.nl

Our plan was to overnight at the small island near the entrance to the Lauwersmeer. So we cast off from De Dream and through the lock, northbound on the Dokkumer Diep. Four kilometers later we found the island and its very sheltered quay, inside a cut on the island's west shore. The protection was important as we were only 7km from the Waddenzee and 18km from the North Sea, a very windy area.

Waterway	From	To	KM	Hours
Slotergat	Sloten	Slotermeer	1.4	0.3
Slotermeer			3.0	0.4
Ee river	Slotermeer	Woudsend	1.3	0.2
Woudsender Rakken	Woudsend	Heegermeer	2.0	0.3
Heegermeer	De Rakken	Heeg	1.2	0.2
Wijde Wijmerts	Heeg	IJlst	5.0	0.8
Draai/Geeuw	IJlst	Sneek	4.0	0.8
Houkesloot	Sneek	Sneekermeer	4.0	0.5
Sneekermeer	Houkesloot	Terherne	5.0	0.7
Prinses Margriet Kanaal	Terherne	Grou	7.0	0.9
Pikmeer	Grou	Goëngahuizen	4.0	1.0
Goengahuistersloot	Goëngahuizen	Veenhoop	4.5	1.0
Hooidamsloot	Veenhoop	Earnewald	2.0	0.5
Lange Sloot/Rogsloot	Princenhof	Warten	9.0	2.0
Lang Deel/Van Harinxma/ Harlingertrekvaart	Warten	Leeuwarden	16.0	2.5
Dokkumer Ee	Leeuwarden	Dokkum	22.5	6.0
Dokkumer Ee	Dokkum	Lauwersmeer	16.5	2.5

Lauwersmeer

The little island (150 meters wide and 450 meters long) was our private domain until late in the day, when two sailboats and a motorcruiser joined us, so we eagerly walked the small footpaths that we found through the underbrush. We saw new species of birds here in the seaside location. In the afternoon we dinghied over to the western shore where there is a small sandy beach, for a bit of wading and swimming. This would be our last night in Friesland; the border of Groningen province is in the middle of the channel on the east side of the island.

We used that channel the next day, continuing up the western arm of the lake to the narrow strip of land that separates the lake from the Waddenzee, then east to the town of Lauwersoog (lauwers-view).

Lauwersoog is the most northerly fishing port in the Netherlands; it was created only in 1969, when the Lauwersmeer was sealed off from the sea; the previous port was at Zoutkamp, 15km inland. The Robbengatsluis is the sea lock; the Vissershaven, filled largely by Danish fishing boats, is on the sea side of the lock. Jachthaven Noordergat is on the inside, just across the road from the fishing fleet, the fish auction warehouse and other services, including a supermarket.

Out the sea lock and across the Waddenzee are the Frisian barrier islands. A "...wad" is a mudflat, and so the name is appropriate, it is a sea of mudflats. We will not be going out into the Waddenzee. Neither Carol nor I care much for open-water boating; seasickness in my case, outright fear in hers! We have been told that others have found the Waddenzee to be smoother and nicer than the IJsselmeer, but of course it depends on the winds and tides. To do it you need an up-to-date chart and tide table to plan the trip, and then watch the weather. The channel is well marked but many places outside of the channel dry out at low tide and the current can run at several knots. Note: Dutch Customs agents walk the docks looking for foreign flagged boats and checking their registration papers.

There are, of course, ferries from Lauwersoog carrying tourists out to the islands. Another option is to simply walk. Not on water, but through it. Trudging through muck is a pastime for the Dutch, who call it wadlopen. A popular route is across a shallow stretch of the Waddenzee from Holwerd to Ameland island, a route to the west of the Lauwersmeer. The straight-line distance is about 8km, through mud and sometimes water that is waist deep. Having experienced an unexpectedly (and scary) fast-moving tide a couple of times on the rocky coast of Brittany, this is definitely not for us.

More to our liking was a quiet dinner at the restaurant Waddenzeezicht. We follow the dictum that fish is best when eaten close to the source, and that certainly describes Lauwersoog. We had a fine view of sunset on the sea as we enjoyed our meal of local fish. Afterward a walk on the sea dike to the west gave us a good dose of salt air.

Reitdiep

The next morning we were headed inland again, to the city of Groningen. The chart shows a total distance of about 46km. According to the ANWB Wateralmanak, the speed limit on the first half is 9 km/hr and on the second half is 6 km/hr; those are the speeds that I would use anyway. There is only one lock, near the city. So I estimated about seven hours travel time. We left the dock at 08:00 and that would put us at Groningen by 15:00. The schedule for the many bridges leading into Groningen is restricted after 16:00, so that gave us just an hour of grace.

The only potential stop would be at Zoutkamp, but there isn't much to see or do in the town itself. In order to not arrive at Groningen much later than 15:00, we decided not to stop. We did go very slowly as we passed through the lock there (which is labeled "Staat open", stays open) and viewed the boats moored on both sides of the river.

The first hour of the day was in the Lauwersmeer. We took the "scenic route" rather than the direct channel down the middle of the lake. This took us close by the reeds and grass which are prevalent around the lake, so that we could see the birds. A motorboat is not the best vehicle for birdwatching, but we could see them swooping about over the reeds, or perched on a tall stalk.

The waterway led us into a funnel, as the river Reitdiep slowly drew in its banks. We arrived at Zoutkamp in two hours, as planned, and followed the twists and turns of the river across the flat plain of far northern Holland. It was a pleasant ride but the waterway is not as scenic as the Dokkumer, the view is one of nonstop fields, with almost no farmhouses or trees or windmills to add some interest.

It wasn't until we reached Garnwerd, about ten kilometers north of the city, that we found a village with a windmill, De Meeuw, a row of moored sailing barges and motorboats, and a potential stop for lunch. We had eaten as we traveled so we didn't stop. We also were not delayed at the bridge which had to be opened for us, as it is located in an unusual (for this river) straight stretch; we could see the bridge well in advance and called on the VHF, so it rose up just as we approached.

The next bridge was a fietsbrug, a cyclists bridge, that swings to open. The operator had told us on VHF that it would be open. We then told him that we would stop at the quay before the next bridge, which would have to open for us, so that we and Johnnie could have a brief walk. As it turned out, we were ready to go again just as a boat bound in the other direction came through the open bridge. The remote bridgekeeper could see us on a surveillance camera and asked by radio if we were ready; when I replied yes, he held the bridge for us. Drivers waiting for the bridge to close didn't seem upset by the short delay, it's part of daily life. The operator sounded like a young man, and he spoke excellent English.

He also operated the Dorkwerdersluis lock on the south side of the Van Starkenborghkanaal intersection. We watched for barge traffic and dipped behind a large towboat/barge rig as we crossed and then entered the open lock, green light showing. We radioed our thanks for his very helpful service.

Under a new remote jurisdiction, we waited for a few minutes at a wooden pier as the next double drawbridge (Zernikebrug) prepared to open. The Dutch do like to use a variety of designs for their bridges, at least in part because there are so many different authorities which build and operate the bridges. These two bridges presented a low, straight, smooth steel face to us, painted starkly white. A large circular white steel plate covered the hinge mechanism. The smoothness and simplicity of the design was very unusual, compared to the intricate designs of older bridges and the clever lifting mechanisms of the newer ones. This design is like an abstract sculpture, but one as created by an engineer.

The next two bridges were just the opposite, totally utilitarian steel I-beam spans. We passed easily under the first bridge with no need to open, but the second had only 0.90m clearance, so we had a short wait. Next up was a low Spoorbrug, a railway bridge, on a tightly-specified operating schedule. We were just in time for the 14:20-14:28 opening period.

Groningen

The city began just after this bridge, with a row of square apartment buildings on the west side and a long row of woonboten on the east bank. Straight ahead we could see the tall brick cylindrical water tower, a very handsome landmark. As soon as we passed through the bridge in front of the tower both sides of the river were lined with moored barges, both liveaboards and working commercial barges, an informal barge museum stretching into the city. Carol was pleased to see the family laundry line on a sailing tjalk, with towels and tee-shirts grouped by color, two white, two orange, two blue, one yellow, just as she would have done it.

The entrance to the city center is at the Plantsoenbrug, where the canal straight ahead is the Noorderhaven, permanent home of dozens of barges, some rafted three abreast. That is a sight which would attract any boater but we avoided it for now, instead turning south toward the Zuiderhaven.

Our intention for mooring was to pass through the city and go on to the east side, either at the Oosterhaven or the Groninger Motorboat Club; the latter had been highly recommended for its friendly staff, excellent facilities and good security. But as we exited the Museumbrug we saw a space available at the west bank of the Zuiderhaven. We quickly pulled over and tied up on the Sluiskade to think about it; we liked the location and decided to stay. There were no services available and the location is wide open, right in the city center, so I will explain why we chose this spot.

First of all, it is right in the center of the places that we wanted to visit; we could walk to the Noorderplantsoen, the park at the northwest corner of the city center, and to the Groninger Museum and the Noorderlijk Scheepvaartmuseum. It was a longer walk to the Martini tower, but that is not close to the marinas either. The Vismarkt, home of street markets, is at the physical (and cultural) center of the city just a few blocks away.

Second, we are used to being self-sufficient onboard. We rarely connect to shore power, even when it is available; we can operate on battery power overnight. We have a wastewater tank, albeit a small one, so we don't have to discharge overboard. Third, we have a dog who is a little smaller than medium size but he can put up a very fierce defense of his territory when necessary; don't step onto our boat unannounced!

Perhaps it is difficult to explain that, while it should be obviousby now that we really enjoy the opportunity to moor alone on a quiet island, we also like to be in the thick of things in a city. Our location in Groningen was perfect, we could watch pedestrians on the quays and boats on the canals, as well as rowers, from the modern club dock straight across the canal.

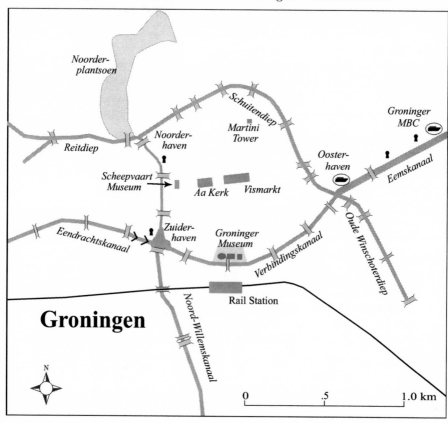

As soon as we had tied up we walked back up the canal and then three blocks east to the Vismarkt. The Tuesday market is open from 09:00 to 17:00; we were late in the day for the best fresh produce but we did find some vegetables and a great mushroom vendor.

On our way to the market we had walked quickly by two of the main buildings of interest in Groningen, the Aa Kerk and the Korenbeurs (corn exchange.) So after our tour through the street market we took some time to view these buildings. We had seen the beautiful tower of the Aa church as we had come down the canal and we had looked forward to touring the interior. We found it striking, tall walls and arches finished in white with brick trim, set off with dark wood altar, organ and choir.

I had expected that the Noorderlijk Scheepvaartmuseum (Northern Maritime Museum) would front on the canal but instead it was in the middle of a tightly-packed block between the Aa Kerk and bridge over the canal, on our route to and from the market. I planned to return there the next morning, while Carol shopped at the smaller Wednesday market. noordelijkscheepvaartmuseum.nl

Our mooring was at the southwest corner of the inner canal ring, roughly a rectangle surrounding the city center. Only a small portion of the original star fortifications remain; a map dated 1649 shows an outer ring with 17 star points, surely the most of any of the forts that we have visited. The city has been built over all except the four stars remaining at the northwest corner, now transformed into a large city park, the Noorder-plantsoen.

A panoramic view of the city is the main attraction of the famous Martini Tower. The citizens of Groningen often refer to the tall Martinikerk tower as *d'Olle Grieze* (Old Grey One), perhaps as opposed to "The better-looking one". The tower of the Aa Kerk is very beautiful, even as the building itself is a typical red-brick structure with gray tile roof. The two open open decks at the top give the tower a light, airy feeling and the pale-yellow vertical lines of brick connecting the levels add to the "reaching for the sky" appearance. I often use church towers as a reference point while walking in the cities; the streets and alleys may twist and turn, so an occasional glimpse of a church spire can help keep me on track. As long as it's the right one, that is why I pay attention to the design.

For dinner we were back at our pizza ways again, the Napoli Pizzeria came highly recommended by a local couple and was just a short walk up the quay from our mooring. It's a long way from Groningen to Napoli, but we did get transported there for a while. napoligroningen.nl

Wednesday morning went as planned, after an early morning walk in the Noorderplantsoen park Carol and Johnnie had an enjoyable shopping tour of the smaller market, while I learned something of the barging history of Groningen and northern Holland. In the afternoon we walked the circuit of the inner canal ring, starting at the Noorderhaven.

Cruising the Canals & Rivers of the Netherlands

On this trip I kept thinking that I had never seen so many boats in one place, then along came another to top the previous record-holder. Now I think that the Noorderhaven is in first place. On the south quay the (relatively) smaller barges are lined side-by-side, bow to the quay, at a slight angle. On the north side the larger barges lay parallel to the quay, 1, 2 or 3 deep. This is not a classic barge museum, this is the home base of everyday barges used for work and home.

As the Schutendiep curves and turns southeast, the line of woonboten began, the rows of floating residences filling both sides of the canal. Then came the Restaurant 't Pannekoekschip Groningen, a very large two-masted sailing barge converted to a very large pancake restaurant. We didn't try the food.

We saw the Oosterhaven across the water and decided that our choice of a mooring had been a good one. From there we turned west but had to leave the canal, because along the Verbindingskanaal the backyards of residential buildings go to the water, there is no canalside street or path. So we walked along a tree-shaded boulevard, two lanes with a very wide grass median used largely by dog-walkers. We were enjoying the view of the typical Dutch townhouses and apartment buildings when we were startled by the sight of an open steel staircase, painted salmon-pink, stretching across a bay of the canal to a very strange structure rising from the water.

We expected a modern museum here, but the Groninger Museum was far beyond our mental picture. The museum opened in 1994 with the goal of creating more than just a shell for the display of modern art, but to be a work of art itself, a principle that was then becoming more common in contemporary museum architecture. The architects have created a work of art, literally an island, in the middle of a rather mundane city.

The museum consists of three buildings, each its own island in a widened section of the canal. The west structure is a low silver cylinder, then two sharp-edged cubes flanking a tall rectangle and on the east an abstract assemblage of shapes, difficult to define as a building. Carol thinks it resembles a container ship hit by a typhoon in the South China Sea, with some of the containers hanging precariously over the edge. It may look like a ship, but a very strange one; the hull is not dingy gray as on a ship, it is covered with rows of blue, white and pink designs much like the bathroom wallpaper had been in our Paris apartment (it was there when we arrived!)

On the south side, across the canal, are the busy rail and bus terminals and a long block of large brown buildings with hundreds of identical square windows. A fitting bland counterpoint to the wild design of the museum structures.

Inside the museum are the works of a wide range of contemporary artists, the most well-known being Andy Warhol and Jeff Koons. Unfortunately the exhibits were closed for renovation at the time, so we were only able to enjoy the exterior view. We did this from all angles, including walking across the canal from the museum plaza, on a footbridge, for the wide panoramic view from the station. groningermuseum.nl

For dinner we again walked to the Vismarkt plaza, to a traditional European urban coffeehouse/restaurant the Huis de Beurs, named for the Corn Exchange, which it faced. Carol enjoyed the Gevulde aubergine (stuffed eggplant) while I had the Lamsschenkel (lamb shank); both were very good, along with some wheat beer. huisdebeurs.nl

The next day was the turn-around point, from here on south towards Belgium and France. There are two more star forts that I had wanted to visit, Bourtange and Coevorden, but both are close to the German border, well off of the direct route south, and will have to wait for another trip, perhaps combined with a cruise in northwestern Germany.

From our mooring on the Zuiderhaven we headed straight south, immediately entering the Noord-Willemskanaal. Our first task was the eight opening bridges through the southern section of Groningen, accomplished with little delay. I had set no particular destination for this day, as there are many canalside mooring spots marked on the charts.

Just past the southern limit of the city of Groningen a narrow, shallow (1.0m depth) channel leads west into the Paterswoldsemeer, a lake offering moorings at five isolated islands as well as three jachthavens. This is a popular cruising area for small boats, right next to the city. There is also a mooring section on the canal; some travelers on barges stop here rather than in the city; a bus stop is within walking distance.

Drenthe

This point is the border of Groningen and Drenthe provinces; from here south to Meppel we will be in Drenthe, a large and relatively unpopulated province of northeastern Holland.

The Noord-Willemskanaal is a pleasant route, it winds a bit and widens occasionally, with the usual Dutch countryside views of flat green fields and flocks of sheep; in one field, black sheep were prevalent. The highway which parallels the canal is often some distance away and behind the trees. There are three locks and 22 opening bridges in the 28-kilometer length of the canal, so passage requires that the skipper not be in a hurry. It took us the full day to arrive at the west side of Assen.

Assen

We had taken a brief look at the Assen passantenhaven, at the point where the main canal sweeps to the west and a dead-end branch leads straight south into the city. It is a large, square man-made harbor, in the midst of a residential complex. The location is strange, far from the city center or from any facilities or shops. We could have stopped here because we didn't plan to visit the city nor did we need any services or supplies, but there was still traveling time left in the day. We returned to the canal route for another 6km and tied up on the west bank, at the official end of the Noord-Willemskanaal, south of the Brug Asserwijk. Despite being on the fringe of the city, the immediate area was open and along our quay was a small wooded area, perfect for dog walks. We enjoyed a quiet overnight here.

The TT Circuit Assen is one of the most famous motorcycle racing circuits in the world; it is regarded as the "Cathedral of Motorcycle Racing". This would be heaven for our friends John in the USA or Nigel in the UK. For us, we were interested in something much more minor, an unexplained cone-shaped mound of earth across the canal from our mooring. The shape itself was unusual in the otherwise flat parkland, but the mystery was the two-dozen stone chairs set randomly on the mound. Obviously a memorial of some sort, but we couldn't learn more, short of flagging-down a passing car to ask the driver. Neighboring boaters were of no help, and in fact showed little interest. Carol and I both have curiosity about things like this, but sometimes we can't get a resolution.

For the next two days we traveled south on the Drentsche Hoofdvaart (main canal), an apt name for the main waterway across the center of northeastern Holland. From Assen it is literally as straight as an arrow for 14km, then it continues as basically a straight line, with just a few curves to match slight contours of the land, for a total of 42km from Assen to Meppel. There are six locks and thirty opening bridges along the way. This is one of the longest straight-line waterways in the Netherlands, with the most locks and bridges as well. Some people dread this trip.

But it is not as boring as it might seem. The canal is lined by poplar trees and many farmhouses, as well as occasional villages and towns, so there is always something to be seen. The bridges vary in style, another point of interest for me. The Dutch light exists even here, well away from the large bodies of water. We saw it often, under the many bridges, reflecting off the water and onto the underside of the bridge structure, in a dappled and rippling manner.

Near the end of the first day we stopped at a very convenient Shell fuel dock in the town of Dieverbrug, then noticed a Vietnamese restaurant and adjacent visitor's quay. We stopped there and enjoyed a good dinner at the restaurant Hui Mao, followed by a walk around the town, which included a chat with several of the locals, in Dutch/English.

Meppel

Another day on the same canal brought us into Meppel by late afternoon. We went into the jachthaven for a pumpout but were directed to a mooring on the quay of a dead-end canal, across the water from a long block of newly-constructed shops and apartments, the facades finished in a variety of shapes and pastel colors. It was a change from the usual Dutch brick buildings, one that we enjoyed. We didn't walk into the town and had dinner onboard.

On a previous car trip through the Netherlands we had seen the Hunebeden, a line of dolmen sites stretching from just south of Groningen, east of Assen and down as far as Emmen; they are located mostly along highway N34. The sites are too far east of the canal to visit by bicycle, so we had reserved a Citroen rental car for a day of exploring on Sunday. They let us have one of their "occasions", a Citroen C3 Pluriel (a modern version of the venerable Deux Chevaux.) We put the top down on a beautiful day and had a wonderful ride through the countryside; the feel of zipping along in a breezy car was quite a change from the slow travel on the canal.

The definition of dolmen is: "a prehistoric megalithic tomb typically having two large upright stones and a capstone, thought to have been used as a tomb". We had lived for a few years near several sites in Brittany, France and they had intrigued us. This was a good opportunity to see them again. We found six of the dozen sites shown on the Michelin highway map.

The arrangements for the rental car had been done as we cruised down the Hoofdvaart. A Google search brought us to the Citroen dealer's website and from there we used the mobile phone to speak (in English) with a manager who offered us the perfect car for our excursion, at a very reasonable cost and the ability to return the car Sunday night by dropping the keys through the mail slot.

Waterway	From	To	KM	Hours
Reitdiep	Lauwersmeer	Groningen	46.0	7.2
Noord-Willemskanaal	Groningen	Assen	28.0	8.4
Drentsche Hoofdvaart	Assen	Meppel	42.0	15.3

Overijssel Province

Zwartsluis

It was an easy ten kilometers the next morning into Overijssel province on the Meppelerdiep to Zwartsluis, no locks or bridges and just a couple of commercial barges to avoid, with no trouble. We had missed the National Tugboat Days, which I am sure we would have enjoyed (well, at least I would; Carol could spend the time at the market.) We tied up on the town quay at 10:00 and walked around the corner to an outdoor table at Horeca Centrum De Albatros for our usual coffee. There are boatyards and chandleries here, it is a nautical town offering many services to boaters.

Zwolle

But we didn't stay, circling back around an island and through the floodgate to the Zwarte Water, the 17km river route into Zwolle. That city is an important center of the Netherlands, often used as a base by visitors on a boat search; highways and waterways run west to Amsterdam and Zuid Holland, north to Friesland and south to Limburg. For us it will be the gateway to the river IJssel and on south to Belgium. And of course it is a star fort, which I need to investigate.

We had decided to do something at Zwolle that we had never done in France, even though that country is the home of Michelin and offers many Michelin-starred restaurants. We would have dinner at De Librije, now a three-star (top grade) restaurant. In fact we had made reservations long before and had planned to rent a car if we had to, if we were not able to be there on that date by boat. It turned out to be just right, we arrived in early afternoon on the day before that of our reservation. This will be a big hit in our dining budget, but we have been saving up for it with all those pizzas!

We docked on the quay at Rodetorenplein, inside the star fort singel and just down the block from our destination restaurant, which of course we went to check out immediately even though it was closed on that day. Doing so we walked past two red brick towers, these may be the *rode toren* for which the area is named.

Those towers were the only structures that may have been part of the original fortifications. We circled the central city on the star fort singel, as usual this made a pleasant park for a stroll, but there were no ramparts or gates that we could find. Our mooring was quiet on Monday evening, even though we were in a medium-sized city. We did take note, however, of the banner over one of the shopping streets warning, in Dutch and English, *Zakkenrollers Actief* "Beware of Pickpockets".

Tuesday was a rest day, with just a brief walk to see some of the shops. Most of the day was spent in chairs on the back deck, watching the passing boats and pedestrians, saving our strength for the dinner.

165

Jonnie and Thérèse Boer and the team of De Librije served us the "Menu Tradition Qualité", tailoring the dishes and the serving size to our wishes. A brief listing of our favorites:

Goose-liver, oyster, Oloroso sherry and ginger

Raw North Sea langoustines with Oloroso mayonnaise, cucumber juice, horseradisch and roasted with verbena

Turbot, North Sea crab, squid, quinoa and fennel

Giethoorns lamb neck with lemon and lambjus, with pickled herring

I suppose that a restaurant critic would find something to criticize, but we were very happy and considered the expense a good value. After all, we aren't going to do this every week; maybe never again. librije.com

Kampen

We didn't rush off the next morning, as we needed a bit of rest after our major dinner experience. Then we moved to the city of Kampen, northwest on the IJssel river, downstream and away from our direction of travel. It's a star fort, so I thought that it wasn't too far to go out of our way, even though the curves of the river stretched the straight-line distance of 11km to an actual distance of 16km on the water. The curves did offer pleasant views over the flood plain and into the small towns.

Two bridges over the IJssel at Kampen interested me, in their difference. The first was a modern cable-suspension bridge; we have seen quite of few of these on this trip. They are always strikingly beautiful despite, or more likely because of, their simple functional design, accomplished with an eye for appearance. The second was a much older bridge, a *hefbrug* span lifted straight up by a massive cable and pulley system; it was attractive as well, but in an entirely different way. We saw that bridge in the evening, lighted along its length and around the pulleys, looking like a carnival ride.

The city itself is a nice sight from the water; the gray walls, tower and roof of the church stand above the rows of red tile roofs and brick gables. A row of two- and three-masted sailing barges lined the waterfront.

By noon we were tied up at the Oude Buitenhaven. Their excellent facilities include new spotlessly-clean toilets, showers and laundry room, with washer, dryer and ironing board. We didn't meet the harbormaster but we did see a notice posted that he had recently been selected as Harbormaster of the Year for the Netherlands; we could see why, this is a well-run and well-maintained facility. www.wsvdebuitenhaven.nl

The Oude Buitenhaven was originally part of the singel around the west side of Kampen; although the first section of the singel has been filled and is now occupied by office buildings and a warehouse, a two-block walk brought us to the city park based on the singel. The parkland arcs almost back to the river on the south end of the city, so that the park frames the west side as the river frames the east side. No ramparts remain except two gates, the Broederpoort and the Cellebroederspoort. They are similar to the two-spire brick structures that we have seen in other cities, but these are larger buildings than most, heavy, thick structures. The Broederpoort in fact is large enough to support four tower spires, one at each corner of the thick block of the center building. As usual, the park was a very pleasant place for a walk, with ducks and swans on the ponds and a variety of trees shading the paths.

We entered the city center through the Cellebroederspoort and followed the Burgel, a non-navigable canal that mimics the arc of the outer singel. At Broederstraat we could see the Broederpoort gate down the street to our left; we turned right to go out to the IJsselkade, which took us back north to the haven. Along that quay we enjoyed yet another informal museum of classic sailing barges, then at the haven we took a better look at the Kamper botters which we had seen as we came in off the river. These included a replica of the *Kamper Kogge*, a wooden ship whose improvements in seaworthiness greatly enhanced international trade in the 14th century.

After a rest on the boat, we walked just a few steps for dinner. We ignored the *Slender You figure salon* and went directly to the *Sirtaki* Greek restaurant for some simple dishes, a big change from the previous night's dinner but delicious and well-served. grieks-sirtaki.nl

That evening I used Google Earth to look at our next-day cruise on the river and realized that we could have easily biked to the Roggebotsluis, on the Randmeren route, which we had passed through three weeks earlier. We had traveled a few hundred kilometers since then, but it's only 4 km away.

IJssel river

The river Gelderse IJssel, commonly called just the IJssel, was to be our next adventure. An Englishman whose boat was moored near ours had just come down the river (in this case "down" means north.) He told us to expect a current of 3 to 4 km/hr. We made our plans for an over-the-ground speed of 6-7 km/hr and picked Deventer as our stop for the night. It is necessary to do some planning as you can't just stop anywhere on the river; even where a riverfront quay is provided, as at Deventer, overnight mooring is prohibited.

The chart showed these potential stopping points (distance from Kampen): Hattem (18km)

Wijhe (31km)

Veessen (34km)

Terwolde (44km)

Deventer (49km)

The last was a reasonable destination, between 7 and 8 hours travel. Other than Hattem, it is the only place on the list with a haven that is well off the river, inside a lagoon. Also, Deventer is on my star fort map, so that is where we stopped.

It was now late in June and the weather was becoming hot. Our two days on the IJssel brought temperatures of 35°C (95°F), several degrees hotter than any day on this trip. But it was comfortable while we were underway on the river.

I had made notes of the four ferry crossings to watch for, by kilometer distance. We passed under three high bridges between Hattem and Zwolle; they were to be the last for the day. The next bridge is south of the jachthaven at Deventer. So it was a day of wide open skies on a broad river. Because of seasonal flooding the river plain is wide, the widest that we have experienced since the Randmeren.

There was more traffic than we had seen in many days, as this is a major connecting route, the only north-south waterway east of the Amsterdam-Rijnkanaal. At some of the tighter curves, barges on the IJssel will frequently show a "Blue Board" to indicate that they wish to pass starboard-to-starboard rather than the usual port-to-port, so as to be in a part of the river with more favorable current and/or depth. Other barges will respond with their own blue board, indicating that they will comply. Most cruising boats don't have this apparatus and simply move to accommodate the barges.

Deventer

The day was uneventful and we turned into the jachthaven 2km north of Deventer a little past 17:00. www.jachthavendeventer.nl

We found the sign "Bezoekers" (visitors) and tied up there until the harbormaster directed us to a pontoon. Johnnie was ready for a walk in the grass, which was plentiful around the small lake. We had kept ourselves fed and refreshed while on the river, so we soon set off by bicycle to visit the city.

Of course there was a bicycle path, which followed the river bank and the road, named IJsselkade. After passing under a railroad bridge over the river we came to an end of the star fort singel; we took the bikes on a narrow dirt path that wound along the singel, soon coming to paved paths through a park. As we have learned to expect, there were no noticeable ramparts or even berms, just a very nice place for a bike ride or a walk.

We had no interest in visiting the rest of the city of Deventer and were off early the next morning, crossing into Gelderland province as we left the city behind.

Waterway	From	To	KM	Hours
Meppelerdiep	Meppel	Zwartsluis	10.0	1.2
Zwarte Water	Zwartsluis	Zwolle	17.5	2.5
Zwolle-IJsselkanaal	Zwolle	IJssel river	3.0	0.6
IJssel river	Spoolde	Deventer	34.0	7.1

Doesburg

We were hoping to reach Arnhem by noon the next day. This meant that we passed by the star fort town of Zutphen without stopping and we approached Doesburg, yet another star fort town. We pulled into the passantenhaven, named Doesburg's Goed, which I think might mean "Doesburg's Best". I would rate it as "pretty good".

Again the schedule was a dog walk, then a bike ride to view the singel. As usual no fortifications to see but our first view across the singel included a handsome shingle-style home with a tall sloping roof, with the spire of a church tower rising behind, a perfect picture that I didn't take. We soon returned the bikes to the boat and took Johnnie with us for a walk along a dirt path on the star points, for walkers only. It wound through dense woods and was a nice departure from the mostly open countryside. We were glad that we stopped here.

Arnhem

Arnhem is the city at the southern end of the river IJssel, but there is no access from the IJssel. To stop at Arnhem we made a 330° turn to our right, joining the downstream flow of the Neder-Rijn river. Three kilometers later we entered the Haven van Malburgen, the commercial barge docks with two jachthavens near the entrance. The first is a sailing and motorboat club which welcomes visitors, however we chose the second, Jachthaven Valkenburg, because it is located further away from the wash of the river.

www.restaurant-valkenburg.nl

We had arrived just after noon and first ate lunch onboard, then walked west along the river to the John Frost bridge. That is the "Bridge Too Far", the prized bridge over the Rhine that the allies could not take from the Germans in September 1944. Operation Market Garden was meant to end the war quickly, after the Normandy invasion and the liberation of Paris. It failed due to the disregarding by the Allies of intelligence from the local Dutch people and by technical failures. The story is very interesting and generally well-known. For a good overview go to: www.market-garden.info

I was curious to see the actual site. The best way to see this, I had been told, would be from the Sint-Eusebiuskerk tower, 93 meters high, a short distance northwest of the bridge. The church itself is worth a visit on its own, but the main attraction for the me was the glass-enclosed elevator inside the church which lifts visitors to an observation level in the tower, "Het hoogtepunt", the high point of Arnhem. There the view shows clearly all significant locations of troops and activity, especially if you have brought along the map from the market-garden website. eusebius.nl

Cruising the Canals & Rivers of the Netherlands

An elevator of this sort is not one Carol's favorite things, so she toured the market at the Kerkplein (church plaza) with Johnnie while I was up in the air. They returned to the boat with bags of fresh produce while I pursued my interest further in the "Battle of Arnhem Information Center" at the north end of the John Frost bridge.

I had seen some very dark clouds coming in from the west when I was in the tower. The rain had begun while I was in the museum and by the time I reached the boat I found Johnnie curled up in his bed. He wouldn't budge to say hello, Tibetan Terriers hate rain. Carol had our dinner well in hand and we settled in for the night.

Rhine

The rain continued through the night and into Sunday as we set off to the southeast, still traveling upriver. Just as we left the haven a huge Rhine river cruise ship came out of the rain, headed east from Rotterdam or Amsterdam. It seemed that we waited five minutes as the ship passed, then we fell in behind it. This wasn't so bad, visibility was poor but I could easily see the stern of the ship and so didn't worry too much about other traffic, although I did ask Carol to keep a watch for any boats coming from our left at the IJssel intersection.

The Pannerdenskanaal is a canal in name only, actually it is a branch of the Rhine, 10.5km long, which itself splits to become the Neder-Rijn and the Gelderse IJssel rivers. We would follow this waterway to the junction with the Waal river, just 1.5km from the German border. As on the Lek, all along the river there are groins sticking out into the river. In this section they seem to be more aggressive, jutting out from both sides and leaving a seemingly narrow center for traffic. At the end of the canal we made another sharp turn back to our right, this time about 350°, onto the Waal. Inside that sharp point are the ruins of a fort, obviously this would have been an important strategic defense position.

We left the shelter of the ship as it continued up the Rhine and quickly got a ride from the river, a big change from three days of going against the current. We cruised along easily at 12 km/hr, on the limestone-laden gray waters of the Rhine main stream. There was a constant flow of barges coming toward us, sometimes two abreast as one barge passed others. The river is wide and the rain had eased, so visibility was adequate and we had no trouble staying clear of traffic.

Nijmegen

That is, until we approached the city of Nijmegen. I was staying well to the right side of the river, following on the rear starboard quarter of a sand barge. Coming around a curve toward us were three barges, small, medium and large. The largest barge was almost in the center of the river, no problem there, but the other two were blue-boarding and just clearing the groins on our side. In retrospect I guess I would have known what to do, since there wasn't much choice, but at the time it helped that the barge ahead steered to port and I followed as we passed between the larger barge and the other two. It wasn't difficult but it did help to have a leader who was used to such things.

That, and the rain, convinced me to abandon my plans to make a stop at Nijmegen, for a brief visit to that city. Lindenberghaven is the city marina, located just beyond the bridge that we went under just after the traffic adventure. I would have had to cross over quickly to enter the haven, then do it again as we left. The poor weather made it easy to choose to just continue on, also this was no day to be walking around on city streets.

The bridge is the same one that was captured by the US 82nd Airborne Division during Operation Market Garden (there are only two bridges over the river at Nijmegen, this road bridge and a rail bridge further west.) I recognized the shape from the pictures that I had seen; the basic structure of the bridge remains as it was built in 1936. The Lindenberghaven is ideally located for the visit I had in mind, which was to walk to the top of Valkhof park, situated on a hill above the haven, for a panoramic view over the Waal river and the bridge. There was no panoramic view on this day, so that will have to wait for a later trip.

We continued along the industrial waterfront, passing a long line of barges moored at warehouses and factories (HJ Heinz is one of them.) There is a tourist waterfront also, right next to the haven. From there the Pancake Boat offers river cruises and, of course, pancakes. At the base of the rail bridge is the Waalhaven, for commercial barges.

A thumb of grassland jutting into the river is the landmark for the entrance to the Maas-Waalkanaal, our path south to the river Maas. It required another sharp turn back, this time to our left, across river traffic. I used the recommended procedure for such crossings, to go on beyond the turn and then circle back, leaving plenty of space to pick the best time for entering the other lane of traffic.

One kilometer down the canal we came to the huge Sluis Weurt complex, two locks side-by-side with an island between. These are huge locks, 16 meters wide and 266 meters long; that's three US football fields (or 2.5 European football pitches) in length. We were monitoring the lock's VHF channel and called to identify ourselves to the lockkeeper. She told us to wait for a barge coming from behind us, then follow it in. We used the rungs of a ladder to secure bow and stern lines, after inspecting the sturdiness of the rungs selected. I'm not sure if this is allowed, but no one complained, if indeed they noticed. It worked well for us, as it had in the past.

Cruising the Canals & Rivers of the Netherlands

The bridges on this 13km canal are all 10 meters high and the second lock stays open, so we completed the passage in a little less than two hours. And as we entered the Maas river the rain stopped and a bright sun broke through in the southwest. We entered our last province, Limburg.

Waterway	From	To	KM	Hours
IJssel river	Deventer	Doesburg	45.0	8.9
IJssel river/Neder-rijn	Doesburg	Arnhem	25.5	4.1
Pannerdenskanaal	Arnhem	Waal river	13.0	2.0
Waal river	Pannerdenskanaal	Nijmegen	19.0	1.6
Maas-Waalkanaal	Nijmegen	Maas river	13.0	1.9
Maas river	Maas-Waalkanaal	Mookerplas	5.0	0.7

Limburg

Mookerplas is the only overnight mooring on the Maas river after Nijmegen. There are riverfront quays at Mook (east side of river) and Cuijk (west side of river, 3km upstream from Mook) but both of these prohibit overnight mooring. If they prohibit mooring on the river overnight, it's probably not a good idea anyway.

As I was hoping, we easily found the low mooring posts on the north shore of the lake, about 1km from the river. On this Sunday night there were no other boats in sight, as well as no dock, pontoon or other facilities, just a bank covered with high grass and a few trees, with a narrow paved road beyond. It looked perfect for us, since we just wanted to tie up, take a long dog walk down the road, enjoy a quiet dinner aboard and have a restful evening. And that is just what happened, a very pleasant night.

Limburg province is the long narrow strip of land on both sides of the Maas river, squeezed in between the hillsides of Belgium and Germany. The province is centralized along the river, as evidenced by municipalities with names such as Horst aan de Maas, Peel en Maas, Maasgouw and Maastricht. The river flows almost due north through the province; our trip picks up the river just as it turns to the west, later becoming the Bergse Maas and Amer, on which we had cruised weeks earlier.

The flow in the river has been tamed by locks, so we were anticipating facing a current of 3 to 5 km/hr, significantly less than we had encountered on the IJssel and Waal. For planning purposes I used an average speed over the ground of 8 km/hr. Planning is necessary, as there are limited choices for overnight stops off the river. When we left our mooring on the Mookerplas, we joined the river at kilometer 164; the chart showed jachthavens at kilometer posts 152, 133, 122 and 111. The last is at the city of Venlo, about seven hours travel time. The WV De Maas at Venlo came highly recommended, so we selected that as our destination. For one thing, we needed a pumpout, which they offer. A look at the website of the yacht club and of the adjacent restaurant had sealed the deal. wsv-de-maas-venlo.nl www.brasseriedeadmiraal.nl

Navigating on the Maas is very easy; groins are used only from KM164 to KM 155, the river is a uniform width and the curves are gentle. There is a constant flow of commercial barges and leisure boats (some are actually sailing) but the north and south lanes are respected, all passing is on the starboard side. It is much more peaceful than the Waal.

The surroundings are peaceful as well. The river is lined by trees and flood plains, and just a few towns front directly on the river. Venlo is one of those, in fact the rivers splits the cities of Venlo and Blerick. Even there, grass fields of the floodplain are the view from the river, with the towns set behind concrete levees.

The only lock of the day came at the Sambeek, a double lock alongside a weir. It is the same width as the Weurt lock at Nijmegen, much shorter (at 142 meters, still very long) and about the same rise. At Weurt we had risen about 4 meters, here the rise will be 3.25 meters, not deep enough to raise fears. We fell into a line of leisure boats on the starboard side; a long barge took up most of the port side. The barge skipper allowed the small boats to leave first, in somewhat of a charge forward, so much so that the ferry one kilometer downstream waited for us all to pass before crossing.

Venlo

The jachthaven WSV De Maas is located about 3km north of the city, on the same inlet from the river as a large area of industrial wharves. However the haven is isolated by the flood plain on the east side and a high wooded hill on the west side. (Yes, there are hills in Holland, now that we are in Limburg.) The yacht club is run by volunteers, all friendly and helpful. The facilities are excellent; this is definitely a good choice when on the Maas.

We could have ridden our bikes into Venlo but settled for a walk around the perimeter of the woods, then an evening aboard and a good-enough meat and fish dinner in the Brasserie De Admiraal.

A passing tanker barge caused us to wait at the exit of the haven, for what seemed like a very long time. The big barges look longer when you watch from the side. Then we joined the morning river traffic, a busy flow of barges and small boats in both directions. As on the previous day it wasn't hectic, simply two lanes of traffic. We noticed the passantenhaven in Venlo, a convenient stop at the city center. It is well protected from the river but doesn't offer the facilities which we used at the yacht club. On the other side of the river is the riverfront quay at Blerick, suitable for a day stop but open to the river. Early in the morning there were no visiting boats, just ducks and swans. The landmark to locate this quay is the church steeple, very unusually a tall modern structure, four white columns supporting several platforms, with a clock and bells at the top level.

A few kilometers on, at Tegelen, a relatively tighter curve caused a line of four barges to blue-board, moving well over to our side of the river. We saw them well in advance and made our move to the left-hand lane; it feels strange to be doing this, but it is common practice on the rivers. To add to the excitement, while we were there on the "wrong" side, a car ferry pulled out from the east bank, headed straight across the river. I slowed just a bit, probably didn't have to, and slid through his wake.

That brought us to the Belfeld lock, specifications on the chart exactly the same as the Sambeek lock of the day before. We are old hands at this now, no problem. After that it was a quiet morning of cruising, watching the fields and trees along the shore.

One point of interest was a row of camping cottages at Kessel which stretched for a half-kilometer along the river, each with its own T-shaped dock; we didn't count them, but the number must have approached one hundred. The churches at Steyl, with its double steeple, and Kessel, with its thick square tower, returned to the traditional style after the surprise at Blerick. Then, for the first time in many days, the molen De Grauwe Beer (the Gray Bear) stood straight ahead, on the east side of a curve. I'm sure there must have been others along the Maas that we didn't see, but this was one that couldn't be missed when southbound.

There are very few bridges over the Maas, in fact the last one that we had seen on this day was the Zuiderbrug at Venlo, kilometer 106. So the rail bridge at kilometer 85.5 was a clear signal to move to the east side of the river for the Maas route, through a lock and into Roermond. The west side of the river is the northern end of the Lateralkanaal Linne-Buggenum, a straight bypass on the west of the Roermond lakes.

Roermond

Our destination was at the town; there are marinas scattered around the nearby lakes but we entered the Haven La Bonne Aventure right in front of the town center and docked at the Jachthaven RWV Nautilus, a marina with the full set of services and a central location, including a great view out to the lakes on the west. The haven is behind a dike of the namesake for the town, the river Roer; the banks of the Roer made a good path for a sightseeing walk through town.

On the north side of the Roer is the market plaza; it wasn't market day but there were a half-dozen choices of outdoor cafes. I'm not sure which one we ended up at, but I did like our soup and sandwich lunch.

Roermond's Designer Outlet Centre draws shoppers from Germany and Belgium. It is within easy walking distance of the city center, offering famous names and designer brands at discount. We weren't in the market for shopping, but boaters bound from Holland to France might want to stock up here. Carol limited her shopping spree to the butcher, baker and produce shop, for dinner onboard.

Roermond is a true watersports center; across the Maas from the town itself lies the extensive lake district known as the "Maasplassen", a 3,000 hectare chain of lakes, both large and small. Vast expanses of water provide the ultimate recreation grounds for sailers, rowers, swimmers, anglers, sun worshippers and lovers of nature. There is something for everybody thanks to the wide variety of beaches, marinas and campsites. The lakes and the river are the backdrop for holiday homes, hotels, restaurants and campgrounds. I went off on my bicycle, south along the riverfront, to visit the boat brokerage Krekelberg Nautic at Herten, just to see the boats on sale, located at a huge marina complex. There are a number of good boatyards in this area for winter storage of boats, out of the water.

Our last day of travel in the Netherlands was to the city of Masstricht. The Maas makes some large loops south of Roermond, one of them shortcut by the Sluis Linne, another huge lock. Two kilometers south of that lock we took a brief detour into the Kanaal Wessem-Nederweert, to the boatyard of Jaree Tinnemans, at the town of Heel.

Several years earlier the three of us, Carol, Johnnie and I, had a very enjoyable few hours at this family-operated boatbuilding and repair yard. I was on an assignment from a client, for whom I was doing a barge search. After a wasted day-before chasing around with an unprepared broker, we started fresh with a new broker who brought us here, to inspect the personal barge of Jaree's son, a tjalk which he had converted for family use. The work done was excellent, from the interior woodwork to the external painting, as well as all mechanical, plumbing and wiring installations (the barge was purchased, a great find.) The visit was both business and pleasure; we dropped in on this cruise just to say hello again.

Maasbracht

The canal junction at Maasbracht is three-way, as it is also the northern end of the Julianakanaal. A point of grassland separates the natural Maas river from the man-made canal; the correct channel was easy to spot, as a huge barge laden with bright-red shipping containers of the "K-line" was just coming out of the canal, northbound. (The natural Maas is navigable for a few more kilometers from here, but not all the way to Maastricht.) Behind the barge was what looked to be a brand new Linssen Sturdy yacht, built at the boat and shipbuilding town of Maasbracht. It was either on a test run or a just-delivered boat for, I'm sure, a happy buyer. The ANWB Wateralmanak lists a jachthaven at the factory, they may accept visitors; this is, however, a very industrial area.

For the next four hours we followed the straight cut of the canal, passing through three more locks. The good feature of the Julianakanaal is that the waterway is not enclosed within high dikes; for much of the distance the water level is the same as the surrounding land, or in some places even well above the valley. The view encompasses nearby towns, sand quarries and farm fields, back to the hillsides in Belgium and Germany. As we traveled south the valley (and the borders) closed in on the river. The chart shows no mooring quays or jachthavens along the entire Julianakanaal; even a concrete quay at the town of Berg, which looked to be a possible short-term stop, was walled off by a steel railing, with no gate.

Maastricht

By early afternoon we were at Maastricht, docked in the Oude Bassin (locally called Het Bassin or 't Bassin.) www.tbassin.nl   We had entered through Sluis 20, a welcome return to narrow locks, one that we used alone. We took a slip on the south side of the rectangular harbor, toward the river end, wanting to be near the restaurants and bars, which have tables on the quay, but not directly in front of one. We wanted to enjoy the night life to some extent, but also be able to go to bed early. It was just one long block south to the central Markt Square; we were too late for the Wednesday market (08:00-13:00) but we intend to stay through the Friday market, which includes fish vendors.

The historic heart of the most European city in the Netherlands is two blocks southwest from the Markt square; Vrijthof, a large square with cobblestones, trees and cafes is a vast esplanade, bordered by cafés and restaurants with pleasant terraces, is dominated by two churches: St.-Servaaskerk and St.-Janskerk.

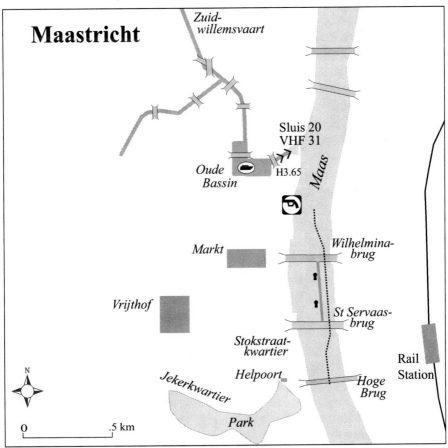

Cruising the Canals & Rivers of the Netherlands

Nearly all of the streets in the area bounded by the Markt square, Vrijthof and the river are pedestrianized, narrow cobblestone alleys. The few streets in this zone which do allow traffic do not have space for parking; the area is wonderful for wandering about, to view the preserved buildings. Cafes with open-air tables are scattered throughout these streets, just as they are at Vrijthof and at the Bassin. If you are walking in the city center and want refreshment, just sit down!

We did just that, at a small cafe with tables in a quiet square on Bredestraat at the main shopping street of the old city, the Wolfstraat. We had coffee and pastry for a late afternoon snack in the square named for the Onze-Lieve-Vrouwe (Our Dear Lady) Basilica, located at the southeast corner of the plaza. Through the trees we could see the tall, flat face of its clock tower, with cylindrical stone towers on each side.

A French couple at a nearby table chatted with us, recommending that we not miss the Stokstraatkwartier (Stokstraat quarter, closer to the river) with its galleries and trendy shops. These turned out as both elegant and far over our shopping budget (let alone our shopping needs; these shops sold things that we might want, but definitely don't need.)

But it was on one of the nearby streets (Havenstraat) that we found Restaurant Rozemarijn, read the menu and made a reservation for the next night. Our fine dining budget just about exhausted for this month, we felt that we could have a good dinner at reasonable cost from their à la carte menu. www.restaurant-rozemarijn.nl

On the way back to our boat we came to Brugstraat and walked out to the middle of the St Servaas bridge for a view of the Maas. This is a massive stone bridge, with seven identical arches and one wide flat span at the eastern shore, over the channel designated for barge traffic. It is widely regarded as the oldest bridge in the Netherlands; construction began in 1280, to replace a collapsed Roman bridge. Strangely, it did not have a name until 1932, it was just "the bridge".

A concrete wall runs north from the bastion at the west end of the flat span, stretching 250 meters north to the Wilhelminabrug. This wall is the passantenhaven; visiting boats moor on the west side of the wall, opposite the busy channel. To the south, upstream, is the Hoge Brug, a modern steel arch supports a suspended footbridge in a single 153 meter span over the entire river, leading from the old city on the west bank to the Centre Ceramique, a cultural district in the modern city on the east bank.

We returned to the west bank, where the Maaspromenade hosts even more outdoor cafes, as well as the Brasserie Bonhomme and the docks of river tour boats. The Wilhelminabrug, a modern bridge of nondescript style, crosses from the Heineken Music Hall on the east bank to the Markt square. and city hall. However, rather than there being a street directly into the square, the bridge splits into two ramps, a V-shape. Inside the V is, in my opinion, an abomination, the Mosae Forum. This is a new retail, residential and business area in the old city center of Maastricht. Their claim is "History and modern architecture stand side by side here between the Market and the Meuse". Well, I wish that they had placed it on the modern side of the river, the east. I do appreciate modern design in architecture, but not this particular one, and certainly not in this location.

We walked quickly north along the river, noting the Coffeeshop Mississippi, a converted barge moored at the quay, and the fuel dock, where we will stop on our way back to the river. In a minute we were back at Sluis 20, where we followed a small park down to the bassin, one level below the streets. After a rest on Orion's deck, we walked over to Le Bon Bassin for drinks and a dozen oysters each. ("Each" means Carol and me; Johnnie was there but he doesn't care for oysters.) www.lebonbassin.nl

Our first stop on the next morning was the Selexyz bookstore in the Dominican church. One block west on Grote Gracht from the Markt square, then south on Helmstraat to the Vrijhof square, we watched on our left for the entrance to the *plein* (plaza) of the Dominican church. We were not surprised that the first thing we saw was the outdoor cafe, Grandcafe Amadeus, in front of the church; we'll make use of that after visiting the bookstore. Inside, it is amazing to find long rows of books under the tall arches and stained glass windows of the nave. A book lover's delight!

From there we walked toward the river on the Grote Staat, a pedestrianized shopping street. We passed through the Stokstraatkwartier again, this time cutting through the interior of the block between Havenstraat and Stokstraat to see the sculptures in this very nice courtyard. We continued south for another three blocks, past the river side of Our Dear Lady Basilica, to the Helpoort, the oldest existing city gate in the Netherlands. The twin towers, built using random fieldstones, date from 1229. It now includes an exhibition about the history of Maastricht as a fortress.

The Helpoort marks the beginning of the city park, which starts at the river and runs west along the old fortifications, the Walmuur. Still preserved, these walls are dominated by towers, shaded by trees and bordered by gardens. The first small lake features fountain jets shooting as high as the stone ramparts, which make a nice backdrop for the water display. Round towers at regular intervals along the wall complete the beautiful scenes.

This theme continues at more small lakes formed by the Jeker, a small river which flows into the Maas. In some places the flow rushes through medieval gates and a narrow channel; at one of these, a water-wheel mill still operates.

A life-size statue of a man with a huge wide-brimmed hat, a cape and a drawn sword reminds us that D'Artagnan was born in Maastricht and died in 1673. The Jekerkwartier is one of picturesque streets with small shops and restaurants, and the Jeker waterways, a quiet and restrained section of the old city. We walked back to the north along various city streets, no longer looking at special attractions, just the handsome homes and neighborhood shops. Eventually we came to streets that we recognized and made our way back to the boat.

After a few hours of rest, we left Johnnie behind to guard the boat and walked to our dinner reservation at the Rozemarijn. We were given a small table near the open kitchen area. We chose "Rilette of duck with duck liver and coffee jelly" and "Baked sweet bread with Livar bacon, onions, chestnuts, mustard and a gravy of veal." Along with wine by the glass, these made a tasty meal for about 80 euros total.

The Friday market consists of "375 stalls with great variety of products: vegetables, cheese, textiles, fish, flowers, clothes, perfumes, jewelry, greeting cards, zippers, leather bags, underwear, lingerie". We were mainly interested in the vegetables, cheese, and fish and went away with a good supply of each. After lunch onboard we left the haven and stopped at the Nautica Jansen fuel dock, then headed up the Maas (soon to be the Meuse) for just five kilometers, pulling off into a lake on the east side with island moorings, for a restful weekend before starting a tour of Belgium.

Waterway	From	To	KM	Hours
Maas river	Mookerplas	Venlo	53.5	7.0
Maas river	Venlo	Roermond	31.0	4.5
Julianakanaal	Roermond	Maastricht	34.0	5.0

Reflections

Reflections on the Trip

"Reflections" is purposely meant to have two meanings: my thoughts about the experiences we had and the sights we saw, as well as the reflections of the famous Dutch Light on the waters and land of the Netherlands.

For us, the trip was a success. We accomplished the basic plan of visiting all twelve provinces of the Netherlands. We did it in 86 days, staying overnight at 62 different places and visiting at least a dozen more for a daytime stop. We traveled a total of 1,459 kilometers. almost forty percent of all of the waterway length in the entire country. A suitable subtitle for this book might be "Around the Netherlands in (a little more than) 80 days".

How did we do on star forts? We came close to 80%, touring the singel of 28 star fort towns out of the 36 on my list. The rest are destinations that I look forward to visiting.

We started the trip on the first day of April, at Vlissingen, and ended the story of our cruise on June 25 at the border of Belgium. The timing was set by various outside factors, but proved to be convenient because it ended just before the busiest season started, the months of July and August. We had very little trouble finding moorings when and where we wanted them. This would not have been true at full season, also we would probably have encountered delays at locks and bridges because of the high volume of pleasure boats on the waterways.

Most other travelers would not want to include such a large scope in such a compressed time schedule, and would most likely want to stay longer in the places that they enjoyed the most. We enjoyed each place, but in different ways and to different degrees; I don't think that there was a single place that we disliked, although of course we liked some more than others.

Here is my personal "Best of..." list:

Best waterfront - Vreeland, on the Vecht river, does not offer a visitor's quay except on the northern edge of the town. This means that the flowers and shrubs of residents' yards run right over the banks of the river. Their own small boats are moored at almost every house, the various styles and shapes adding to the interest of the view. The graceful, symmetrical white structures of the lifting bridge in the middle of town make a beautiful sight next to the handsome white bridgekeeper's building. This is definitely a town where travelers should cruise very slowly and then tie-up on the grassy bank outside of town for a walk along the narrow brick streets past the charming homes. Vreeland is at the top of our "Let's move here" list.

Best isolated island mooring - Spiegelpolder, during our visit, lived up to its name "mirror"; the lake was so smooth that white clouds and blue skies reflected off the waters, as did the orange and pink glow at sunset. The strip of four small islands reminded me of a South Seas atoll, protecting the narrow creeks between the islands and the shoreline. There we could row our dinghy, swim at a sandy beach and enjoy the floating lilypads and the wildflowers on the banks; if we were there later in the season, we would have picked wild blackberries from the vines.

Best natural area - Biesbosch is a similar area except bigger and more varied. We liked the canoe routes and the opportunities to go ashore for a walk along the designated nature walks, or into the woodlands and savanna grasslands.

Best major city - Amsterdam; this probably goes without saying, as this city has so many places to walk, to visit, to sit and drink coffee or beer, to dine. It is justly famous as a city of canals, most of them lined by barges and small boats as well as by rows of classic buildings, ranging from beautiful to interesting.

Best medium city - Utrecht is similar to Amsterdam but on a smaller, toned-down scale. It feels safer, more relaxed, it would be a great city to live in.

Best city to winter onboard - two choices, each with a different style: Gorinchem for a quiet, almost boring, small city, centrally located. Maastricht for a vibrant, exciting, medium-sized city. In both places the haven is located right in the center of everything, and welcomes winter-long stays.

Best cruising river - For a small, natural river with countryside views, the Linge. For a medium river, natural but with many beautiful and interesting towns, the Vecht. For a big river with unending views of flood plains and fields of sheep, cattle and small towns, the Maas.

Best Star Fort - Naarden; not surprising, as it was the one that inspired this trip. But it was surprising, after visiting two dozen others, that it is the most original and best preserved, relatively undisturbed by modern life.

Biggest surprises - I shouldn't have been surprised, because I knew to expect to see bicycles, houseboats and rowing shells, but I was surprised by the pervasive sights of bicycles everywhere and used by everyone, houseboats in many more places and in larger numbers than I expected, and the extent of rowing: the wide range of places where people row for sport and the large number of rowing shells that we encountered at these places.

Another surprise: I knew that we would be able to enjoy outdoor cafes, but I didn't know that almost all Dutch towns have outdoor cafes and that most Dutch cities have very, very many outdoor cafes.

Reflections

Most beautiful haven - Blokzijl; a historic town, former Zuider Zee seaport, with the haven for visiting boaters right in the original harbor. Entering through the old flood gates into the widening triangle of the haven, you see the vista of the town and a wide range of boats, from sailing barges to modern white motorboats, spread out in front of you. The docks line the edges of the scene, so that visitors can enjoy the view right from the deck of their boat.

There is something to be said, that the weather in Holland can change quickly and is not always pleasant. On our cruise we had mostly days of beautiful golden sunlight; with occasional brief passing showers, and just a few rainy days. Springtime proved to be an ideal time to see the beauty of all parts of this wonderful country. Each day was a little bit longer, so that we could be out sightseeing, or just walking, well into the evening hours.

Finally, the wonders of "Dutch Light". The famous Dutch Light isn't a myth to me. It can be absolutely stunning here sometimes, making even the most mundane thing into a thing of beauty! The main difference between Dutch light and other light is the water; horizontal water reflects the light, doubling the landscape. The land is flat, so the reflection remains the same view.

The light compares to the desert light which we know well at our home in the southwestern USA. Desert light is crystal clear but hazy in the distance; there it is diffused by dust particles. In Holland it is diffused by water in the atmosphere, clouds and droplets too small to form clouds. There is so much water surface, which reflects the light, as the earth reflects it in the desert.

The difference, of course, is that at home we are used to mountains, buttes and mesas rising above the land, and the colors are shades of gray, brown and dull red. Traveling through the Netherlands is a total change of scene, one that we enjoyed tremendously.

Cruising the Canals & Rivers of Europe

Tom Sommers' EuroCanals Guides

Waterways of the Netherlands (2010 edition) includes maps, color photos and route suggestions for all waterways in the Netherlands.

Country Guides: Guides for the inland waterways include a detailed listing of all navigable waterways, indexed to an overall map. The listings include waterway length, minimum draft, minimum bridge clearance, number of locks and minimum lock size. These Guides are useful for planning.

> Waterways of France
> Waterways of Southwestern France
> Waterways of Brittany
> Waterways of Belgium
> Waterways of England
> Waterways of the Netherlands
> Buying a Barge in The Netherlands
> Waterways of Germany

Canal/River Guides: For the major waterways

> France: Canal de Bourgogne
> Rivers Lot, Seine, Rhône, Saône
> Canal du Midi
> Canal du Nivernais
> Canal entre Champagne et Bourgogne
> Germany: Berlin By Boat

EuroCanals Guides 2011: A compilation of canal guide e-books, seminars and articles published from 2000 to 2010. On CD-ROM for PC-Windows or Mac OS-X.

To Order or for more information regarding the EuroCanals Guides, Go To:

www.eurocanals.com

CPSIA information can be obtained at www.ICGtesting.com

263695BV00001B/84/P